MCSD Test Success:
Visual Basic 6
Desktop Applications

MCSD Test Success™:
Visual Basic® 6
Desktop Applications

Michael McKelvy

San Francisco • Paris • Düsseldorf • Soest • London

Associate Publisher: Richard Mills
Contracts and Licensing Manager: Kristine O'Callaghan
Acquisitions & Developmental Editor: Denise Santoro
Editor: Jane Ross
Project Editor: Julie Sakaue
Technical Editor: TK Herman
Book Designer: Bill Gibson
Electronic Publishing Specialist: Kate Kaminski
Project Team Leader: Shannon Murphy
Proofreader: Andrea Fox
Indexer: Blythe Woolston
Cover Designer: Design Site
Cover Illustrator/Photographer: Jack D. Myers, Design Site

SYBEX is a registered trademark of SYBEX Inc.

Test Success is a trademark of SYBEX Inc.

Screen reproductions produced with Collage Complete.
Collage Complete is a trademark of Inner Media Inc.

Microsoft, the Microsoft Internet Explorer logo, Windows, Windows NT, and the Windows logo are either registered trademarks or trademarks of Microsoft Corporation in the United States and/or other countries.

SYBEX is an independent entity from Microsoft Corporation, and not affiliated with Microsoft Corporation in any manner. This publication may be used in assisting students to prepare for a Microsoft Certified Professional Exam. Neither Microsoft Corporation, its designated review company, nor SYBEX warrants that use of this publication will ensure passing the relevant exam. Microsoft is either a registered trademark or trademark of Microsoft Corporation in the United States and/or other countries.

TRADEMARKS: SYBEX has attempted throughout this book to distinguish proprietary trademarks from descriptive terms by following the capitalization style used by the manufacturer.

The author and publisher have made their best efforts to prepare this book, and the content is based upon final release software whenever possible. Portions of the manuscript may be based upon pre-release versions supplied by software manufacturer(s). The author and the publisher make no representation or warranties of any kind with regard to the completeness or accuracy of the contents herein and accept no liability of any kind including but not limited to performance, merchantability, fitness for any particular purpose, or any losses or damages of any kind caused or alleged to be caused directly or indirectly from this book.

Library of Congress Card Number: 99-61813
ISBN: 0-7821-2432-1

Manufactured in the United States of America

10 9 8 7 6 5 4 3 2

To my wife, Wanda, and my children, Laura and Eric, for their love and support, and for their patience during the long hours of the project.

Acknowledgments

A book like this is not the effort of a single individual; it takes a talented team of people to create a book that is useful for the reader and is a quality publication. I would like to thank all the members of the team that helped me put this book together. First, the editorial team at Sybex—Denise Santoro and Julie Sakaue; second, our editor—Jane Ross; and our technical editor—TK Herman. Next, I would like to thank the production team that gets the book ready for the printer—Kate Kaminski and Shannon Murphy. Finally, I would like to thank my daughter Laura for helping me organize some of the research material for this book.

Contents at a Glance

Table of Contents

Introduction

Corporate America is facing a major challenge in finding information workers to handle all of the computer-related tasks that are critical to almost every business. Part of the challenge is ensuring that the people who are hired are well qualified for the job. One of the methods of determining an individual's qualifications is through certification. There are a variety of certifications for different types of computer-related jobs.

For developers, one of the most significant certifications is the Microsoft Certified Solution Developer (MCSD) certification. This certification, the first of its kind in the industry, gives developers the opportunity to showcase their skills and familiarity with Microsoft platforms and development tools. The industry response has been significant. MCSD certification provides a way for developers to prove their skills, adding credibility to their job applications and promotions.

To achieve MCSD certification, you need to pass Exam 70-100, "Analyzing Requirements and Defining Solution Architectures," as well as an exam on Distributed Applications Development and an exam on Desktop Applications Development. For the Desktop Applications Development you can choose either Visual Basic, which this book covers, or Visual C++.

Your Key to Passing Exam 70-176

This book provides you with the key to passing Exam 70-176, Designing and Implementing Desktop Applications with Microsoft Visual Basic 6.0. Inside, you'll find information relevant to this exam together with practice questions, all designed to make sure that, when you take the exam, you are ready.

Understand the Exam Objectives

To help you prepare for certification exams, Microsoft provides a list of exam objectives for each test. This book is structured according to the objectives for Exam 70-176, which is designed to measure your understanding of using Visual Basic in the desktop environment.

Review sections and over 400 study questions allow you to quickly learn the information that you need for each objective and for the exam itself.

This enables you to prepare for the exam efficiently and effectively. However, to be truly prepared for the exam and for real-world programming, you should study Visual Basic in depth and have some hands-on programming experience.

Get Ready for the Real Thing

More than 150 sample test questions prepare you for the test-taking experience. These are multiple-choice questions that resemble actual exam questions. If you can pass the Sample Tests at the end of each unit and the Final Review at the end of the book, you'll know you're ready.

Is This Book for You?

If you are interested in preparing for the Visual Basic Desktop Applications exam, this book is for you. The exams are written at a survey level, discussing many different topics in general terms and a few topics in specific terms. This book is designed to give you the information you need to pass the exam and to complement your understanding without overburdening you with unnecessary detail.

 Many of the objectives for the Visual Basic Desktop Applications exam overlap with the objectives for the Visual Basic Distributed Applications exam. However, all objectives for the Desktop Applications exam are covered in their entirety in this book.

Understanding Microsoft Certification

Microsoft offers several levels of certification for anyone who has or is pursuing a career as a network professional working with Microsoft products:

- Microsoft Certified Professional (MCP)
- Microsoft Certified Solution Developer (MCSD)

- Microsoft Certified Systems Engineer (MCSE)

- Microsoft Certified Systems Engineer + Internet (MCSE+I)

- Microsoft Certified Professional + Internet

- Microsoft Certified Professional + Site Building

- Microsoft Certified Trainer (MCT)

The one you choose depends on your area of expertise and your career goals.

Microsoft Certified Professional (MCP)

This certification is for individuals with expertise in one specific area. MCP certification is often a stepping stone to MCSD and/or MCSE certification. By passing one certification exam, you become an MCP.

Microsoft Certified Solution Developer (MCSD)

The MCSD certification identifies developers with experience working with Microsoft operating systems, development tools, and technologies. To achieve the MCSD certification, you must pass four exams:

1. Analyzing Requirements and Defining Solution Architectures

2. Desktop Applications Development (either Visual Basic or Visual C++)

3. Distributed Applications Development (either Visual Basic or Visual C++)

4. Elective

Possible electives include the following:

- Application Development with Microsoft Access for Windows 95

- Implementing a Database Design on Microsoft SQL Server 7.0

- Developing Applications with C++ Using the Microsoft Foundation Class Library

- Designing and Implementing Web Solutions with Microsoft Visual InterDev 6.0

- Designing and Implementing Web Sites with Microsoft FrontPage 98

Microsoft Certified Systems Engineer (MCSE)

The MCSE certification identifies network professionals with significant experience working with Microsoft operating systems, and BackOffice tools. You need to complete all of the steps required for certification. Passing the exams shows that you meet the high standards that Microsoft has set for MCSEs.

The following list applies to the NT 4.0 track. Microsoft still supports a track for 3.51, but 4.0 certification is more desirable because it is the current operating system.

To become an MCSE, you must pass a series of six exams:

1. Networking Essentials (waived for Novell CNEs)
2. Implementing and Supporting Microsoft Windows NT Workstation 4.0 (or Windows 95)
3. Implementing and Supporting Microsoft Windows NT Server 4.0
4. Implementing and Supporting Microsoft Windows NT Server 4.0 in the Enterprise
5. Elective
6. Elective

Possible electives include the following:

- Internetworking with Microsoft TCP/IP on Microsoft Windows NT 4.0

- Implementing and Supporting Microsoft Internet Information Server 4.0

- Implementing and Supporting Microsoft Exchange Server 5.5

- Implementing and Supporting Microsoft SNA Server 4.0

- Implementing and Supporting Microsoft Systems Management Server 1.2

- Implementing a Database Design on Microsoft SQL Server 6.5

- System Administration for Microsoft SQL Server 6.5

Microsoft Certified Trainer (MCT)

As an MCT, you can deliver Microsoft-certified courseware through official Microsoft channels. The number of exams you are required to pass depends on the number of courses you want to deliver. Certification is granted on a course-by-course basis.

In addition to passing exams for the courses that you want to deliver, you must also attend a trainer skills course that is approved by Microsoft. You must also demonstrate that you have prepared adequately for each new class. This can be done by either attending the class or completing a self-study checklist and sending it to Microsoft.

For the most up-to-date certification information, visit Microsoft's Web site at www.microsoft.com/train_cert.

Preparing for the MCSD Exams

To prepare for the MCSD certification exams, you should try to work with the products as much as possible. In addition, a variety of resources from which you can learn about the products and exams are available:

- You can take instructor-led courses.

- Online training is an alternative to instructor-led courses. This is a useful option for people who cannot find any courses in their area or who do not have the time to attend classes.

- If you prefer to use a book to help you prepare for the MCSD tests, you can choose from a wide variety of publications. These include study guides, such as the Sybex *MCSD Study Guide* series, which cover the core MCSD exams and key electives.

 For more MCSD information, point your browser to the Sybex Web site, where you'll find information about the MCP program, job links, and descriptions of other quality titles in the Sybex line of MCSD-related books. Go to http://www.sybex.com and click on the MCSD logo.

Scheduling and Taking an Exam

Once you think you are ready to take an exam, contact Sylvan Prometric Testing Centers at (800) 755-EXAM (755-3926) or Virtual University Enterprises at www.vue.com/ms. They'll tell you where to find the closest testing center. Before you call, get out your credit card because each exam costs $100 at time of writing.

You can schedule the exam for a time that is convenient for you. The exams are downloaded from Prometric to the testing center, and you show up at your scheduled time and take the exam on a computer.

Once you complete the exam, you will know right away whether you have passed or not. At the end of the exam, you will receive a score report. It will list the areas that you were tested on and how you performed. If you pass the exam, you don't need to do anything else—Prometric uploads the test results to Microsoft. If you don't pass, you must pay again in order to schedule to take the exam again. But at least you will know from the score report where you did poorly, so you can study that particular information more carefully.

Test-Taking Hints

If you know what to expect, your chances of passing the exam are much greater. The following are some tips that can help you achieve success.

Get There Early and Be Prepared

This is your last chance to review. Bring your book and review any areas about which you feel unsure. If you need a quick drink of water or a visit to the restroom, take the time before the exam. Once your exam starts, it will not be paused for these needs.

When you arrive for your exam, you will be asked to present two forms of ID. You will also be asked to sign a piece of paper verifying that you understand the testing rules and that you will not disclose the content of the exam to others.

Before you start the exam, you will have an opportunity to take a practice exam. It is not related to Visual Basic and is simply offered so that you will have a feel for the exam-taking process.

What You Can and Can't Take in with You

These are closed-book exams. The only thing you can take in is scratch paper provided by the testing center. Use this paper as much as possible to diagram the questions. Many times diagramming questions will help make the answer clear. You will have to give this paper back to the test administrator at the end of the exam.

Many testing centers are very strict about what you can take into the testing room. Some centers will not even allow you to bring in items like a zipped purse. If you feel tempted to take in any outside material, beware that many testing centers use monitoring devices such as video and audio equipment (so don't swear, even if you are alone in the room!)

Prometric Testing Centers take the test-taking process and the test validation very seriously.

Test Approach

As you take the test, if you know the answer to a question, fill it in and move on. If you're not sure of the answer, mark your best guess, then "mark" the question.

At the end of the exam, you can review the questions. Depending on the amount of time remaining, you can then view all of the questions again, or you can view only the questions about which you were unsure. Double-check your answers, just in case you misread any of the questions on the first pass. (Sometimes half of the battle is in trying to figure out exactly what the question is asking you.) You may find that a related question provides a clue for a troublesome question.

Be sure to answer all questions. Unanswered questions are scored as incorrect and will count against you. There is no penalty for guessing. Also, make sure you keep an eye on the remaining time so that you can pace yourself accordingly.

If you do not pass the exam, note everything that you can remember while the exam is still fresh on your mind. This will help you prepare for your next try. Although the next exam will not be exactly the same, the questions will be similar, and you don't want to make the same mistakes.

After You Become Certified

Once you become an MCSD, Microsoft kicks in some goodies, including the following:

- A one-year subscription to the Microsoft Beta Evaluation program, which is a great way to get your hands on new software. Be the first kid on the block to play with new and upcoming software.

- Access to a secured area of the Microsoft Web site that provides technical support and product information. This certification benefit is also available for MCP certification.

- Permission to use the Microsoft Certified Professional logos (each certification has its own logo), which look great on letterhead and business cards.

- An MCP certificate (you will get a certificate for each level of certification you reach), suitable for framing, or sending copies to Mom.

- A one-year subscription to *Microsoft Certified Professional Magazine*, which provides information on professional and career development.

How to Use This Book

The Visual Basic exams are mostly conceptual, rather than applied. However, the exercises in this book are designed to reinforce some of the important topics on this exam, especially those topics where implementation detail will be tested. To address the wide range of topics on this exam, many Microsoft applications and development tools have been referenced in this book. To do all of the exercises in this book, you must have the following software installed:

- Windows Operating System selected from the following configurations:
  - Windows 95/98
  - Windows NT Workstation
- Microsoft Access 97 (version 8) with the Northwind sample database installed.
- Microsoft Visual Basic 6 at a default installation.
- Microsoft Internet Explorer 4. Note that all exercises and screen shots in this book assume that the Active Desktop is not installed with IE 4.

All of the exercises in the book assume that products have been installed according to the defaults and no consideration is given for additional customizations that you have made on the installation.

As you work through this book, you may want to follow these general procedures:

1. Review the exam objectives as you work through the unit. (You should check the Microsoft Train_Cert Web site to make sure the objectives haven't changed.)

2. Study a unit carefully, making sure you fully understand the information.

3. Complete all hands-on exercises in the unit, referring to the text so that you understand every step you take.

4. Answer the study questions at the end of the unit. (You will find the answers to these questions in Appendix A.)

5. Note which questions you did not understand and study those sections of the book again.

To learn all of the material covered in this book, you will need to study regularly and with discipline. Try to set aside the same time every day to study and select a comfortable and quiet place in which to do it. Good Luck!

About the Author

Michael McKelvy

Michael McKelvy is the founder and president of McKelvy Software Systems, Inc., a software development firm in Birmingham, Alabama, specializing in the development of database applications for a variety of businesses. Mike has also written a number of books on programming in Visual Basic, including the *Visual Basic 5 Study Guide* and the *Visual Basic 6 Desktop Applications Study Guide*, both from Sybex.

How to Contact Sybex

Technical Support   support@sybex.com

Web site   www.sybex.com

To find information on this book on the Sybex Web site, click Catalog, then type **2432** in the search field and press Enter.

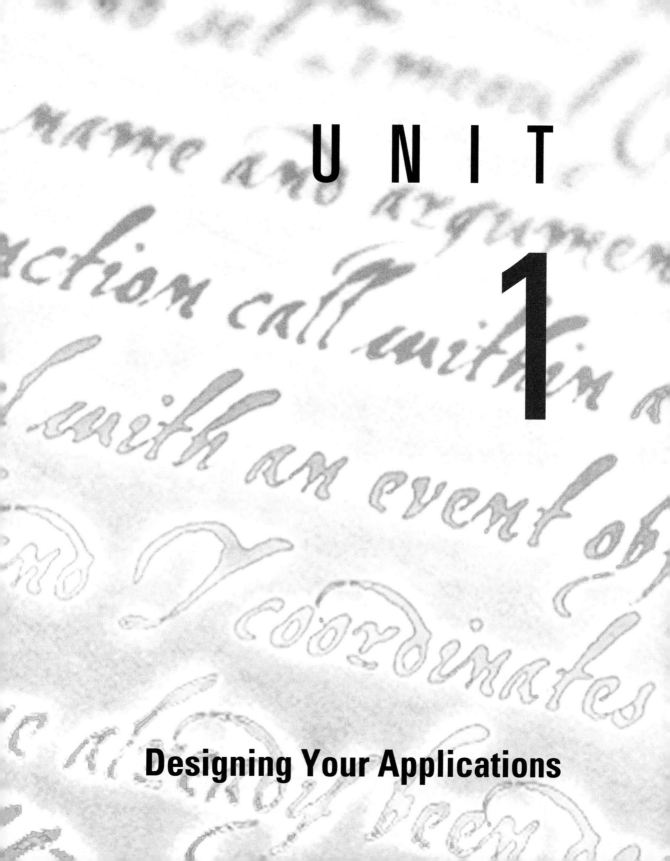

UNIT

1

Designing Your Applications

Test Objectives: Deriving the Physical Design

- Assess the potential impact of the logical design on performance, maintainability, extensibility, and availability.

- Design Visual Basic components to access data from a database.

- Design the properties, methods, and events of components.

Exam objectives are subject to change at any time without prior notice and at Microsoft's sole discretion. Please visit Microsoft's Training & Certification Web site (www.microsoft.com/Train_Cert) for the most current exam objectives listing.

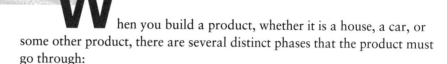

When you build a product, whether it is a house, a car, or some other product, there are several distinct phases that the product must go through:

- Concept

- Design

- Construction

- Maintenance

Programs are just like any other product that you build. The concept is an idea for solving a business problem. Design is how you create the program to solve the problem. Construction is writing the code and creating the forms and components. Maintenance is fixing bugs and adding new features.

The design of the program has a major impact on the construction, performance, and maintenance of the program. A good design will save you a lot of effort in creating and maintaining the program, while a bad design will cause you many headaches throughout the life cycle of the program.

Assess the Potential Impact of the Logical Design on Performance, Maintainability, Extensibility, and Availability

When you are creating the design of your application, there are a number of factors that you need to consider:

- Which functions of the program will be reused in other programs?

- How many developers will be working on the program?

- Does the entire application reside on a single machine or will it span multiple computers?

- How often do you expect to make enhancements to the program?

The answers to these questions will have a major impact on the design of the program. For example, if you need to accommodate multiple programs accessing a function, you may want to place the function in an ActiveX server instead of in the application itself.

Designing Maintainable Code

One of the key goals of any program design is to make the program as easily maintainable as possible. While this is very important when you will be performing all the maintenance activities on your own program, it is even more important if others will be maintaining the program. A poorly designed program is difficult to maintain and results in wasted time and money in program support. There are several key elements to designing a maintainable program:

- Place redundant code segments in a procedure or function instead of having multiple copies of the same code.

- Make use of classes to encapsulate data and functions for a particular business or programming object. This is useful in stand-alone applications and essential in client/server or Web-based applications.

- Use naming conventions for variables and controls. This makes the code easier to read and makes much of your program self-documenting.

- Declare all variables and, if possible, declare them as specific data types. This makes your code easier to maintain and helps eliminate errors by allowing the debugging tools in Visual Basic to check for mismatched data types and misspelled variable names.

- Use comments to describe the function of a class, procedure, or segment of code. Well-commented code is much easier to maintain.

Using Naming Conventions

To make it easier to read your code, you should use naming conventions to identify the type of control or variable that is represented by a name. Microsoft has recommended naming conventions for use in Visual Basic programs. The naming conventions for variables and controls are summarized in Tables 1.1 and 1.2 respectively. Whether you use Microsoft's conventions or your own, the important point is to establish and use a naming convention, particularly in a multiple developer environment.

T A B L E   1.1
Variable Naming Conventions

Data Type	Suggested Variable Prefix
String	str
Integer	int
Long	lng
Single	sng
Double	dbl
Currency	cur
Date	dte
Boolean	bln
Variant	var

T A B L E   1.2
Control Naming Conventions

Control Type	Suggested Prefix
Text Box	txt
Label	lbl
Command Button	cmd

TABLE 1.2 *(cont.)*	**Control Type**	**Suggested Prefix**
Control Naming Conventions	Form	frm
	Frame	fra
	Image	img
	Picture Box	pic
	Timer	tmr
	Combo Box	cbo
	List Box	lst
	Data Control	dat

Tables 1.1 and 1.2 do not give a complete list of variable data types or control types. You can find more information on naming conventions in the Microsoft Visual Basic documentation.

Forcing Variable Declaration

To declare a variable for use, you use a Dim, Public, or Private statement, typically at the beginning of a procedure. These statements inform Visual Basic to reserve space for the variable. By adding the As clause to the declaration statement, you can identify the type of data that will be stored in the variable. If, at a later point in your program, you try to assign the wrong type of data to a variable, Visual Basic generates an error that you can trap and use to correct the situation. The following code shows examples of variable declarations:

```
Public iSecLevel As Integer    'Security level
Public iMaxUsers As Integer    'Maximum users allowed
Public sSystemID As String     'System ID
```

```
Public sSysPassword As String 'System Password
Dim sINIReturn As String, sMessage As String
Dim iDemoCheck As Integer
```

Forcing variable declaration causes Visual Basic to check each variable name that is used in your program to ensure that it was declared before it was used. This helps you find typographic errors, such as misspelling the name of a variable. To force variable declaration, you set the Require Variable Declaration option on the Editor page of the Options dialog box shown in Figure 1.1. You can access this dialog box by choosing the Options item from the Tools menu.

F I G U R E   1.1

Setting the Require
Variable Declaration
option

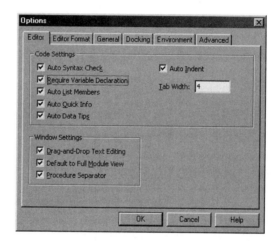

When this option is set, Visual Basic automatically places the Option Explicit statement at the beginning of every new form or module created in your program. To force variable declaration in existing modules or forms, you can manually add this statement in the Declarations section of the module or form.

Commenting Your Code

Comments provide an easy way to describe the functions of the code within the code itself. By providing comments, you make it easier for yourself or another programmer to understand what the program is doing. This makes maintenance much easier. You indicate a comment in Visual Basic by prefacing the statement with a single quotation mark (') or with the letters

Rem. Either of these indicates to Visual Basic that the text following is a comment and not to be compiled or run. If you are using the standard colors in your editor, comments are typically shown in green on your screen. The following code shows an example of comments in a program:

```
'Close error object
Set oErrorLog = Nothing
'Close databases
MainDB.Close
TempDB.Close
'Unload forms
For I = Forms.Count - 1 To 0 Step -1
    If Forms(I).Name <> "frmMain" Then
        Unload Forms(I)
    End If
Next I
Unload frmMain
'Exit the program
End
```

Designing for Code Reuse

Creating reusable code is tightly integrated with creating maintainable code. To create code that is easy to maintain, you place functions and procedures in modules and classes. This makes them easy to test. The smaller size of the individual pieces makes it easier to find the areas of code where an error occurs or the area that needs to be modified to add a new function. Placing code in standard modules or class modules also makes the code reusable. If a function you need is in a class file, you simply add the class to your new project and begin writing code using the class object.

The following are several suggestions for making your code reusable:

- Place generic functions and procedures in a standard module.

- Use class modules to encapsulate data and tasks for a particular business object or programming object.

- If you use a group of controls (e.g., navigation buttons for a database application) in multiple projects, consider creating a custom control.

- For forms that can be used in multiple projects (e.g., splash screens, Login screens, and About boxes) create properties of the form to handle information from multiple projects. This makes the form generic and easy to use in multiple programs.

Designing for Performance

Another major consideration for most programs is the performance of the program on the user's machine. Some of the decisions that you need to make about performance involve which compiler options to use. This topic is covered in detail in Unit 11, "Debugging Your Application." However, there are several other techniques you can use in your design to get the optimum performance from your program:

- Define objects as a specific type. This makes the creation of the objects faster.

- Limit the instances of objects to only those you need. Each object instance that you create adds overhead to your program. For example, don't create an employee object for each of the 1000 employees in the application if you will only be accessing one employee at a time.

- For database applications, use queries to create recordsets containing only the information you need. Don't create a recordset of every order in the system if you are only looking at the orders for one customer.

- Use specific data type variables where possible. Variant data type variables have a lot of overhead.

- Test, test, test. This is the only way to measure the performance of a program.

Design Visual Basic Components to Access Data from a Database

One of the most common tasks for Visual Basic programmers is creating programs that view and manipulate information in a database. With each version of Visual Basic, the tools for working with databases have become more powerful, giving the programmer the ability to write more powerful programs.

Since the introduction of class modules in Visual Basic 4, programmers have been able to create components, including components for accessing data. Visual Basic 5 extended this capability by introducing the ability to create ActiveX controls. Visual Basic 6 extends the capabilities once again by providing the ability to set up controls and classes as data sources and data consumers.

When you begin designing a component for database access, you need to approach the design with the same thought you put into designing the overall program. To design the component, you need to consider the following:

- What task will the component perform?

- Will the component be reused in other programs and how will it be reused?

- Will the end user need access to the capabilities of the component?

- How can you make the component easy to maintain?

The first decision you will have to make in creating a data access component is which type of component to use. If the component does not need to provide a visual interface to the outside world, you should probably use a class module to create the component. If the component will be displaying data or providing a data source for bound controls, you will need to create the component from a UserControl.

Creating Components from Class Modules

There are two common uses of class modules in a data access program:

- To create a business object to retrieve specific data from a database and to provide it to programs requesting the data

- To encapsulate the data-access functions of a program to ease program maintenance and error handling

For many client/server programs, you need to create a number of business objects that access specific data. For example, you may need to create an employee object that retrieves information about a specific employee from a database and provides the information to the client program. Then, depending on the application and the permission level of the user, the user could view and/or modify the data. The component would need methods that retrieved the data from the database and could store changed information back to the database.

The properties of the component would need to store and provide access to the various pieces of information about the employee, such as name, department, address, phone, and possibly salary. Such a component would also need to work with any security components to ensure that only authorized users see sensitive data. A component of this type would be created from a class module and compiled into an ActiveX server so that multiple programs could use the object. By having multiple programs access the data through the same component, you realize the objectives of code reuse and ease of maintenance.

The other common use of class modules is to encapsulate the functions required for data access. Using a class module allows you to create a generic routine for opening a database or a recordset. This generic routine can include all the error-handling code that is necessary for the data-access methods. Then, for each database or recordset that you need to open, you set the properties and call the methods of the class to perform the functions. This eliminates the need for redundant data-access code and error handling throughout your program. The following code listing shows a simple class for opening databases:

```
Option Explicit
'This class handles the chores of opening a database
'and returning a database object. The DBOpen property
'indicates whether the operation was successful.
Dim m_WS As Workspace, m_DB As Database, m_bDBOpen _
As Boolean

Private Sub Class_Initialize()
'Set the initial workspace to default
Set m_WS = DBEngine.Workspaces(0)
'Set the initial DBOpen flag to false
m_bDBOpen = False
End Sub

Public Property Get CurDataBase() As Database
'If the database is open, return the database object
```

```
If m_bDBOpen Then
    Set CurDataBase = m_DB
Else
    Set CurDataBase = Nothing
End If
End Property

Public Property Get DBOpen() As Boolean
DBOpen = m_bDBOpen
End Property

Public Sub OpenDB(sDBName As String, Optional bExcl, _
 Optional bReadOnly, Optional sOptions)
Dim bOpenOK As Boolean, sMessage As String, sPassword _
As String
On Error GoTo DBOpenErr
'Initialize variables
bOpenOK = True

'Check for missing parameters and set default values
If IsMissing(bExcl) Then bExcl = False
If IsMissing(bReadOnly) Then bReadOnly = False
If IsMissing(sOptions) Then sOptions = ""

'If a database is already open, close it
If m_bDBOpen Then
    m_DB.Close
    m_bDBOpen = False
End If

'Attempt to open the database
Set m_DB = m_WS.OpenDatabase(sDBName, bExcl, bReadOnly, _
 sOptions)

'Set the database flag to indicate whether it was opened
'succesfully
```

```
If bOpenOK Then
    m_bDBOpen = True
Else
    m_bDBOpen = False
End If

Exit Sub

DBOpenErr:
    Select Case Err.Number
        Case 3031  'Password required or incorrect
            sMessage = "This database requires a password."
            sMessage = sMessage & "Please enter the"
            sMessage = sMessage & " correct password or"
            sMessage = sMessage & " click Cancel to "
            sMessage = sMessage & "abort opening the "
            sMessage = sMessage & "database."
            sPassword = InputBox(sMessage, _
            "Password Entry")
            If sPassword = "" Then
                'If user cancels, proceed without opening
                'the database
                bOpenOK = False
                Resume Next
            Else
                'Attempt to open the database with the
                'input password
                sOptions = ";pwd=" & sPassword
                Resume
            End If
    End Select
    Resume Next
End Sub
```

Creating Data-Bound Components

One of the new features of Visual Basic 6 is the ability for class modules and ActiveX controls to be data sources and data consumers. This means that you can write a class or control that can serve as the data source for data-bound controls in your program. In addition, classes and ActiveX controls can be bound to a data control, making it easier to work with the data in the recordset created by the control.

To design a data-bound component, you must first determine whether the component will be a provider or a consumer of data. While it is possible to create a component that is both a provider and a consumer, your components will typically be one or the other.

When you set out to create a data source, make sure you have a good understanding of the ActiveX Data Objects (ADO). You can only create a data source using ADO; this cannot be done with DAO or RDO. In creating a data source, the key design decision is whether the component will access a specific set of data or whether the component will be a generic component where the user can specify the data to be retrieved. After you make this decision, you can define the properties for getting database name and path information to the component and the properties for allowing other components to retrieve data from the data source. You also need a method that enables the component to open the target database and recordset.

There are a few more design decisions involved in creating a data consumer control. In this case, you need to determine which properties of the control will be bound to a data source and which of the properties will be the default property. You may also need to create properties of the component that allow the user to specify recordset fields to attach to the various properties of your component.

Design the Properties, Methods, and Events of Components

Visual Basic 6 gives you the ability to create a number of different program components. Using different structures in Visual Basic, you can create ActiveX controls and ActiveX documents. Using class modules, you can create ActiveX servers. For each of these components, you will need to know how to create properties, methods, and events.

The properties of a component enable you to store information in the component. In the case of a control, this information might be used to determine the appearance of the control. For other components, the properties contain the information about a business object, such as the social security number of an employee.

The methods of a component allow the component to take action on the data stored in the properties. A control might have a Move method used to reposition the control to another point on a form. A component such as an employee object might have a method for calculating payroll and tax information.

Events of a component are a means to let your main program know that something has occurred. An event can be used to notify the program of a change to a piece of data or to notify the program of the completion of a long task.

Properties, methods, and events of a component are all handled through code procedures in the component. Also, the use of custom properties and methods is not limited to controls and classes. You can also create custom properties and methods for the forms you use in your program. Using properties and methods for a form provides a safe and convenient means to pass information to and from a form and to work with the information.

Determining the Design of the Component

In creating a component, you need to first determine the design of the component, before you begin implementation. While this seems obvious, it is often tempting to immediately start coding a component without taking time to do a real design. The key elements of component design involve answering the following questions:

- What information is needed by the component to perform its tasks? This is the information that will be passed to the component in the form of Property Let and Property Set procedures.

- What information is output by the component for use by client applications? This is the information that is returned by the component through the Property Get procedures.

- What actions must the component perform on the information it has? These actions define the methods of the component.

- Does the component need to notify the client application of the completion of a task or the occurrence of an error? Notifications that the component needs to make determine the type of events that the component will provide.

To illustrate how to design a component, consider how you would handle payroll for an employee. To determine what to pay an employee, you need to have information about the employee's rate of pay, the hours worked in the pay period, the tax status of the employee, and any payroll deductions that might need to be made. These items of information are the input to the component and your component needs Property Let procedures to allow the information to be input to the component.

The main task performed by the component is the determination of gross pay, taxes to various entities, total deductions, and net pay. This task identifies that you need a method (possibly more than one) to perform the calculation and Property Get procedures to return the values calculated. If you want your component to handle printing the check for the employee or creating a tax deposit form, you need to create methods for these tasks as well.

Finally, you may want your component to notify the user that the calculation is completed so that data can be reviewed before the check is printed. If you include an event procedure in your program, you can raise the event when the payroll calculation is complete. The client application can then respond to the event by displaying a notification to the user.

The design is the first step in creating the properties, methods, and events of a component. After you have completed the design, you need to implement the elements of the component. The following sections provide a brief review of the creation of properties, methods, and events.

Creating a Property in a Component

A property of a component is a public interface that allows the component to communicate with an external program. The properties that you create for a component are similar to the intrinsic properties of the controls that you use to create the user interface of your program. A property that you create can be read/write, read-only, or write-only. The properties you create can be set in code using an assignment statement or, if your component is supported in design mode (e.g., a control), through the Properties window.

There are two means of creating a property that is accessible by an external program:

- Create a public variable.

- Create a property procedure.

While it is quicker and easier to create a property using a public variable, this is not the recommended means. The drawback to using a public variable is that values can be set or retrieved with no processing to ensure the validity of the data being passed. This can lead to runtime errors and to erroneous results in your program. To correctly create a property, you should use a set of property procedures.

Creating a property through a property procedure requires the following steps:

1. Create a private variable in the component to hold the information for use by the component.

2. Create a Property Let or Property Set procedure to assign a value to the internal variable. This procedure enables you to process the information being passed to the component to ensure its validity. Property Set is used for passing objects to the component. Property Let is used for all standard data types.

3. Create a Property Get procedure to allow retrieval of the information from the internal variable.

The following code shows a typical Property Let and Property Get combination:

```
Dim m_lUserID As Long


Public Property Get UserID() As Long
UserID = m_lUserID
End Property


Public Property Let UserID(lNewValue As Long)
m_lUserID = UserID
End Property
```

The simplest way to create the Property procedures for a component is through the Add Procedure dialog box shown in Figure 1.2.

F I G U R E 1.2

Creating a new
property

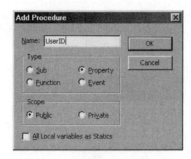

In the dialog box, you specify the name of the property that you want to create and choose the Property option in the Type selection. You also need to set the Scope selection to Public. After you click the OK button, Visual Basic creates the framework of the property. You then need to perform the following steps to complete the creation of the property:

1. Specify the data type for the input to the Property Let procedure and the return data type of the Property Get procedure. These data types should be the same for a given Property Let/Get combination.

2. Declare a private variable in the component to hold the information being passed.

3. Write code in the procedures to set and retrieve the value of the internal variable.

Creating a Method in a Component

When you create a component, you need procedures to handle a number of tasks for the component. These tasks may include calculations that manipulate data, code to retrieve or store information in a database, or code to perform tasks on the component itself, such as moving a control. The procedures for these tasks can be either Sub or Function procedures. The key difference between the two is that a Function procedure returns a value as part of the task. In creating the procedures, you have to make a determination whether the procedure should be public or private. A private procedure is one that is used internally by the component but is not accessible to any external programs or components. A public procedure is one that is accessible by any external programs. Public procedures make up the methods of a component.

Creating a method is very similar to creating a Property procedure. You can create a method by using the Add Procedure dialog box in Visual Basic. To create a method, set the Type option to either Sub or Function, depending on whether you need to return a value, and set the Scope option to Public. After you enter a name for the procedure and click the OK button, the procedure framework is created for you, as shown in Figure 1.3.

FIGURE 1.3

Creating a method in a component

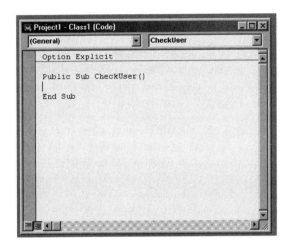

After you create the framework for the method, you need to perform the following steps to complete the creation of the method:

- Add arguments to the Procedure declaration to allow information to be passed to the procedure.

- Write the code necessary to handle the task the procedure will perform.

A completed method is shown in the following code segment:

```
Public Sub SetPermissions(m_DB As Database)
'Retrieve permissions for this user from the input recordset
Dim I As Integer, m_Rset As Recordset, sPermSQL As String
'Set up permissions for current user
If m_lUserID <= 0 Then
    m_iMaxPerm = 0
    Exit Sub
```

```
    End If
    sPermSQL = "Select * From UserPermissions Where UserID = _
              " &m_lUserID
    Set m_Rset = m_DB.OpenRecordset(sPermSQL, dbOpenDynaset)
    With m_Rset
        If .RecordCount = 0 Then
            'No permissions for user
            m_iMaxPerm = 0
        Else
            'Get permissions from file
            ReDim m_bUserPerm(1 To m_iMaxPerm)
            For I = 1 To m_iMaxPerm
                m_bUserPerm(I) = False
            Next I
            .MoveFirst
            Do While Not .EOF
                I = !PermissionID
                If I > 0 And I <= m_iMaxPerm Then _
                m_bUserPerm(I) = !PermissionGranted
                .MoveNext
            Loop
        End If
    End With
    m_Rset.Close
End Sub
```

For a procedure that can only be used within the component, replace the Public keyword in the declaration with the Private keyword. However, public and private are not the only declarations that you can use for a procedure. Another option is the Friend declaration. The Friend declaration enables you to make a property or method available to other modules in the current project (the one in which the class is defined), without making the routine truly public. You can create necessary routines for data conversion or other functions and declare them as Friend. Your program can then use these routines internally, but other programs are not permitted to use the methods or view the properties declared as Friend. The Friend declaration is mainly used in the creation of ActiveX servers.

Creating an Event

The final type of procedure that you need to understand to design and create components is the event procedure. Event procedures allow your components to trigger events that a calling program can respond to. These events are similar to the events in a form or control. To create an event procedure, you must perform two steps:

1. Declare the event procedure, along with the information to be passed by the procedure to the calling program.

2. Write code in your component to raise the event.

The following code shows how an event procedure can be created in a component:

```
Public Event DataRetrieved(ByVal lNumRecords As Long)


Public Sub GetData()
Dim lRecs As Long
'Code to open the recordset
lRecs = rsInformation.RecordCount
RaiseEvent DataRetrieved(lRecs)
End Sub
```

```
STUDY QUESTIONS
```

Assess the Potential Impact of the Logical Design on Performance, Maintainability, Extensibility, and Availability

1. True or False. Your program runs faster if you repeat the code for a function wherever it is needed.

2. _____ are used to encapsulate data and functions of a business object.

3. To help make your program more readable and easier to maintain, you should adopt and consistently use a _____.

4. To help avoid errors, you should _____ all variables prior to their use.

5. A variable with the prefix **str** would contain _____ data.

6. True or False. You should use the default names of controls as they are assigned by Visual Basic.

7. You can designate a line as a comment by placing a _____ character or the letters _____ in front of the line.

8. The _____ statement forces variable declaration in a form or module.

9. To create a generic form, pass information to the form using

_____.

10. Using classes in a program makes the functions easier to

_____ and _____.

11. True or False. In a database application, opening the entire table of a database gives you the same performance as retrieving specific fields and records.

12. True or False. Declaring variables as a specific type reduces overhead compared to declaring them as variant.

Design Visual Basic Components to Access Data from a Database

13. When creating a business object, you typically compile the component into an

_____ to allow multiple programs to use the

component.

14. If your component needs to have a visual interface, you will need to use the

_____ to create the component.

15. Encapsulating data access functions in a class module makes

_____ and _____

easier.

STUDY QUESTIONS

16. True or False. You can create components that are data sources and/or data-bound components.

Design the Properties, Methods, and Events of Components

17. A _____ procedure enables you to pass information to a component. This procedure works with standard data types.

18. To retrieve information from a component, you use a _____ procedure.

19. The _____ procedure is used to pass objects to a component.

20. To hold the information passed to a component, you use an _____.

21. A method is a Sub or Function procedure that is declared in a component with the _____ keyword.

22. True or False. Procedures declared as private can be accessed by other components in the same project.

23. To trigger an event from the component, you use the _____ method.

24.   The key difference between a Sub and a Function procedure is that a
_____ returns a value.

SAMPLE TEST

1-1   Which procedure would you use to pass object information to a component?

    A. Property Get

    B. Property Set

    C. Property Let

    D. Object Set

1-2   Which procedure would you use to retrieve object information from a component?

    A. Property Get

    B. Property Set

    C. Property Let

    D. Object Get

1-3   According to naming conventions, what is the appropriate prefix for a label control?

    A. lbl

    B. lab

    C. l

    D. A prefix is not needed.

1-4   What type of information is contained in a variable with the **int** prefix?

    A. Long Integer

    B. String

    C. Date

    D. Integer

1-5   Which statement is used to enforce variable declaration?

    A. Option Implicit

    B. Force Declaration

    C. Option Explicit

    D. Forcing variable declaration is automatic in Visual Basic.

1-6   Which of the following enhances the maintainability of your code? Check all that apply.

    A. Placing often-used functions in a module

    B. Using the default control names

    C. Using comments in the code

    D. Assigning variables as they are needed instead of declaring them

1-7   Which declaration allows a procedure to be used as a method of a component?

    A. Public

    B. Private

    C. Friend

    D. Event

1-8   Which declaration allows a procedure to be used within a server but prevents it from being called from outside the server?

    A. Public

    B. Private

    C. Friend

    D. Event

1-9 You can create properties and methods for which of the following? Check all that apply.

    A. Visual Basic controls

    B. Classes

    C. Forms

    D. ActiveX controls

1-10 Which of the following data-access methods can be used with a bound component?

    A. Data Access Objects only

    B. ActiveX Data Objects only

    C. Both DAO and ADO

    D. Neither DAO nor ADO

1-11 Which of the following data-access methods can be used to create a data source?

    A. Data Access Objects only

    B. ActiveX Data Objects only

    C. Both DAO and ADO

    D. Neither DAO nor ADO

U N I T

2

Setting Up Visual Basic

Test Objectives: Establishing the Development Environment

- **Establish the environment for source code version control.**

- **Install and configure Visual Basic for developing desktop applications.**

 Exam objectives are subject to change at any time without prior notice and at Microsoft's sole discretion. Please visit Microsoft's Training & Certification Web site (www.microsoft.com/Train_Cert) for the most current exam objectives listing.

Before you can use Visual Basic to write programs, you must install Visual Basic on your system. There are a number of options available when you install the program. This unit covers the basics of installing Visual Basic. It also discusses using version control for your source code and how Visual Basic implements version control through the Visual SourceSafe add-in.

Establish the Environment for Source Code Version Control

When you install Visual Basic, one of the options you can select is to install Visual SourceSafe. Visual SourceSafe is a version control program that is integrated with Visual Basic and the other members of the Visual Studio family.

Visual SourceSafe maintains a database of all the programs that you choose to keep under version control. Once a program has been added to the database, Visual SourceSafe tracks changes that are made to the program and who made the changes. Having this information enables you to roll back changes that create problems and to know who has changed components of your program. This type of information is essential if more than one programmer is working on an application.

Setting Up Visual SourceSafe

Before you can use Visual SourceSafe to track changes in your projects, you need to set it up for use. Visual SourceSafe is typically installed as a program group with Visual Studio or Visual Basic. One of the programs in the group is the Visual SourceSafe Admin program. The Administrator screen, shown in Figure 2.1, enables you to carry out these tasks:

- Manage users.

- Create and modify SourceSafe databases.

- Archive and restore projects.

F I G U R E   2.1

Administering Visual
SourceSafe

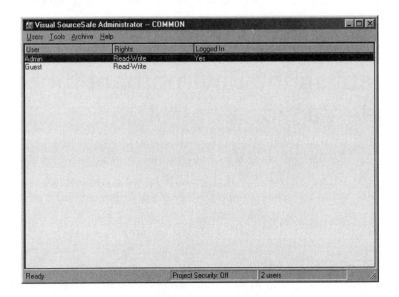

The primary function of Visual SourceSafe is managing users. You must create users in the Administrator program before they can add or retrieve projects in Visual SourceSafe. To add a user, choose the Add User item from the Users menu. Then fill in the username and password (optional) in the Add User dialog box shown in Figure 2.2. You can also choose to give the user read-only access to the repository, meaning that they can look at code but cannot modify it.

F I G U R E   2.2

Adding a user

Adding a Project

When you save a project, Visual SourceSafe asks if you want to add the project to the repository. If you choose Yes, you will be presented with the Login screen for Visual SourceSafe, shown in Figure 2.3. This screen requires you to enter a username, password (optional), and the database where the program is to be stored.

F I G U R E   2.3

Logging into Visual
SourceSafe

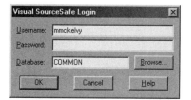

After logging in, you can specify the name of the project and which source folder to use to store the project. This is done in the Add To SourceSafe Project dialog box shown in Figure 2.4.

F I G U R E   2.4

Adding a project

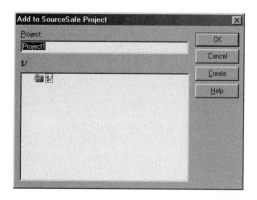

Next you choose the files of your current project to add to SourceSafe. In the Add Files dialog box, shown in Figure 2.5, you can choose to add all files or individual files.

FIGURE 2.5

Selecting the files
to add

Retrieving a Project

When you use Visual SourceSafe, you cannot open projects and files as you normally would without the version control program. If you try to open a project, Visual Basic will open a read-only version of the project and its associated files. To be able to work on the program, you need to check the program out from SourceSafe.

After you open the project, you can choose the SourceSafe item from the Tools menu. This brings up the SourceSafe submenu shown in Figure 2.6.

From this menu, you can check out the files of your project using the Check Out Files dialog box shown in Figure 2.7. This dialog box lets you specify the individual files that you want to check out. Once a file is checked out, you can modify it and later store it back in the SourceSafe repository.

You can also handle project checkouts and other management functions by running SourceSafe itself. The main screen for Visual SourceSafe is shown in Figure 2.8.

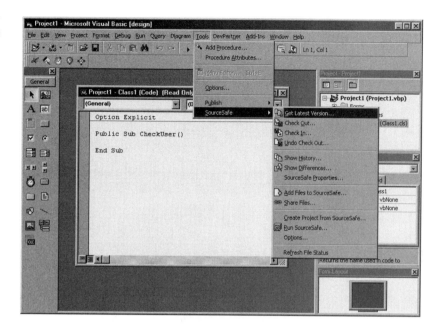

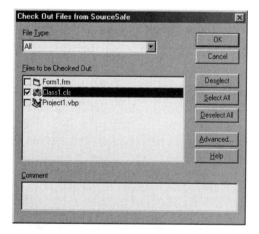

FIGURE 2.8

Visual SourceSafe
main screen

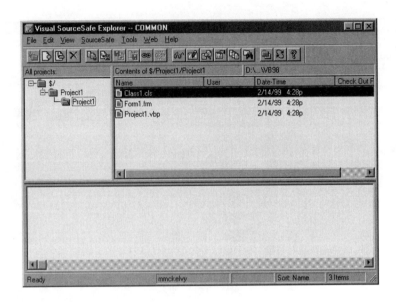

Install and Configure Visual Basic for Developing Desktop Applications

Before you can begin writing programs in Visual Basic, you have to install the Visual Basic program. Installing Visual Basic is similar to installing any other Windows program. There are a number of options available in the installation. In addition to Visual Basic itself, there are several auxiliary programs that can be installed. To use Visual Basic's help features, you need to install Internet Explorer 4 (or higher), if it is not already on your system.

Running the Installation Program

The first step to installing Visual Basic is to insert the CD into the drive. For most systems, this starts the AutoPlay process and automatically begins the installation of Visual Basic. If you do not have AutoPlay enabled, you can start the installation by running the SETUP.EXE program from the root directory of the CD.

After viewing the title screen of the installation, complete these steps:

1. Read and accept the license agreement.

2. Enter your CD key and your name and company information.

3. If you are installing from the Visual Studio CD, select the Product option, then select Visual Basic as the product to install. This step is skipped if you only have Visual Basic.

The next steps of the installation depend on the current configuration of your computer and the version of Visual Basic that you are installing. The steps discussed here assume that you are using the Enterprise Edition. Once you have entered the information for the three steps above, the Setup wizard checks your computer for the correct version of Internet Explorer. If you have version 4.01 or higher, Setup will skip the installation of Internet Explorer. Otherwise, IE 4.01 is installed and you will need to reboot your computer.

Verify the installation of IE 4.01. If you are installing the Enterprise Edition, you will be asked if you wish to install the Distributed Component Object Model (DCOM). DCOM is required if you are planning to create distributed applications, such as n-tier client/server or Internet applications. For desktop-only applications, DCOM is not required.

At this point, you come to the Custom dialog box of the Setup wizard, shown in Figure 2.9.

FIGURE 2.9

Choosing installation options

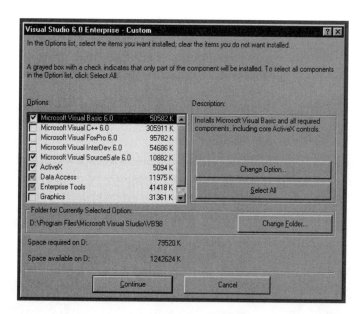

This dialog box lets you select the specific installation options for your computer. You can choose from several options:

Visual SourceSafe This is a version control tool that helps you manage changes between versions of your application. Each component of your application is stored in a repository. As program changes are made, Visual SourceSafe tracks the changes and who made them. Visual SourceSafe is very beneficial for multiple-developer environments.

ActiveX controls This is a group of controls beyond the standard TextBox and Label controls. These controls include data grids, the StatusBar control, Toolbar control, and many other controls. You should install these if you are creating programs that require more than the simplest set of controls.

Data Access This is a group of DLLs required for creating database applications. The DLLs include those required for ActiveX Data Objects, the Data Environment, and ODBC drivers. You can also select to install specific data-access methods, all methods, or none.

Enterprise Tools This group of tools includes the Visual Component Manager, which makes it easier to manage and reuse components that you create in Visual Basic. The group also includes the Microsoft Visual Modeler, which helps you create object models for object-based programs.

After selecting the items you wish to install, click the Continue button to begin the actual installation of files. After the Setup program completes the installation of the Visual Basic files, you will be prompted to install the Microsoft Developer's Network Library. This library contains all the documentation for Visual Basic and all the help files. All of this information is presented in the form of HTML Help, as shown in Figure 2.10.

The next installation screens let you choose to install client tools such as InstallShield and Server components. To install one of these tools, highlight the tool in the dialog box and click the Install button. The final installation screen prompts you to register your copy of Visual Basic 6. Registration provides you with notification of updates and allows you access to the owners'

F I G U R E 2.10

HTML Help for
Visual Basic

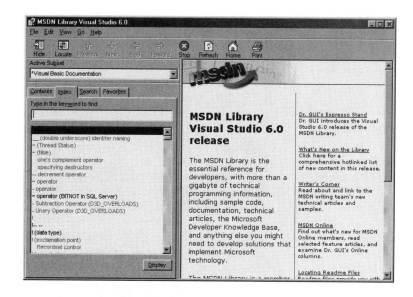

area of the Microsoft Web site. On the Web site, you can find additional custom controls and sample programs. You will also have access to the Microsoft Knowledge Base to help you with troubleshooting your programs.

Configuring Your Environment

After you have installed Visual Basic, you can start the program and begin creating applications. When you first start Visual Basic, you will be asked to choose a project type to create. There are a number of different project templates that you can use to create your applications. After you have chosen the project type, you will be in the Integrated Development Environment (IDE). The default appearance of the IDE is shown in Figure 2.11. You can configure the IDE to suit your needs. Each of the windows in the IDE can be docked or moved to another location on the screen. In addition, you can add other windows and menus to the IDE using the options of the View menu. This allows you to customize the environment to meet your specific needs and preferences.

FIGURE 2.11

Using the Integrated
Development
Environment (IDE)

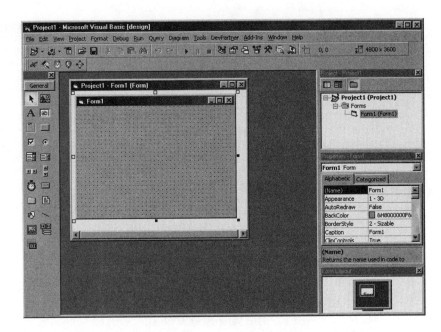

When you first start Visual Basic or when you choose the New Project
item from the File menu, you are presented with the New Project dialog box,
shown in Figure 2.12.

FIGURE 2.12

Choosing a
project type

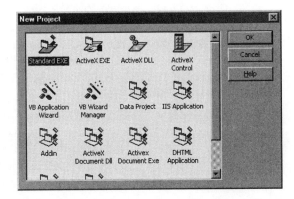

From this dialog box you can choose one of several built-in project templates for creating your applications. For many projects, you will need to add references and controls to these base templates for your particular application. If you have a particular set of references and controls that you use for multiple projects, you can set up your own template. To set up a template, perform these steps:

1. Open a project template closest to the requirements for your project.

2. Add the references and controls that you need to the new project.

3. Save the project in the Template folder under the directory where Visual Basic is installed. The next time you start a new project, your custom template will be one of the options available to you.

Establish the Environment for Source Code Version Control

1. Visual SourceSafe is a tool for providing _____ to your applications.

2. True or False. Using version control is highly recommended in a multiple-programmer environment.

3. Before you can use Visual SourceSafe, you must

_____ .

4. True or False. A password is optional for a user of Visual SourceSafe.

5. The first step to adding a project to Visual SourceSafe is to

_____ .

6. True or False. You must add all files in your project to Visual SourceSafe.

7. After a project is in Visual SourceSafe, you must

_____ the project before you can modify it.

8. The two main functions of a version control program are to

_____ and _____ .

9. After you have modified a project, you should

_____ the files of the project.

10. True or False. You can obtain a read-only copy of a project from Visual SourceSafe.

Install and Configure Visual Basic for Developing Desktop Applications

11. True or False. You must have Internet Explorer 4.01 or higher to use some functions of Visual Basic.

12. For creating distributed applications, you must install _____ with Visual Basic.

13. All help and documentation for Visual Basic is contained in _____ files.

14. True or False. You can move windows of the IDE around to meet your needs.

15. To use a particular set of controls and references for multiple projects, you can save the information as a _____.

SAMPLE TEST

2-1   Which of the following items are required for you to log into Visual SourceSafe? Check all that apply.

     A. Username

     B. Password

     C. Project name

     D. Database

2-2   Which of the following items are functions of the Visual SourceSafe Administrator program? Check all that apply.

     A. Checking in projects

     B. Managing users

     C. Modifying SourceSafe databases

     D. Managing Access databases

2-3   Visual Basic help is contained in which of the following formats?

     A. HTML Help

     B. WinHelp

     C. Access databases

     D. Text files

SAMPLE TEST

2-4 What version of Internet Explorer is required for use with Visual Basic?

    A. Internet Explorer is not required.

    B. Version 3.

    C. Version 4.01 or higher.

    D. Any version will work.

2-5 Which of the following items must be installed with Visual Basic to handle version control?

    A. Internet Explorer

    B. Visual Component Manager

    C. Distributed Component Object Model

    D. Visual SourceSafe

2-6 Which Visual Basic menu helps you manage the windows and toolbars of the IDE?

    A. File

    B. View

    C. Edit

    D. Window

U N I T

3

Developing the
Basic User Interface

Test Objectives: Creating User Services

- **Implement navigational design.**

  - Dynamically modify the appearance of a menu.

  - Add a pop-up menu to an application.

  - Create an application that adds and deletes menus at run time.

  - Add controls to forms.

  - Set properties for controls.

  - Assign code to a control to respond to an event.

 Exam objectives are subject to change at any time without prior notice and at Microsoft's sole discretion. Please visit Microsoft's Training & Certification Web site (www.microsoft.com/Train_Cert) for the most current exam objectives listing.

his unit is the first of five that cover objectives related to creating user services. This unit examines how to create the basic interface design of a program, how to create a menu for your program, and how to manipulate controls to create the interface.

Implement Navigational Design

The user interface is the most important element of most programs. This is because the interface is the part of the program that your users see and with which they interact. In many cases, if the interface is bad, it doesn't matter how well the program works, people will not use it. Therefore, good interface design and implementation is essential for your programs.

One key feature of most user interfaces is the program menu. The menu provides convenient access to most, if not all, the functions and options available in a program. A well-designed menu presents these functions to the user in a logical and well-organized manner.

While Visual Basic allows you to include a menu on any form in your program, most programs have a single menu on the main form of the program. This design is implemented in most of the programs that you commonly use, such as Word, Excel, or even Visual Basic itself. In fact, looking at these other programs gives you some valuable insight into how to design the menu of your own programs. The main menu of Visual Basic, shown in Figure 3.1, illustrates how functions are organized into related groups. For example, the File menu contains items that enable the user to create new projects, to open existing projects, to save files, and to exit the program.

When you design a menu for your program, follow the conventions illustrated in Visual Basic's menu. Try to group your functions into logical categories, such as File, Edit, View, Tools, Window, and Help. Most of these menu categories are in most programs you use. Of course, you are not lim-

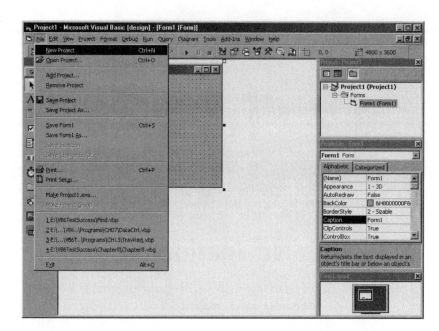

ited to just these categories, but you should use these standard names when you have functions that fit in the categories. Using standard categories makes the interface of your program more intuitive for users.

Creating and Modifying Menus

The tool for creating menus in Visual Basic is the Menu Editor. This editor, shown in Figure 3.2, is the only means of creating both the main menu of your program and any pop-up menus. The Menu Editor enables you to set the properties of each menu item and to organize all the items into a menu hierarchy.

To create a menu item, enter a value in the Name property of the item. The Name is the only required property of a menu item. However, you will also set the Caption property of most items. The Name property is used to identify the menu item to your program. The Name is used as a reference to the item when you make changes to the properties in code. The Caption property contains the text that is seen by the user of the menu.

F I G U R E 3.2

Visual Basic's Menu
Editor

You should set a value of the Caption property of each item in the menu
even if you change the text later in code. Having a value in the Caption
property makes it easier for you to identify individual items while in the
design environment.

As an exercise, follow these steps to create the top-level menu items for a
typical menu:

1. Type **File** in the Caption property of the first menu item, and type
   mnuFile in the Name property.

2. Press Enter to accept the values and move to the next item in the menu.

3. Repeating steps 1 and 2, create several other top-level menus using the
   values in Table 3.1.

4. When you have finished entering the values, click the OK button of the
   Menu Editor to accept the menu. The menu you created should look
   like the one shown in Figure 3.3.

T A B L E 3.1	Caption	Name
Values for Top-Level Menus	Edit	mnuEdit
	View	mnuView
	Tools	mnuTools
	Window	mnuWindow
	Help	mnuHelp

F I G U R E 3.3

Typical main menu for a program

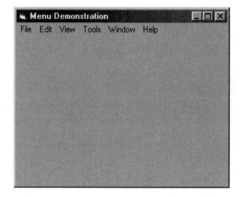

Most menus contain not only top-level items but also one or more levels of submenu items. The Menu Editor makes it easy for you to create these submenus as well. To create a submenu, you create a new menu item below the main-menu item and indent the new item. Each level of indentation in the Menu Editor corresponds to a sublevel of a menu. As an example, perform the following steps to create two levels of submenus below the File menu:

1. Open the Menu Editor in Visual Basic.

2. Click the Edit item in the menu organizer at the bottom of the dialog box.

3. Click the Insert button to create a new item above the Edit item.

4. Click the Right Arrow button to indent the new item and to indicate that it is a subitem of the File menu.

5. Type **New** in the Caption property of the new item and **filNew** in the Name property.

6. Repeat steps 2–5 to add other items. Add three items using Open, Close, and Exit for the Caption properties and filOpen, filClose, and filExit for the Name properties.

7. Click the Open item and use the Insert and Right Arrow buttons to create a subitem of the New menu.

8. Type **Database** as the Caption property and **newDatabase** as the Name property.

9. Repeat steps 7 and 8, typing **Text** as the Caption property and **newText** as the Name property.

When you have finished the steps, the Menu Editor looks like the one shown in Figure 3.4. After you click the OK button of the Menu Editor to accept the changes, your menu will contain two sublevel menus as shown in Figure 3.5.

FIGURE 3.4

Sublevel menus in the editor

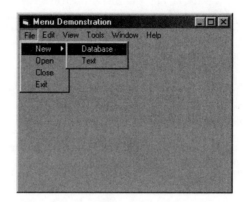

Using these basic steps, you can create any menus you need for your
program.

Dynamically Modifying the Appearance of a Menu

The discussion so far has focused on creating the menu structure for the program. However, another component of creating a good menu is to make it
visually appealing and easy to use. There are some simple steps that you can
take to achieve both of these goals.

Modifying a Menu from the Design Environment

Most menus contain more than a few items. As the list of items for a single
section of the menu, such as the File section, increases, it becomes harder for
a user to navigate. To alleviate this problem, notice that most menus contain
separator bars to break a menu section down into smaller groups. Separator
bars are easy to create in the Menu Editor. To create a separator, insert a
new menu item and place a single hyphen (-) in the Caption property of the
item. Of course, you must also specify a name for the item. A separator bar
item places a horizontal bar across the width of the drop-down menu. This
bar cannot be clicked by the user but serves to provide additional organization to the menu.

To make a menu easier to use, you can provide keyboard navigation capabilities to the menu. This can be accomplished through the use of shortcut
keys and access keys. Shortcut keys are key combinations that immediately
invoke a menu item. A shortcut key for an item is specified in the Shortcut

Key property of the menu item. There are approximately 70 shortcut key combinations that can be used in a menu, but each combination can be used only once. When you specify the shortcut key, the combination is displayed beside the text of the menu item.

If you use a shortcut key that is the same as a Windows shortcut key (e.g., Ctrl+C), the code in your menu item will override the default Windows functionality for your program.

Access keys also enable the user to select menu items with a series of key-strokes. An access key is defined by placing an ampersand (&) in front of a character in the Caption property of the menu item. When an access key is defined for a top-level menu, the user can select the menu by holding down the Alt key and pressing the letter associated with the hotkey. Once the drop-down menu is activated, an item with a hotkey can be accessed by pressing the key. Access keys are indicated in the menu by an underscored character. Figure 3.6 shows the use of separator bars, shortcut keys, and access keys.

FIGURE 3.6

Adding to the appearance and usability of a menu

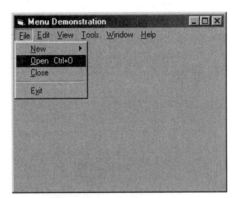

Modifying the Appearance of a Menu from Code

For some applications, the menu is finished when you close the Menu Editor of Visual Basic. However, many programs require you to modify the appearance of a menu while the program is running. This is accomplished by setting some of the properties of menu items with program code.

One of the most common changes made while a program is running is to disable or hide menus or menu items when certain conditions are met. For example, in a word processor program, you do not want the Edit menu available to the user unless a document is open for editing. To accomplish this, you set the Visible property of the Edit menu to False when you are in the Menu Editor or as the program starts. When you set the Visible property to False, the menu and any associated submenus are hidden from view. Then, when a document is opened, you can use an assignment statement to change the Visible property to True, thus displaying the menu for the user. This is illustrated in the following statement:

```
mnuEdit.Visible = True
```

If you want the menu items to be visible but don't want the user to be able to access them, you can set the value of the Enabled property. Setting Enabled to False disables the menu item but leaves it displayed. This effect is indicated to the user by showing the item as gray text instead of black. To allow the user to access the menu, change the Enabled property to True.

Another reason for changing the appearance of a menu is to indicate that certain options have been selected. If you use a menu item to toggle an option on or off, you can indicate when the option is on by placing a check mark to the left of the menu item. To do this, you set the value of the Checked property of the menu item. If the value is True, the check mark is shown; otherwise the check mark does not appear. Figure 3.7 shows the use of the Checked property.

FIGURE 3.7

Indicating the status of an option with the Checked property

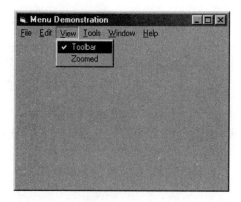

The final change that you can make to the appearance of a menu is to change the Caption property using program code. By changing the Caption property, you can change the text that is shown to the user, as well as changing the access key for the menu item.

Adding a Pop-up Menu to an Application

Pop-up menus are commonplace in many of today's computer programs. These menus provide the user with a way to access menu items that are appropriate to the task at hand. For example, if you right-click in various parts of the Visual Basic interface, you will see a variety of pop-up menus. Right-click on the toolbar and you get a menu that enables you to configure the toolbar to your liking. Right-click a control on a form and you get a menu that lets you move the control or open its Properties window. Figure 3.8 shows an example of a control pop-up menu.

FIGURE 3.8

One of Visual Basic's pop-up menus

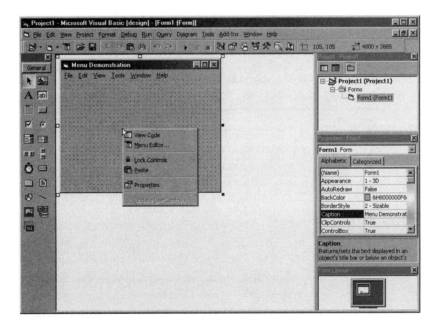

You can create pop-up menus in your programs as well. In fact, you can create a number of pop-up menus to provide the same type of context-sensitive menus that you see in Visual Basic and other programs. For each pop-up menu you use, you need to perform two tasks:

- Create the menu items.

- Invoke the menu in response to a user action.

The first step, creating the menu items, is the same as creating menu items for the main menu bar of a program. You open the Menu Editor and enter the items as part of a menu group. This group can appear on the main menu, or you can set the Visible property of the top-level item to False to have the menu appear only in response to a user action. A pop-up menu can be created from any level of your menu and can have multiple sublevels of menu items.

After the menu is created, it is a simple matter to activate the pop-up menu. The PopupMenu method of the Form object handles all the work for you. You specify the method and the name of the menu item that is the top-level item of the pop-up. As an example, the following code would activate a pop-up menu named popFormat:

```
Me.PopupMenu popFormat
```

When calling the PopupMenu method, you would typically specify the name of the form using the method. However, if you want to use the same form that contains the code, the Me keyword can be substituted for the name of the form.

The real key to activating a pop-up menu is choosing the event that will be used to show the menu. Typically, users expect to see the pop-up menu in response to the click of the right mouse button. You can handle this by placing the code for the PopupMenu method in the MouseDown or MouseUp (typically the MouseUp) event of the form or a control. These events tell you which button was clicked, whether a shift key was pressed, and the location of the mouse pointer when the button was pressed. Knowing the location allows you to activate separate menus for different areas of the form. The following code would be used to display the Format menu when the user clicks the right mouse button on any open area of the form:

```
Private Sub Form_MouseUp(Button As Integer, Shift As _
Integer, X As Single, Y As Single)
If Button = vbRightButton Then
    Me.PopupMenu popFormat
End If
End Sub
```

Adding and Deleting Menu Items

Changing the properties of your menu items is one way to modify the appearance of a menu at runtime. However, in many programs there is a need to add or remove menu items from the menu as the program is run. The most typical applications of this technique are keeping a recently used file list and keeping a list of currently open windows. Each of these tasks adds and deletes menu items at runtime, but each works in a different way.

One method of adding and deleting menus at runtime only works with Multi-Document Interface (MDI) programs. A feature of Visual Basic's menu system enables you to automatically keep track of all the open child windows of an MDI application. The way to handle this is to select a menu item in the Menu Editor, typically the Window item, and to set the WindowList property of the item to True. With this property set, a menu item is added to the menu group each time a child window is opened in the program. As the child window is closed, the menu item is removed. Figure 3.9 shows a typical application of the WindowList feature.

While the WindowList is a convenient way to add and remove menu items, it is limited in its functionality. First, it only shows the open MDI child windows of an application. It does not show any other open windows. Second, you cannot add your own items to the WindowList.

The second method of adding and deleting menu items involves the use of a menu item array. An array is a group of menu items with the same Name property and different values of the Index property. One of the most common uses of a menu control array is to keep a list of the most recently used files for a program. You can see this in programs like Word or Excel where the File menu contains the names of the last three or four files that you accessed.

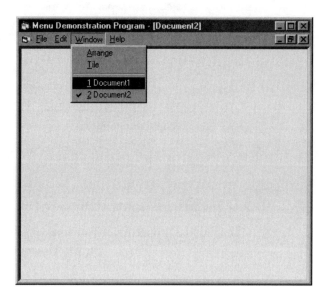

While creating menu items on the fly is not difficult, there are several tasks that you must complete:

- You must create at least one element of the array in the Menu Editor. Visual Basic does not allow you to create a menu item array completely in code. It only allows you to add or remove items from the array. To create the first element of the menu item array, set the Index property of the menu item to zero. This indicates that the item is part of an array, not just a single menu item.

- You must use the Load statement to add items to the array. To use the Load statement, you must specify the name of the control array and the index of the element to be added. This index value must be unique. To ensure that the index value is unique, you can use the UBound property of an array to determine the index of the last element and add one to that value.

- You must use the Unload statement to remove elements from the array. To use the Unload statement, you must again specify the name of the menu item array and the index to be removed. You cannot, however, remove any items in the array that were created with the Menu Editor.

- You can only write code in a single procedure to handle all the elements of the menu item array. The Click event is tied to the Name of the array; however, the index information is passed to the procedure, and you can use a Select statement to handle separate tasks for individual array elements.

The following code shows you how items are added to a menu item array using the Load statement:

```
Dim I As Integer, J As Integer
For I = 1 To 4
    J = filMRUFile.UBound + 1
    Load filMRUFile(J)
    filMRUFile(J).Caption = Trim(Str(I)) & " - File" & _
    Trim(Str(I))
    filMRUFile(J).Visible = True
Next I
```

Adding Controls to Forms

Menus are one of the key elements of your program's interface. Controls are the other key element. The controls of the program are where most of the interaction between the user and the program occurs. For example, the text box enables the user to enter data into the program and can also be used to display results to the user. The command button provides a way for the user to initiate an action. And the Picture box control provides a means for displaying and editing images in your program.

The first step to using controls in a program is to add them to the form. The simplest way to add a control is to double-click the control in the toolbox. This adds an instance of the control to the center of your form. After the control is added, you can move the control to the desired location and change its size using the mouse. A second method of adding a control to a form is to click the control in the toolbox, then click-and-drag the mouse on the form. The control is placed with one corner where you initially clicked the mouse. The size of the control is determined by how far you drag the mouse from the origin. As you drag the mouse, an outline shows you the size of the control that you are creating. In addition, if you rest the mouse, a tooltip will show you the exact size of the control in twips. This is illustrated in Figure 3.10.

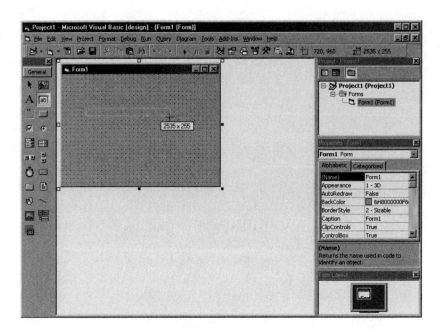

F I G U R E   3.10

Sizing a control with
the mouse

If you are using a scale mode other than twips, the size and position of the
control is displayed in the selected units.

Setting Control Properties

As you add controls to the forms of your program, you control the behavior
and appearance of these controls and of the forms themselves through the
properties of each control. Properties such as Left, Top, Height, and Width
determine the size and position of each control. These four properties, along
with the Name property, are common to every control you use. The availability of other properties depends on the specific control you are using.

While you are in design mode, you change the properties available at
design time through the Properties window of the Visual Basic design environment. This window, shown in Figure 3.11, allows you to easily set the
properties by providing descriptions of the properties, drop-down lists for

any properties that have only a specified set of values, and even dialog boxes for some properties such as Font, or ForeColor and BackColor. All these elements are designed to make it as easy as possible for you to create your programs.

F I G U R E   3.11

Setting control properties in the design environment

Writing Code for Events

While menus and controls make up the user interface of a program, it is the program code that does the actual work in any program you develop. The code of your program can perform any type of task, such as checking the spelling of words in a document or determining the balance of your checkbook. All code in a Visual Basic program is executed in response to an event that occurs in the program. An event can be the start-up of the program, the loading of a form, or an action initiated by a user.

Events are Visual Basic's way of notifying you that the form has received a Windows message from the operating system. These messages can indicate that the user has pressed a key, clicked a mouse button, or taken some other action. The events can also be triggered in response to system events or control events, such as having a specified amount of time elapse. While there are a large number of events available for each control and for forms (take a look at the form event list in the Code window), your program will only respond to events for which you have written program code. All other events are ignored.

Program code can be divided into two major categories:

- Assignment statements are used to set the value of a control's property or of a variable. You saw such a statement earlier in this unit when you modified the appearance of a menu item.

- Control statements, as their name implies, control the flow of a program. These statements include For...Next loops, If...Then...Else...End If structures, and others.

To write code for an event, you must first determine two things:

- To which event you want your program to respond

- What task will be performed in response to the event

The most common event that is used in programs is the Click event. The Click event is the only event supported by a menu item. It is also the primary event for a command button and is available in many other controls. Follow the steps below to create a simple program that adds two numbers together in response to a user clicking a command button:

1. Open a new project.

2. Add three text boxes to the form. Name the text boxes txtInput1, txtInput2, and txtOutput. For each of the text boxes, clear the Text property.

3. Add a command button to the form, and name it cmdAddition. Set the Caption property of the button to Add Numbers.

4. Double-click the command button to open the Code window as shown in Figure 3.12. (You can also open the Code window by clicking the View Code button in the Project window or by pressing F7.)

5. Make sure that cmdAddition is showing in the Object list (the left-hand list) of the Code window and Click is showing in the procedure list (the right-hand list).

FIGURE 3.12

Writing code in the
Code window

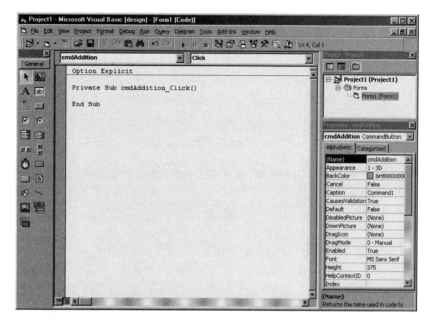

6. Add the following code to the window:

```
Dim sngInput1 As Single, sngInput2 As Single
Dim sngOutput As Single
sngInput1 = Val(txtInput1.Text)
sngInput2 = Val(txtInput2.Text)
sngOutput = sngInput1 + sngInput2
txtOutput.Text = sngOutput
```

7. Click the Run button on the Visual Basic toolbar. Then enter a
number in each of the input text boxes, and click the command
button. The results of the addition are shown in the output text box.

Implement Navigational Design

1. The _____ and _____ properties of the menu item determine whether an item is accessible by a user.

2. True or False. The Name property of the menu item determines the text that is seen by the user.

Dynamically Modify the Appearance of a Menu

3. You can change the menu item text and its associated hotkey by modifying the _____ property in code.

4. The letter for a menu item's hotkey is preceded by the _____ character.

5. True or False. You can change the value of a menu item's shortcut key from code.

6. The _____ property of the menu item is often used to indicate a selection made by the user by placing a check mark next to the item.

7. True or False. Menu items created with the Menu Editor can be moved to other menus using program code.

8. True or False. Your program can have only a single menu bar.

9. True or False. Each form in your program can have only a single menu bar.

10. To hide a menu from the user, you set its _____ property to False.

11. True or False. When you hide a menu item, all its subitems are also hidden.

12. True or False. The Index property of a menu item is used to set its position in the menu.

Add a Pop-up Menu to an Application

13. True or False. A pop-up menu cannot appear as an item on the main menu bar of a form.

14. A pop-up menu can be displayed using the forms _____ method.

15. True or False. A pop-up menu is automatically displayed when the user clicks the right mouse button.

16. True or False. A pop-up menu can contain subitems.

17. The _____ property determines the text seen by the user for a pop-up menu item.

18. True or False. A form can have only one pop-up menu.

19. True or False. Right-clicking the mouse is the only action that will invoke a pop-up menu.

Create an Application That Adds and Deletes Menus at Run Time

20. The _____ property is the same for each menu item in a control array.

21. True or False. You can create all the elements of a menu item control array in code.

22. The elements of a menu item control array are distinguished by the value of the _____ property.

23. To add elements to a control array, you use the _____ statement in your code.

24. True or False. All menu items in a control array share the same event code.

25. To remove items from a control array, you use the _____ statement in your code.

26. True or False. Using code, you can remove control array items that were created with the Menu Editor.

27. To have your menu automatically track open child windows, you need to set the _____ property of a menu item.

28. True or False. You can set up a menu item to track all open windows of your program.

Add Controls to Forms

29. True or False. You can add a control to your form by double-clicking the control in the toolbox.

30. You control the position of a control using the _____ and _____ properties.

31. True or False. You can add controls to your form at runtime using program code.

32. True or False. Controls added to your form at design time can be removed by program code.

33. Controls you add with program code cannot be seen by the user until you change the value of the _____ property.

34. True or False. Forms are the only containers you can use for a control in your program.

35. True or False. Controls provide the only means by which a user can interact with your program.

Set Properties for Controls

36. The size of a control is controlled by the _____ and _____ properties.

37. The position of a control is always specified in relation to the _____ corner of the control's container.

38. True or False. The properties of a control that you set at design time cannot be changed at runtime.

39. The _____ and _____ properties determine the colors used by the control.

40. True or False. In the design environment, you can simultaneously modify the properties of multiple controls of the same type.

41. True or False. In the design environment, you can simultaneously modify the properties of multiple controls of different types.

42. Most controls have the _____ property, which determines whether the user will see the control on the form.

43. The default property of a control is also known as its _____ property.

Assign Code to a Control to Respond to an Event

44. True or False. You must write code for every possible event a control can receive.

45. You can detect keystrokes in the _____, _____, and _____ events.

46. The _____ and _____ events enable you to determine whether a control key was pressed with a keystroke.

47. The _____ and _____ events tell you which mouse button was pressed.

48. True or False. Program code in an event procedure can consist of only a single line of code.

49. True or False. You can call an event procedure from other parts of your program.

SAMPLE TEST

3-1 What is the purpose of the Checked property?

    A. To place a check box next to the menu item

    B. To verify that the menu item is valid

    C. To display or hide a check mark next to the menu item

    D. To show or hide the menu item

3-2 Which of the following statements are true of pop-up menus? Check all that apply.

    A. A pop-up menu can have multiple levels.

    B. A pop-up menu can also be displayed as part of the main menu.

    C. The pop-up menu is automatically invoked by clicking the right mouse button.

    D. You can have multiple pop-up menus on a form.

3-3 How do you invoke a pop-up menu?

    A. Visual Basic does it automatically for you.

    B. Use the Load command and specify the Menu name.

    C. Use the PopupMenu method of the form.

    D. Use the ShowMenu command with the Pop-up option set.

3-4 Which Form events tell you which mouse button was clicked? Check all that apply.

    A. MouseDown

    B. Click

    C. MouseUp

    D. Keypress

3-5   Which property enables a menu item to keep a list with the names of MDI child windows?

    A. Index

    B. WindowList

    C. ShortcutKey

    D. Visible

3-6   What types of windows can be tracked automatically by Visual Basic? Select all that apply.

    A. Dialogs

    B. Standard windows

    C. MDI parent windows

    D. MDI child windows

3-7   Which property enables your code to distinguish between the elements of a menu item array?

    A. Caption

    B. Index

    C. Name

    D. ShortcutKey

3-8   How do you add elements to the menu item array through code?

    A. Use the Add method of the menu items collection.

    B. Use the Load statement.

    C. Change the Name and Index property of another menu item.

    D. Use the Add method of the form.

3-9 Which of the following statements about menu item arrays is false?

   A. You must create at least one element of the array in design mode.

   B. You cannot delete any elements that were created in design mode.

   C. You can delete all but the first element of the array.

   D. All array elements share the same event procedure.

3-10 How can you determine the last index value in a menu item array?

   A. Check the value of the Count property.

   B. Check the value of the UBound property.

   C. Check the LBound property.

   D. Use a loop to step through all the elements to find the Index of the last one.

3-11 Which of the following is a valid way to add a control to a form? Check all that apply.

   A. Double-click the control in the toolbox.

   B. Drag the control from the toolbox to the form.

   C. Select a control, then click-and-drag the mouse on the form.

   D. Right-click the form to bring up a list of controls to add.

3-12 Which properties of a control determine the position of the control within its container?

   A. Left and Top

   B. Right and Bottom

   C. Left and Width

   D. Height and Width

3-13 Where is the position of the upper-left corner of a control measured from?

  A. The upper-left corner of the form

  B. The lower-right corner of the form

  C. The upper-left corner of the control's container

  D. The lower-right corner of the control's container

3-14 Which of the following statements is the correct way to change the Text property of a text box?

  A. `Set Text = "New Value"`

  B. `ChangeText(txtInput, "New Value")`

  C. `txtInput.Text = "New Value"`

  D. `txtInput.Change "New Value"`

3-15 Which of the following is true for control event procedures?

  A. You must write code for every event that a control supports.

  B. The code for an event procedure must be at least two lines long.

  C. You only write code for events that you want your control to respond to.

  D. You can only write code for the Click event of a control.

3-16 What actions can cause events in a program?

  A. User actions

  B. System changes

  C. Program code

  D. All of the above

U N I T

4

Creating Data Input Forms
and Dialog Boxes

Test Objectives: Creating User Services

- **Create data input forms and dialog boxes.**

  - Display and manipulate data by using custom controls. Controls include TreeView, List-View, ImageList, Toolbar, and StatusBar.

  - Create an application that adds and deletes controls at run time.

  - Use the Controls collection to manipulate controls at run time.

  - Use the Forms collection to manipulate forms at run time.

Exam objectives are subject to change at any time without prior notice and at Microsoft's sole discretion. Please visit Microsoft's Training & Certification Web site (www.microsoft.com/Train_Cert) for the most current exam objectives listing.

Unit 3 covered the basics of creating a user interface for your program using standard controls. You also saw how to create and modify menus for your program. This unit extends the discussion of user interfaces by showing you how to use more advanced controls to add more functionality to your programs.

Create Data Input Forms and Dialog Boxes

In this unit, you will see how to use the TreeView, ListView, ImageList, Toolbar, and StatusBar controls. In addition, this unit covers some advanced coding techniques that enable you to add and delete controls at runtime and discusses how to manipulate controls and forms through the use of collections.

Displaying and Manipulating Data Using Custom Controls

The standard controls in Visual Basic enable you to create a wide variety of user interface designs. However, on many occasions other interface elements are required to make the interface both visually pleasing and easy to use. This is particularly true when the interface displays and manipulates large amounts of information. One group of controls that comes with Visual Basic provides you with a variety of tools to handle these more advanced interfaces. This set of tools is called the Windows Common Controls. The controls are contained in a single OCX file and consist of eight separate controls:

TreeView   Displays information in a hierarchical tree, like the left panel of Windows Explorer.

ListView   Displays information in a multicolumn list, like the right panel of Windows Explorer.

Toolbar   Lets you create the push-button toolbars that you see in most programs.

StatusBar   Allows you to present information to the user in a concise manner.

ProgressBar   Allows you to keep the user informed of the progress of a long operation.

ImageList   Provides an easy way to manage the images that are used by several of the other controls.

TabStrip   Allows you to create multiple pages on a single form, with each page being accessible by pressing a tab.

ImageCombo   Allows you to display a list of items, each with its own icon and with multiple indentation levels.

To use any of these controls, you must add the controls to the toolbox. To do this, right-click the toolbox and select the Components item from the pop-up menu. This brings up the Components dialog box shown in Figure 4.1. In this dialog box, you can select any available components by placing a check mark in the box next to the name of the control.

F I G U R E 4.1

Adding tools to the
toolbox

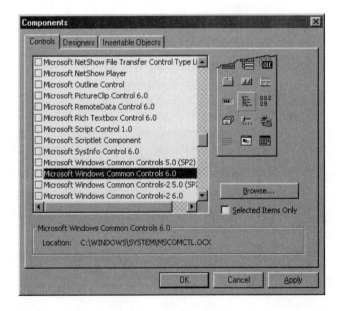

After you add the controls to the toolbox, you can add instances of the controls to a form in the same manner that you add standard controls. You can then set the properties of the controls and write code for their events.

Managing Images on Your Form

The first control that this unit explores is the ImageList control. This control does not have any user interface component of its own. Instead, the Image-List control is used to provide images for other controls such as the Tree-View, ListView, and Toolbar controls. The ImageList control can be completely set up from the design environment, or you can add images to the control with code. Unless you have specific needs to work with code, you should set up the ImageList control from the design environment. In addition to making it easier to set up the control, this method has the advantage of placing all the images in the form definition file, eliminating the need to distribute separate image files with your program.

Setting up the ImageList Control To begin setting up the ImageList control, you need to place an instance of the control on your form. Once you add the ImageList to your form, change the Name property of the control to something meaningful. This name is used in code and is used by any control that references the ImageList. After setting the Name property, click the button next to the Custom property to bring up the property pages as shown in Figure 4.2. This is the easiest way to set up the ImageList control. To manage the images, click the Images tab of the property pages.

The images of the ImageList control are contained in a collection of List-Image objects. The name of the collection is ListImages. Each object in the collection has four key properties that you will use in your program:

Index Specifies the numeric position of the object within the collection. The Index property of the ListImages collection starts with one and continues to the number of objects in the collection.

Picture Contains the image that is stored for the ListImage object.

Key Is a text string that uniquely identifies the image. The Key property can be used to refer to the image instead of having to use the Index of the collection.

Tag Allows you to associate other data with the image. This property is not used by Visual Basic itself, so you can set the value to anything that would be useful to you in your program.

FIGURE 4.2

Adding images to the
ImageList control

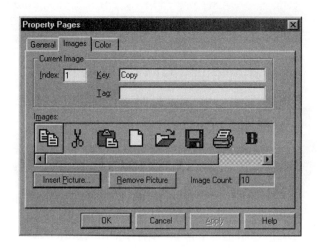

Adding a Picture to the ImageList Control   To add a picture to the
ImageList control, follow these steps:

1. Click the Insert Picture button in the dialog box.

2. Select a picture from the Select Picture dialog box. You can select from
   bitmaps, icons, JPEG files, etc.

3. After you select the picture, it will be displayed in the property pages
   of the ImageList. At this point, you can set the Key and Tag properties
   for the ListImage object. Notice that the Index property is set for
   you automatically.

To remove an image from the ImageList control, simply select the image
and click the Remove Picture button in the dialog box.

As stated previously, you can also manage the images in the ImageList
control using program code. The management of the images is handled
through three methods of the ListImages collection:

Add   Adds a new ListImage object to the collection.

Remove   Deletes a ListImage object from the collection.

Clear   Removes all ListImage objects from the collection.

To add pictures to the ImageList control, you use the Add method and specify the following:

- The index of the picture (optional parameter)
- The Key property, which specifies a unique identifier for the picture (also an optional parameter)
- The picture to be included

The picture source can be the Picture property of another control, such as an Image or PictureBox, or you can load a picture from a bitmap file using the LoadPicture command.

To remove one of the images, you use the Remove method of the collection and specify the index or key of the image to be removed.

Displaying Data with the TreeView Control

One of the controls you can use for displaying large amounts of data is the TreeView control. This control enables you to arrange information in a hierarchical structure that not only displays the data but also indicates the relation between the different levels of data. You are probably familiar with the directory tree that is shown in the left-hand panel of Windows Explorer. This is an example of the TreeView control.

When you use the TreeView control to display data, in addition to displaying data and its relations, you also give the user the ability to modify the view of the data. The TreeView control allows the user to expand and collapse branches of the tree to show as much or as little detail as desired, as shown in Figure 4.3. This capability can be very useful in many types of applications. For example, if you were listing all the attendees of a school, you might set up the first level of branches as the grades in the school. The next level would be the teachers in each grade, and the last level would show the students in each class. A user could then expand the branches of the tree to show all the teachers in a single grade, then all the students in a particular class.

In the TreeView control, each piece of information is displayed in an object called a node. In addition to displaying the data itself, you can set properties of the nodes to display pictures for the data and to display check boxes next to the data. The check boxes allow the user to select particular nodes for processing, and the pictures enable you to provide visual cues to the user about the data or about functions.

FIGURE 4.3

Using the TreeView
control

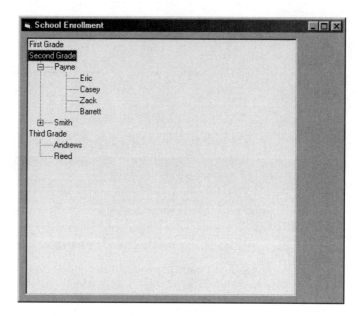

Creating the TreeView Control   The first step to using the TreeView control is to place an instance of the control on a form. You can then set the general properties of the control to determine how it will look and how it will behave. Some of the key properties of the TreeView control are as follows:

ImageList   Specifies the name of the ImageList control that contains the pictures used for the nodes of the tree.

Indentation   Specifies the number of twips that each level of the tree hierarchy is indented from its parent node.

LabelEdit   Specifies how the user can edit the label of the tree node. If the property is set to automatic, the user can click on the node label and begin editing. In this case, the BeforeLabelEdit event is fired when the user clicks on the node. If the property is set to manual, the user can edit the label only after the StartLabelEdit method has been invoked. In this case, the BeforeLabelEdit event is fired after the method is run.

LineStyle   Determines whether lines are drawn between root nodes or not. The default is not to draw the lines. In either case, the control draws lines between parent and child nodes.

Sorted Determines whether the root nodes of the tree are sorted alphabetically. There is also a Sorted property for each node of the tree that determines whether the child nodes of a given node are sorted.

Style Determines which combination of the following are displayed by the TreeView control: images, text, lines, and plus and minus signs to indicate the expansion of branches.

CheckBoxes Determines whether a check box is placed next to each node of the tree.

These properties are typically set using the property pages of the control, while you are in the design environment. The property pages are shown in Figure 4.4. You can also set most of these properties from program code.

FIGURE 4.4

Setting the TreeView properties

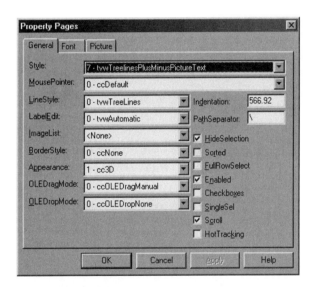

Creating the Nodes of the Tree You may have noticed in the property pages of the TreeView control (shown in Figure 4.4) that there was no provision for adding nodes to the tree. This is because all the nodes of the TreeView control must be added and deleted using program code. Each node of the tree is a separate object that is contained in the Nodes collection of the control. The Nodes collection is managed using the same methods you saw for the ImageList control. These are Add, Clear, and Remove. If you are getting the idea that collections play an important part in the programming of many controls and projects, you are correct. A good understanding of collections is essential to working with Visual Basic.

To add a node to the Nodes collection, specify the name of the TreeView control, the name of the collection, the Add method, and values for several parameters. The general syntax of the Add method is shown in the following code:

```
TreeView.Nodes.Add relative, relationship, key, text, _
image, selectedimage
```

Of these parameters, only the Text parameter is required. However, if other parameters prior to Text are omitted, their places must be held by commas. Each of these parameters specifies information about the node, as summarized here:

Relative   Specifies the Key value of the node to which the added node is related.

Relationship   Specifies the type of relationship that exists between the new node and the node specified in the Relative parameter. There are five possible settings for the Relationship property. The key one of these is the tvwChild setting, which specifies that the node being created is a child of another node.

Key   Specifies a unique identifier for the new node.

Text   Specifies the text to be displayed in the node.

Image   Specifies the index of an image in the ImageList control that is associated with the TreeView control. This image is shown whenever the node is visible unless the node is the selected node and the SelectedImage has been specified.

SelectedImage   Specifies the index of an image in the ImageList control that should be displayed when the node is selected.

To remove a node from the tree, you specify the Remove method of the Nodes collection and the Key value of the node to be removed.

Using the ListView Control to Handle Data

The ListView control is another control that enables you to display and manipulate large amounts of data. The ListView control provides you with four ways to display data items:

Icon   Displays each item as text with a large icon.

Small icon   Displays each item as text with a small icon.

List   Displays each item as simple text.

Report   Displays each item with a number of columns of detail data.

You can see each of these views of data by looking at the directory listings shown in the My Computer application of Windows 95/98. Of the four views, the report view is by far the most flexible and useful for displaying data. The report view enables you to define a number of columns for displaying detailed information related to each item listed in the first column of the ListView control. The other views only display this main piece of text.

Creating a ListView Control   To use the ListView control, you have to create an instance of the control on your form. Once this is done, you can use the property pages to set the basic properties of the control. The General page of the property pages (shown in Figure 4.5) lets you set which of the four types of view you want to use for displaying your data. This is set using the View property of the control.

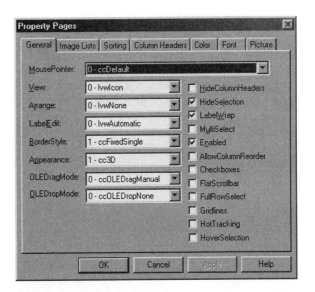

In addition to the View property, you can set a number of other properties which specify how the ListView control looks and behaves. Some of the key properties are as follows:

Arrange   Specifies whether items are aligned along the left edge of the control or the top edge of the control or are not aligned.

HideColumnHeaders   Specifies whether column headers are shown. This property only affects the report view of the ListView control.

LabelWrap   Determines whether the label of an item is wrapped to additional lines if the length of the line is greater than the icon spacing defined by the operating system. This option only affects the icon views of the ListView control.

MultiSelect   Specifies whether the user can select multiple ListItems in the ListView control, similar to the MultiSelect property of the ListBox control.

Checkboxes   Specifies whether check boxes appear next to the items of the list.

Creating Columns for a Report View   After you set the general properties of the ListView, you need to create the columns for the report view. In the design mode, you can create columns using the Column Headers page of the property pages. This page is shown in Figure 4.6.

FIGURE 4.6

Creating columns

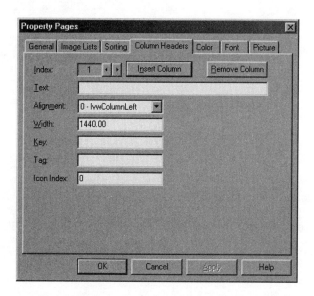

The columns of the report view are created by setting up ColumnHeader objects in the ColumnHeaders collection of the ListView control. Each ColumnHeader object defines one column of the control. Each ColumnHeader is identified by an index (from one to the number of columns) and the text that is displayed to the user. To create a new ColumnHeader, click the Insert Column button on the page. Notice that an index value is automatically assigned. Enter the text that will appear in the column header into the Text property. In addition, there are five other properties that you can set for each column:

Alignment   Specifies whether the text is left or right justified or centered in the column header.

Width   Specifies the width of the column.

Key   Specifies a string that uniquely identifies the column.

Tag   Contains text that you can use in your programming. The value of the Tag property is not used by Visual Basic.

IconIndex   Specifies the icon from the ImageList control that should be displayed in the column header.

You will need to create a column header for each column that you want to include in the report view of your data.

Adding Data to the ListView Control   After setting up the general appearance of the control and adding the column headers that you need for the List-View control, you need to add the data to be displayed. The data for a ListView control is contained in a collection of ListItem objects. These List-Items are managed in a manner similar to the nodes of the TreeView control. ListItems are added to and removed from the ListItems collection using the Add, Remove, and Clear methods.

Each ListItem that you create contains a Text property. This Text property is the only thing that is displayed if you are not using the report view of the ListView control. If you are using the report view, the information in the Text property is displayed in the first column of the ListView control. Each ListItem object also contains a collection of SubItems. The SubItems contain the information that is displayed in the other columns of the report view. There is a SubItem for each column in the ListView, other than the first column.

To create a ListItem with information in multiple columns, follow these steps:

1. Create an instance of the ListItem object by declaring a variable as a ListItem.

2. Add the instance of the ListItem to the ListItems collection using the Add method and specifying a value for the Text property.

3. Set the values for each SubItem in the ListItem object.

The following code shows how to do this for an order-entry system. The display for the system is shown in Figure 4.7.

```
Dim liOrderItem As ListItem
Set liOrderItem = lvwOrders.ListItems.Add(, , "Gloves")
With liOrderItem
    .SubItems(1) = 4
    .SubItems(2) = 10.50
    .SubItems(3) = Val(.SubItems(1)) * Val(.SubItems(2))
End With
```

FIGURE 4.7

Using ListView to display orders

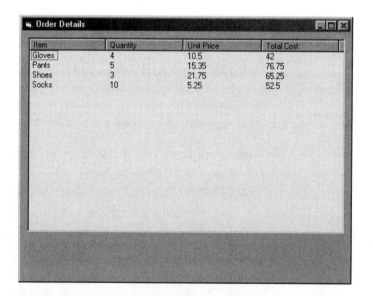

Item	Quantity	Unit Price	Total Cost
Gloves	4	10.5	42
Pants	5	15.35	76.75
Shoes	3	21.75	65.25
Socks	10	5.25	52.5

Using a Toolbar as an Alternative to Menus

You have probably noticed that most programs today contain toolbars in addition to menus. These toolbars provide the user with one-click access to the most commonly used functions of a program. While you can have only one menu on a form, you can create multiple toolbars for a form. You can even allow the user to customize the appearance of the toolbar, which is difficult to do with a menu.

While the Toolbar control handles most of the creation of a toolbar for your program, you also need an ImageList control on the form. The ImageList control provides the images that appear on the Toolbar buttons. Therefore, in order to create a toolbar, you need to set up two controls on your form.

The creation of an ImageList control was covered earlier in this unit.

Setting up the Toolbar Control   After placing an instance of the Toolbar control on your form, you can open the property pages, shown in Figure 4.8, to set up the toolbar. There are three properties that identify ImageList controls. These properties indicate which ImageList control is used for the main picture on the toolbar buttons, which to use for disabled buttons, and which to show when the mouse is positioned above a button. The drop-down lists for each of these properties contain the names of all ImageList controls on the current form. You can use the same ImageList control for all three properties or use a separate ImageList control for each one.

FIGURE 4.8

Setting general properties for a toolbar

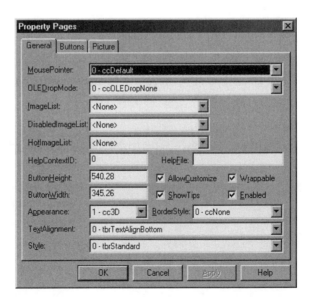

In addition to specifying the ImageList properties of the toolbar, the General page of the property pages lets you specify other properties as follows:

BorderStyle   Causes the toolbar to be displayed with a single-line border or no border (default).

Appearance   Causes the toolbar to be shown as a three-dimensional (default) or flat bar.

TextAlignment   Determines whether text on the toolbar button is placed below or to the right of the picture on the button.

Style   Determines whether the toolbar appears as a standard or flat toolbar.

ButtonHeight and **ButtonWidth**   Specify the size of the buttons in the toolbar.

ShowTips   Specifies whether the tool tip information entered in the ToolTips property of the Button object is displayed.

Wrappable   Specifies whether the toolbar creates a second row of buttons if there is insufficient space for all the buttons on a single row.

AllowCustomize   Specifies whether the user is allowed to customize the toolbar.

Creating Toolbar Buttons   After you have set the general properties of the toolbar, you are ready to create the actual buttons of the toolbar. Like the Nodes collection of the TreeView control and the ListItems collection of the ListView control, the Toolbar control uses a collection to manage the buttons shown in the bar. The collection is named Buttons, and the individual objects are Button objects.

To create the buttons for your toolbar, you need to access the Buttons page of the property pages, shown in Figure 4.9. To add a button, click the Insert Button command button of the dialog box . This sets up a new button for you and automatically sets the value of the Index property.

For each new button, you need to set the following three properties:

Image property   Specifies the picture to be shown on the button.

Key property   Specifies the name by which the button is referenced in code.

Style property   Specifies the appearance and behavior of the button.

FIGURE 4.9

Adding buttons to the
toolbar

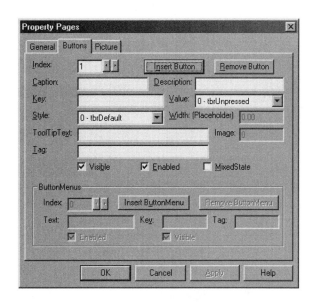

The Style property is the one that controls how the button looks and behaves. For most of your buttons, choose the Default style. This produces a standard toolbar button that the user can press to launch a task. There are a total of six styles of toolbar buttons that you can create in a toolbar. These styles are summarized below. An example of each of the styles is shown in Figure 4.10.

tbrDefault   Creates a standard button that can be clicked to launch a task.

tbrCheck   Creates a two-state button, such as the Bold button, that turns an option on or off and indicates the status of the option by the appearance of the button.

tbrButtonGroup   Creates one button of a group that allows a single option to be selected from the group. An example is the group of alignment buttons that allow the user to choose right-justified, left-justified, or centered alignment.

tbrSeparator   Creates an empty button with a width of eight pixels and provides a space between groups of buttons.

tbrPlaceHolder   Provides a space on the toolbar for other controls, such as a combo box, that can be used for providing multiple options.

tbrDropdown   Creates a drop-down menu that is shown when the button is pressed. The items of the menu are created with the ButtonMenu portion of the Toolbar dialog box.

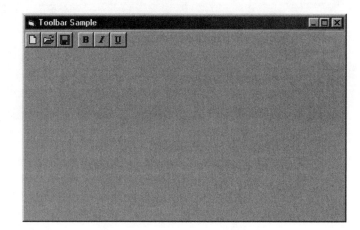

There are several other properties that you can use to customize the buttons of the toolbar. These properties are summarized in Table 4.1.

	Property	Description
TABLE 4.1 Optional Button Properties	Caption	Specifies the text that will appear on the face of the button. If only a Caption is specified (no Image property), the text appears in the center of the button. If an Image and Caption are both specified, the text appears below the picture in the button.
	Description	Provides a description of the button for the user, if customization of the toolbar is allowed.
	Value	Sets or returns the current state of the button. The value is 0 if the button is not pressed; 1 if the button is pressed.

T A B L E 4.1 *(cont.)*	**Property**	**Description**
Optional Button Properties	Width	Specifies the width of the button for the Placeholder style only. For all other button types, the width is ignored.
	Tag	Assigns other data to the button for use in your program.
	ToolTipText	Specifies the text that is displayed when the user pauses the mouse over the button. This text is displayed only if the ShowTips property of the toolbar is set to True.

Writing Code for the Toolbar Of course, creating the toolbar is only half the task of using it in your program. In order to make the toolbar functional, you have to add code to the events of the toolbar. The events and your code are what enable the toolbar to perform tasks when the user clicks a button.

The key event of the toolbar is the ButtonClick event. This event is fired whenever the user presses a button on the toolbar. The event passes an object reference to the button that was pressed. You can use the Key or Index property of the passed button to determine which button was clicked and to take the appropriate action. The following code uses the Key property to determine the button pressed and to call a menu-item Click procedure. The reason for using the menu procedures is that, in many cases, the function of the button is the same as the function of a menu item. Calling the menu item's procedure instead of repeating the code makes maintenance of the program easier.

```
Private Sub tlbSample_ButtonClick(ByVal Button As _
MSComctlLib.Button)
Select Case Button.Key
    Case "New"
        filNew_Click
    Case "Print"
```

```
        filPrint_Click
    Case "Bold"
        fmtBold_Click
End Select
End Sub
```

Displaying Status Information with the Status Bar

The final control covered in this unit is the StatusBar control. This control is typically located at the bottom of a form and displays various information about what is happening in a program. Like the other controls discussed, the parts of the StatusBar control are objects that are managed by a collection. In the case of the StatusBar control, each object is a Panel and the collection is the Panels collection.

After you have placed an instance of the StatusBar control on your form, you can set some of the general properties of the control. The Align property determines where the status bar is located. The typical position is at the bottom of the form, but the Align property allows you to set the control to be located at the top of the form, the bottom of the form, or on either side of the form. Another property is the Style property. This property determines whether the status bar contains a single line of text or shows multiple panels of information.

If you plan to have multiple panels of information, the easiest way to set up the panels is through the property pages shown in Figure 4.11. For each panel that you create in the status bar, the key property is the Style property. The Style property determines what information the panel contains. The available settings of the Style property are summarized below:

sbrText   Allows you to insert the text to be displayed. The panel will display the information contained in the Text property of the Panel object or will display the bitmap contained in the Picture property. This is the only setting that allows you to modify the information in the panel.

sbrCaps   Displays "CAPS" in the panel. When Caps Lock is on, the text is shown in normal text. When Caps Lock is off, the text displayed is dimmed.

sbrNum   Is similar to the sbrCaps option, except that this panel style displays "NUM" to indicate the status of the NumLock key.

F I G U R E   4.11

Adding panels to the
status bar

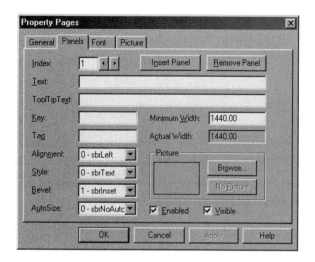

sbrIns   Is similar to the sbrCaps option, except that this panel style displays "INS" to indicate the status of the Insert key.

sbrScrl   Is similar to the sbrCaps option, except that this panel style displays "SCRL" to indicate the status of the Scroll Lock key.

sbrDate   Displays the current date.

sbrTime   Displays the current time.

sbrKana   Is similar to the sbrCaps option, except that this panel style displays "KANA" to indicate the status of a special setting used for handling Katakana characters in Japanese language programs.

In addition to the Style property, there are several other properties that control the appearance of each panel of the status bar. These are as follows:

Text   Specifies the text that will be displayed in the panel. This property is only valid with the sbrText style of panel.

Picture   Specifies the bitmap to be displayed in the panel. Like the Text property, this property is only valid with the sbrText style.

ToolTipText   Specifies the text to be shown if the user rests the mouse cursor on the panel.

Key   Contains a text string that uniquely identifies the panel in the collection.

Bevel   Determines whether the panel has a raised, indented (default), or flat appearance.

MinWidth   Specifies the minimum width of the panel.

Autosize   Controls how the panel is sized, while observing the minimum width constraint. This property has one of three settings:

sbrNoAutoSize   Causes the panel size to be set to the size specified in the MinWidth property.

sbrSpring   Causes the panel to occupy the remaining space in the status bar after all other panels have been sized. If more than one panel uses the sbrSpring setting, the remaining space is shared equally among these panels.

sbrContents   Causes the panel size to be adjusted to fit the contents of the panel, whether text or picture or both.

Adding and Deleting Controls at Run Time

In Unit 3, you saw how you could add and delete menu items using menu item arrays. These arrays allowed you to modify the appearance of the menu using program code. You can do the same thing with the controls on your forms. Working with control arrays enables you to add and delete some of the controls on your forms while the program is running. However, this is not the only advantage of using control arrays. Some of the other advantages of using control arrays are as follows:

- You can use a program loop to easily change the properties of all the controls in the array.

- The code for all the controls is contained in a single procedure, making code maintenance easier.

- Adding controls in the design environment is easier, making it more convenient to change the form design to meet changing user needs.

Of course, the key advantage of the control array is the ability to add and delete controls at runtime. This capability enables you to create data-entry forms that change as the data structure of a file changes. You can also write custom dialog boxes that allow a flexible number of inputs or are flexible in the data they display.

In addition to using control arrays, Visual Basic now gives you the ability to add a control to a form using code, without having to create an array. Using the Add method of the Controls collection, you can create a new control entirely from scratch.

Creating the Control Array

A control array is a group of controls of the same type that all have the same value for the Name property. Each control in the array is a fully functional instance of the control, and each control can have different property values from all the other controls. The thing that distinguishes the individual controls in the array and distinguishes an array element from a single control is the value of the Index property. If a control has a value in the Index property, the control is part of an array. Also, each control in an array must have a unique value for the Index property.

The initial element of a control array must be created in the design environment. There are two ways to create the first element of the control array. First, you can select a control, copy it by pressing Ctrl+C, then paste it back on the form by pressing Ctrl+V. Visual Basic then asks you if you want to create a control array. If you respond Yes, the second control is added to the form and the Index property of both controls is set. By default, the Index property of the first control is zero, although you can start a control array with any positive integer value.

The second method of creating the first element of a control array is to set the value of the Index property.

No matter which method you use to create the first element of the control array, all other elements of the array must be of the same type and have the same name as the first element. Which of these methods you use depends on how you want to use the control array. If you are using the array to make property setting and coding easier, you can use the copy-and-paste method. If you are planning to load controls from code, you will probably set the Index property, ensuring that the number of fixed elements in the control array is as small as possible.

NOTE Control arrays should be zero-based, meaning that the first element of the array should have an Index property value of zero. Additional elements of the array should be numbered consecutively. While Visual Basic does not enforce this, failing to follow this convention can cause problems in your programs.

After you have created the initial elements of the control array, you can add more elements in the design mode or with program code. If you are adding elements in the design mode, the easiest way to add another element is to copy an existing element and paste the copy to a new location on the form. In this way, the new element has all its properties (except Index, Left, and Top) set to the same values as the source element. This is very convenient for producing a group of identical controls, such as blank text boxes.

Adding Controls at Run Time

The big benefit of control arrays is the ability to add and delete elements at runtime. You add controls to the array using the Load statement. This statement specifies the name of the array and the element number that you wish to add. The Load statement is illustrated in the following code:

```
iUpper = txtMember.UBound + 1
Load txtMember(iUpper)
```

The code uses the Ubound property of the array to determine the highest index number currently in the array. By adding one to this value, you are assured that your new Index value is unique.

There are four properties of a control array:

Count   specifies the total number of elements in the array.

Item   returns a reference to a specific element of the array.

LBound   specifies the lowest index value of the array.

UBound   specifies the highest index value of the array.

Note that these properties are properties of the array itself, not of the individual controls in the array. To refer to an individual control, you specify the name of the array and the index value of the specific element, as shown in the following code:

```
txtMember(0).Text = "This is the first element."
```

When adding new elements to a control array at runtime, you must meet two specific criteria or an error will occur. These criteria are as follows:

- The control array must already exist. You cannot create the initial element of the array at runtime.

- The Index value specified in the Load statement must be unique.

After you have created the control using the Load statement, you can set its properties like any other control on your form. One important property to set is the Visible property. When the Load statement is used, it creates an instance of the control in memory but does not display the control. If you do not set the Visible property to True, the control cannot be seen by the user. Also, the properties of the newly added control are based on the properties of the first element of the array, so you need to adjust the position of the new element or it will be displayed in the same location as another control.

Deleting Controls from the Array

Removing controls from the array is very similar to adding the controls. To remove controls you use the Unload statement. With this statement, you specify the name of the array and the element to be removed. For an element to be removed from a control array without error, it must meet two criteria:

- The Index value must be valid.

- The element must be one that was added at runtime. You cannot remove a control-array element that was added in the design environment.

The Unload statement is illustrated in the following code:

```
iUpper = txtMember.UBound
Unload txtMember(iUpper)
```

Using the Controls Collection to Manipulate Controls at Run Time

Earlier in this unit, you saw how collections were important in handling the nodes of the TreeView control, the items of the ListView control, and the images of the ImageList control. An understanding of collections is very valuable in writing Visual Basic code. There are two other collections that are important, not only for your programming, but also for passing the certification exam: the Controls collection and the Forms collection.

The Controls collection provides a way to manage and manipulate each control on a particular form. Using the Controls collection, you can do the following:

- Modify a specific property of every control, such as Font or ForeColor.

- Work with database routines to create a generic data-access form or data-display routine.

- Show or hide specific types or groups of controls.

- Add new controls to the form.

There is a Controls collection for each form that you have in your program.

Understanding Collections and Arrays

Control arrays and the Controls collection both work with groups of controls. However, these two entities are not related, and it is important to understand the differences between the two. The following lists highlight the key features of the Controls collection and a control array so you can understand how they are different.

Control Arrays   A control array has the following characteristics:

- All elements of a control array are the same type of control.

- All elements of a control array have the same name.

- The Index properties of the control are set when the control is created and cannot be changed.

- The elements of a control array share the same set of event procedures.

- In code, an element of the control array is referenced by its name and Index property as shown in the following example:

```
cmdNavigation(1).Caption = "First Record"
```

Controls Collection   The Controls collection has the following characteristics:

- The Controls collection contains all controls on a form regardless of type.

- The Index value of an element in the collection is determined by when the control was added to the form.

- The elements of the Controls collection can have different names.

- There are no events associated with the Controls collection.

- In code, a member of the Controls collection is referenced by its index within the collection as shown in the following example:

```
Debug.Print Controls(0).Name
```

Changing Controls with the Controls Collection

One use of the Controls collection is to make a change to each of the controls on a form. For example, you might want to allow the user to change the foreground and background colors of the controls. To accomplish this, you would allow the user to pick two colors (probably using a common dialog-box control), then set the ForeColor and BackColor properties of each control on the form.

The method for working with the Controls collection is to use a For…Each loop. This variation of a For loop runs once for each item in a collection. The following code shows how a For…Each loop would be used to change the colors of all controls:

```
Dim chgControl As Control
For Each chgControl In Controls
    chgControl.ForeColor = vbBlue
    chgControl.BackColor = vbWhite
Next chgControl
```

Since this code is working with the Controls collection of the form on which it resides, you do not have to specify the form name with the Controls collection. To make the change to another open form, you would need to specify the form name; for example, frmMember.Controls.

Changing Specific Controls

Not every control has the same properties. In the example above, it was assumed that each control on the form had a ForeColor and BackColor property. However, many controls, such as a command button, do not have these properties. If you ran the above code on a form with a command button, you would encounter an error. There are two ways of handling this:

- Trap and handle the errors as they occur.

- Only operate on specific controls.

Error trapping is discussed in Unit 7, "Completing an Application."

The first step in working with specific controls is to determine the type of control that is being accessed. Visual Basic has a specific function for determining the type of a control: the TypeOf statement. The TypeOf statement cannot stand by itself in code but is used as part of a logical condition in an If statement as illustrated in the following code:

```
If TypeOf chgControl Is CommandButton Then
    chgControl.Font.Name = "Times New Roman"
    chgControl.Font.Bold = True
End If
```

Each control in Visual Basic has a type constant that can be used with the TypeOf keyword to determine if the current control is of a particular type. You can access a list of these constants in the VB library using the Object Browser, as shown in Figure 4.12.

FIGURE 4.12

Accessing constants using the Object Browser

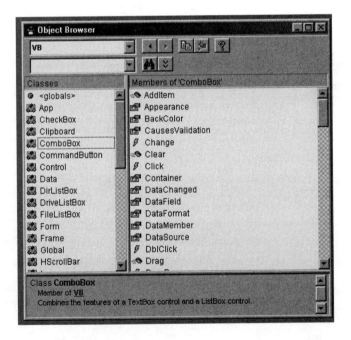

Using the TypeOf clause and a series of If statements, you can handle processing for multiple types of controls. The following code shows how you would set the ForeColor property of text boxes and labels, but ignore all other controls:

```
Dim chgControl As Control
For Each chgControl In Controls
    If TypeOf chgControl Is TextBox Then
        chgControl.ForeColor = vbRed
    ElseIf TypeOf chgControl Is Label Then
        chgControl.ForeColor = vbRed
    End If
Next chgControl
```

Using code such as this eliminates possible errors that occur from trying to set properties for controls that do not support them, such as setting a Font property for a Line control.

Adding Controls to a Form

In Visual Basic 6, you now have the ability to add a control to a form without having to create a control array. This ability gives you even more flexibility in the design and implementation of forms. To add a control to a form, you use the Add method of the Controls collection. Working with this method involves three basic steps:

1. Declare a variable to hold the reference to the control.

2. Use the Add method to create the instance of the control.

3. Set the properties of the control to position it on the form and make it visible to the user.

The following code shows how to add a text box to a form using the Add method:

```
Dim otxtNew As TextBox

Private Sub cmdAddControl_Click()
Set otxtNew = Controls.Add("VB.Textbox", "otxtNew")
With otxtNew
```

```
            .Visible = True
            .Text = "New Control"
            .Width = Me.TextWidth(.Text) + 200
            .Height = Me.TextHeight(.Text) + 50
            .Top = 50
            .Left = 50
      End With
      End Sub
```

Using the Forms Collection to Manipulate Forms at Run Time

Like the Controls collection, the Forms collection is a specialized collection that is automatically maintained by Visual Basic. The Forms collection contains a reference to every form that is currently loaded in your program. This means that the contents of the Forms collection changes throughout the operation of your program. Forms are added to the collection whenever you use the Load statement to load a form into memory. Forms are removed from the collection when you use the Unload statement.

As you probably know, the Load statement is implicitly invoked when you use the Show method to display a form that is not loaded.

There are several primary uses of the Forms collection in a program. The most common uses are to do the following tasks:

- Change the common properties (such as Font) of all loaded forms.

- Determine if a specific form is loaded.

- Ensure that all forms are explicitly closed prior to exiting a program.

As with the Controls collection, you can use a For…Each loop to work with the members of the Forms collection. If you are looking for a particular form, you can identify the form by its Name property. The following code illustrates the use of the For…Each loop to unload each open form in an application before closing the main form and exiting the program.

```
Dim frmLoaded As Form
On Error Resume Next
```

```
'Unload forms
For Each frmLoaded In Forms
    If frmLoaded.Name <> "frmMain" Then
        Unload frmLoaded
    End If
Next I
Unload frmMain
'Exit the program
End
```

STUDY QUESTIONS

Display and Manipulate Data by Using Custom Controls

1. The _____ control handles graphics images for use in other controls.

2. The _____ object contains the data that is displayed in the TreeView control.

3. The _____ view of the ListView control enables you to display multiple columns of data in the list.

4. The objects of the Toolbar control are called _____ objects.

5. The graphic in a ListImage object is contained in the _____ property.

6. True or False. You must add all the pictures you are going to use in the ImageList control while in Design mode.

7. The _____ method removes all the objects in a collection.

8. To remove a ListImage object from the ImageList control, you must specify either the _____ or _____ value with the Remove method.

9. The information displayed in a TreeView control is contained in the
_____ property of the Node object.

10. To create a child node, you must set the _____ to
the value _____.

11. True or False. You can only have two levels of branches in a TreeView control.

12. When relating one node of a TreeView to another node, you must specify values for the
_____ and _____
properties.

13. The _____ property of the ListView control
determines whether the user can select multiple items at once.

14. To define the columns of the ListView control, you create
_____ objects.

15. The information in the first column of a ListView control is contained in the
_____ property of the ListItem.

16. Information for the other columns of a ListView control is contained in the
_____ collection of the ListItem object.

17. True or False. You can change the view of a ListView control from code.

18.   The _____ property of the Button object determines the appearance of the button in the toolbar.

19.   To show tool tips in the toolbar, you must set the value of the _____ property to True.

20.   The _____ and _____ properties determine what appears on the face of a toolbar button.

21.   To create a series of buttons where only one can be pressed at a time, you set the Style property of the button to _____.

22.   True or False. The user can change the configuration of the toolbar while the program is running.

23.   For the Node, ListItem, ListImage, and Button objects, the _____ property provides an easy means of identifying individual objects.

24.   Code for launching program tasks is placed in the _____ event of the ToolBar control.

25.   True or False. The status bar can display only one piece of information at a time.

26.   The information in the status bar is contained in a _____ object.

S T U D Y   Q U E S T I O N S

27. The _____ style of a status-bar panel is the only one whose contents can be changed in code.

28. The _____ and _____ properties determine what is displayed in an sbrText style of panel.

29. True or False. The information in the sbrCaps style of panel is handled automatically by your program.

Create an Application That Adds and Deletes Controls at Run Time

30. True or False. All the controls in a control array must be of the same type.

31. The individual elements of a control array are identified by the _____ property.

32. True or False. Controls in a control array must be sequentially numbered.

33. True or False. All controls in a control array share the same event code.

34. True or False. You can add the first element of a control array to a form using program code.

35. The _____ statement is used to add an element to a control array from code.

36. The _____ property must be set for a newly added control to allow the user to access it.

37. True or False. Using code, you can only remove controls from the control array that were added at runtime.

38. The _____ property of the control array tells you the highest index number in the array.

39. True or False. When you add a new control to an array from code, it is automatically given a unique ID number.

Use the Controls Collection to Manipulate Controls at Run Time

40. True or False. The Controls collection is the same as a control array.

41. True or False. All the controls in the Controls collection must be of the same type.

42. A _____ loop is used to access each control in the Controls collection.

43. The _____ property of a control is used to uniquely identify controls in the Controls collection.

44. To determine which type of control you are working with, you need to use the _____ statement.

45.   True or False. If you try to set a nonexistent property of a control, an error occurs.

46.   True or False. You can remove controls from the Controls collection using the Remove method.

47.   True or False. There are no events associated with the Controls collection.

48.   True or False. There is only one Controls collection in each program.

Use the Forms Collection to Manipulate Forms at Run Time

49.   You add forms to the Forms collection using the _____ statement.

50.   True or False. The Forms collection references each form in a project.

51.   The _____ property of a form is used to distinguish an individual form.

52.   True or False. You must use the TypeOf statement to determine if a form supports a particular property.

53.   True or False. The For…Each loop is the only way to loop through all the forms in a program.

54.   The _____ statement is used to remove a form from the Forms collection.

SAMPLE TEST

4-1 Which style of Toolbar button allows you to select only one button from a series of buttons?

    A. tbrDefault

    B. tbrCheck

    C. tbrButtonGroup

    D. tbrDropDown

4-2 All of the following statements are true about toolbars except:

    A. You can only have one toolbar on a form.

    B. Toolbars can be positioned anywhere on the form.

    C. Toolbars can be customized by the user.

    D. Toolbar buttons can display both text and images.

4-3 Which properties of a Node object must be set to relate it to another Node? Check all that apply.

    A. Relative

    B. Text

    C. Key

    D. Relationship

4-4 Which property of a ListItem object contains the information shown in all views of a List-View control?

    A. Text

    B. Key

    C. Index

    D. SubItem(1)

SAMPLE TEST

4-5   Which object is used to define the columns of a ListView control?

    A. ListItem

    B. SubItem

    C. Column

    D. ColumnHeader

4-6   What is the limit on the number of SubItems in a ListItem object?

    A. One

    B. No Limit

    C. 10

    D. SubItems are limited by the number of columns defined for the ListView control.

4-7   Which views display the detail information of a ListItem that is contained in the SubItem array? Check all that apply.

    A. Icon view

    B. Report view

    C. Small icon view

    D. List view

4-8   Which of the following restrictions about adding a control to a control array at runtime is not true?

    A. You must set the Visible property of the control to make it accessible to the user.

    B. The control array must already exist.

    C. The Index value must be the next sequential number after the upper bound of the array.

    D. The Index of the new control must be unique.

4-9 Which of the following are properties of a control array? Check all that apply.

    A. Count

    B. LBound

    C. Index

    D. Name

4-10 Which of the following statements can be used to change the value of a property in an element of a control array?

    A. `txtMember.Top = 120`

    B. `txtMember(0).Top = 120`

    C. `txtMember.0.Top = 120`

    D. `txtMember0.Top = 120`

4-11 Which of the following statements is True?

    A. You can remove an element of a control array that was created in design mode.

    B. You can remove all but the first element of a control array.

    C. You can only remove control array elements that are added at runtime.

    D. You cannot remove control array elements.

4-12 Which of the following does the Forms collection contain?

    A. All forms in a project

    B. MDI Child forms only

    C. The currently active form

    D. All forms currently loaded by the program

4-13   Which of the following statements is True? Check all that apply.

    A. Forms are added to the Forms collection when they are loaded.

    B. Forms are added to the Forms collection using the Add method.

    C. The contents of the Forms collection can change during the execution of your program.

    D. A form is removed from the Forms collection when it is hidden.

4-14   Which of the following is True of the Controls collection? Check all that apply.

    A. All controls in the collection have the same Name property.

    B. The controls in the collection can be of different types.

    C. The collection contains all the controls in your entire program.

    D. The collection contains all the controls on a form.

4-15   What is the purpose of the TypeOf statement?

    A. To determine if a control has a particular property

    B. To determine the type of control being accessed

    C. To verify that a data type is correct for a control property

    D. To determine if a control exists on a form

4-16   Which type of statement is used to access all the controls in the Controls collection?

    A. For...Next

    B. If...Then...Else

    C. Do...Loop

    D. For...Each

4-17 Which of the following code segments can be used to process all the open forms in a program? Check all that apply.

A.
```
For I = 0 To Forms.Count
    Debug.Print Forms(I).Name
Next I
```

B.
```
For All Forms
    Debug.Print Form.Name
Next Control
```

C.
```
For Each chgForm In Forms
    Debug.Print chgForm.Name
Next chgControl
```

D.
```
For I = 0 To Forms.UBound
    Debug.Print Forms.Item(I).Name
Next I
```

UNIT

5

Writing Code for Your Applications

Test Objectives: Creating User Services

- **Write code that validates user input.**

  - Create an application that verifies data entered at the field level and the form level by a user.

  - Create an application that enables or disables controls based on input in fields.

- **Write code that processes data entered on a form.**

  - Given a scenario, add code to the appropriate form event. Events include Initialize, Terminate, Load, Unload, QueryUnload, Activate, and Deactivate.

 Exam objectives are subject to change at any time without prior notice and at Microsoft's sole discretion. Please visit Microsoft's Training & Certification Web site (www.microsoft.com/Train_Cert) for the most current exam objectives listing.

Data validation is one of the most important and often one of the most overlooked aspects of programming. Data validation is the process of making sure that data entered into a program is as correct as possible. Data validation is important for two reasons:

- To maintain the integrity of information in a database
- To avoid errors in your program

Write Code That Validates User Input

One of the first things to realize about data validation is that you cannot prevent incorrect entries by a user. A user can still type in the wrong name, enter the wrong date, or make other input errors. What you are trying to do with data validation is to limit the type and severity of errors that a user can make. The following list shows some of the tasks that you can handle with data validation:

- Ensure that a user enters a number instead of letters.
- Make sure that a date is valid, e.g., that the user cannot enter 2/29/99.
- Notify the user of an unusual entry, such as someone's age that is greater than 120.
- Limit choices so that the user always enters Yes/No instead of possibly Y/N or True/False.
- Make sure that all required data is entered for a new record.

In addition to these general tasks, data validation can be used to enforce company business rules, such as the size of a raise, the minimum age for new hires, etc.

Verifying Data in an Application

There are various validation techniques that you can use in your programs and most programs make use of several of these techniques. First, you can handle some types of data validation through your choice of controls. If there are a limited number of choices for a data-entry field, you could use a group of option buttons to allow the user to pick a single item from the choices. If you have more than a few choices, you may want to use a list box or combo box to let the user select the particular item. By limiting the user's choices to ones that you know are valid, you guarantee that a valid entry is made. Figure 5.1 shows a data-entry form that makes use of option buttons and lists.

When using a group of option buttons, make sure you set a default value in case the user forgets to make a choice.

FIGURE 5.1

Using option buttons and list boxes to enforce data validation

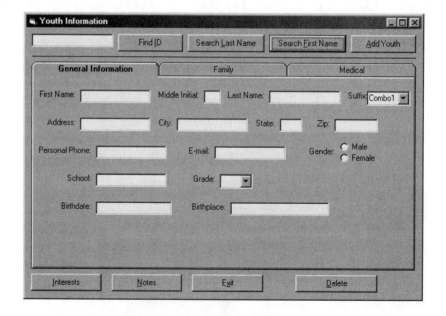

Other examples of how controls are used to enforce data validation are as follows:

- A check box can be used to handle True/False choices.

- A scroll bar can be used to handle numeric choices within a specific range.

- The date picker control can be used to ensure that a valid date is entered.

A second method of handling data validation is through the use of code in the events of certain controls. For example, if you are using a text box for input, you can place code in the KeyPress event that checks for numeric keys. If the key value is not a number, the keystroke is ignored. This code is illustrated below.

```
Private Sub txtAge_KeyPress(KeyAscii As Integer)
If KeyAscii >= 48 And KeyAscii <= 57 Then
        'Numeric key is OK
Else
        If KeyAscii = 46 Then
            'Decimal point is ok
        Else
            'Ignore keystroke
            KeyAscii = 0
            Beep
        End If
End If
End Sub
```

The other methods of data validation involve evaluating the information that is input by the user and taking action based on the input. The actions can be one of the following:

- Issuing an error message

- Not allowing the user to leave an invalid field

- Showing and hiding controls based on the input

Validating Information at the Field Level

Field-level validation means that the data in each field is checked after the user enters the data and before the user is allowed to move to another field. Prior to version 6 of Visual Basic, this type of validation was difficult to implement. You had to place code in the LostFocus event of each control to be validated, and even then there were problems.

Visual Basic 6 introduced a new event and a new property that together make handling field-level validation easier and more reliable. These new code elements are as follows:

Validate event   Fires before the focus shifts from the current control to another control.

CausesValidation property   Informs a control receiving focus that it should fire the Validate event of the previous control.

These two elements work together. The Validate event of a control is only fired if the CausesValidation property of the next control that receives the focus is set to True. By placing code in the Validate event of a control, you can check the input of the control and force the focus to stay on the current control if the input is incorrect. Fortunately, the default value of the CausesValidation property is True, so you usually don't have to remember to set the value. The only problem you may encounter is with controls that don't support the CausesValidation property.

One example of the use of the Validate event is to ensure that text boxes are not left blank when the user enters a new record. The following code shows how to use the Validate event of a text box to check for missing information and to force the user to enter a value.

```
Private Sub txtMember_Validate(Cancel As Boolean)
Dim sInput As String
sInput = txtMember.Text
If Len(sInput) = 0 Then
        MsgBox "Field cannot be left blank", vbExclamation _
+ vbOKOnly, "Validation Error"
        Cancel = True
End If
End Sub
```

The key to making the Validate event work is properly setting the Cancel parameter. If your validation code fails, you need to set the Cancel parameter to True. This indicates to the program that the validation failed and that the focus should remain in the current control.

One exception to the rule of having the CausesValidation property set to True for all controls is when you have a command button that is set up to discard changes to data or to exit the screen without saving the data. For this type of command button, you should set the CausesValidation property to False, to avoid forcing the user to enter valid information that you are going to discard anyway.

Validating Information at the Form Level

Field-level validation alone cannot handle all the validation tasks for an application. In many cases, whether one field is valid depends on the data in other fields on the form. This type of validation is difficult if not impossible to implement at the field level. To handle this type of validation, you must perform the validation after all the data for a form has been entered and before the data is saved. This is known as form-level validation.

There is no specific event, method, or property that handles form-level validation. Instead, you must depend on your coding skills to handle these tasks. The most common way of enforcing form-level validation is to write a function that performs the following tasks:

- Checks the validity of each required field

- Displays a message for an invalid input

- Sets the focus to the control containing the invalid information

- Returns a value that indicates whether the validation failed

This function would be called by the routine that saves the data from the form. If the validation function failed, the save function would be canceled. A typical location for the call to the validation function is in a command button Click event. The following code shows an example of a form-level validation function.

```
Public Function CheckData() As Boolean
Dim sCheckName As String
CheckData = True
sCheckName = txtFirst.Text
```

```
      If Len(Trim(sCheckName)) = 0 Then
            MsgBox "First Name cannot be blank.", vbExclamation _
+ vbOKOnly, "Data Check"
            txtFirst.SetFocus
            CheckData = False
            Exit Function
      End If
      sCheckName = txtLast.Text
      If Len(Trim(sCheckName)) = 0 Then
            MsgBox "Last Name cannot be blank.", vbExclamation _
+ vbOKOnly, "Data Check"
            txtLast.SetFocus
            CheckData = False
            Exit Function
      End If

      End Function

      Private Sub cmdSave_Click()
      If Not CheckData Then Exit Sub
      'Save the data
      End Sub
```

Enabling and Disabling Controls in an Application

A final method of handling data validation is to keep the user from entering information that is not required or is invalid. An example of this is the menus that you encounter with word processing or other programs. The Edit menu of these programs is typically hidden from the user when no document is open. This prevents the user from attempting to run a copy or paste operation when there is no valid data to work with.

You can do the same thing with the controls on your form. Using properties of the controls, you can prevent the user from entering information or even seeing the control if particular conditions are not met. The key properties are as follows:

Visible   Determines whether the user can see a control. To hide a control, set the Visible property to False.

Enabled   Determines whether a user can interact with a control. To allow the user to see the control but not to enter data, set the Enabled property to False.

Locked (text box only)   Determines whether the user can modify the contents of a text box. To prevent modification of the data, set the Locked property to True.

The data entry form shown in Figure 5.2 uses an array of text boxes for user input. The text boxes are locked to prevent modification of the data until the user clicks the Edit or Add buttons on the form. At this point, data entry is allowed. The code below shows how the program unlocks the controls when the Edit button is clicked.

```
Private Sub cmdEdit_Click()
Dim I As Integer
If Index = 0 Then
        'Edit button was pressed, unlock controls
        For I = txtMember.LBound To txtMember.UBound
           txtMember(I).Locked = False
        Next I
End If
End Sub
```

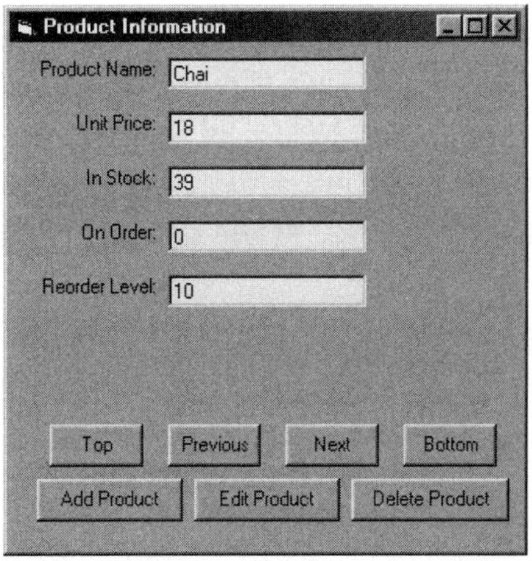

FIGURE 5.2

Unlocking controls in a form using the Edit button

The same effect can be achieved using the Enabled property of the controls and, in fact, using the Enabled property is the only way to lock out controls besides the text box. The only drawback to using the Enabled property is that a disabled control appears grayed out and may not be easy to read if the user needs to view the information from the control.

Write Code That Processes Data Entered on a Form

Events are the elements of a form or control that tell the object when to take an action. An event of a form or control is fired when the operating system sends a message that something has happened in the program. This can be a notification of a keystroke, a mouse click, movement of the form, resizing the form, or a host of other events. Visual Basic has an event for each of the messages to which a form or other object can respond. If you want your program to take some action in response to the event, you write code in the event procedure.

While there are a host of events for forms and controls, there are specific events that occur as the form loads and unloads. These events can be used to initialize information during startup or to make sure all tasks have been handled before a form is closed. Also, it is important for you not only to know what the events are and their functions but also to have an understanding of the order of firing for the events. The order in which events fire can make a difference to how your program performs.

Coding Events That Occur When a Form Loads

When you use the Load statement to place a form in memory or use the Show method to display a form, a series of events can occur. Each of these events is in response to different messages being sent by the operating system. The five key events that can occur when a form is loaded or displayed are as follows:

Initialize   Is triggered once when the form is initially loaded. Any of the following situations can trigger the Initialize event:

- When a property or method of the form is referenced by another part of the program

- When an object variable is used to create a new instance of the form

- Automatically when the form is loaded by the Load command or the Show method

Load   Is triggered only once when the form is first loaded. The Load event can be triggered by the following actions:

- When the Load command is issued to load the form into memory

- Automatically when the Show method is used to display a form that was not previously loaded

Activate   Is triggered when the form receives focus from another form in your application. It is also triggered when the form is initially shown using the Show method.

Resize   Is triggered when the form is initially loaded or when the size of the form is changed. The Resize event can be triggered by the user dragging the border of the form, by changing the Height, Width, or WindowState properties in code, or by the user clicking the Minimize or Maximize buttons.

Paint   Is triggered when a form is initially displayed. It also occurs whenever a part of the form needs to be refreshed, such as when part of the form has been covered up by another form.

As stated earlier, you also need to know the sequence in which the events occur. As you can see from the above list, several events occur when the form is initially loaded. The proper sequence of events on the first load of a form is Initialize, Load, Activate or Resize, and Paint. It should be noted that the Activate event does not fire the first time a form is loaded if there is code in the Resize event.

Coding Events That Occur When a Form Unloads

Just as there are multiple events that occur when a form is loaded, there are multiple events that occur when a form is closed. The events that occur on closing a form are as follows:

QueryUnload   Is triggered when the form is closed using the control menu, the Close button, or the Unload command. The QueryUnload event allows you to determine the method by which the form was closed. This event also allows you to cancel the unloading of the form.

Unload   Is triggered when the form is closed using the control menu, the Close button, or the Unload command. The Unload event always occurs after the QueryUnload event.

Terminate   Is triggered only when all references to the form are destroyed, either by being set to Nothing or by an object variable going out of scope. The Terminate event occurs after the Unload event.

Deactivate   Is triggered when the focus is transferred to another form or program.

Write Code That Validates User Input

1. You can use the following controls to limit the choices available for user input:

_____, _____,

_____, and _____.

2. The _____ event can be used to prevent a user from entering letters in a text box.

3. True or False. You can force a text box to ignore a keystroke by setting the KeyAscii parameter of the KeyPress event to zero.

4. The _____ control is the best choice for handling True/False or Yes/No choices in a user interface.

Create an Application That Verifies Data Entered at the Field Level and the Form Level by a User

5. The _____ event can be used to check the data entered by a user and prevent them from exiting the control if certain criteria are not met.

6. True or False. Validation of each field on a form is an automatic function of Visual Basic.

7. The _____ property forces the program to fire the _____ event of the control that would lose focus.

8. Checking data for each control as information is entered is called
_____ validation.

9. True or False. You can check the validity of data in each field by placing code in the Lost-Focus event.

10. Checking all the data on a form before the record is saved is called
_____ validation.

11. To avoid forcing validation when a user clicks a Discard button, set the
_____ property of the button to
_____.

12. Validation of all the data in a form should be performed in a
_____.

13. True or False. It is a good idea to place the code that validates data is in the routine that saves the data.

Create an Application That Enables or Disables Controls Based on Input in Fields

14. To hide a control, set the _____ property of the control to _____.

15. To leave a control showing on the form but to prevent a user from interacting with the control, set the _____ property to

_____.

16. The _____ property of the text box can be used to prevent a user from modifying the data in the text box.

17. True or False. Disabling a control can make the information in the control difficult to read.

Write Code That Processes Data Entered on a Form

18. The first event triggered when a form is loaded is the _____ event.

19. The _____ event is fired when a user sets the Height or Width properties of the form.

20. The _____ and

_____ events only occur once when the form is loaded.

Given a Scenario, Add Code to the Appropriate Form Event

21. If part of a form is covered and then displayed, the

_____ event is triggered.

22. True or False. The Activate event only occurs when the form is loaded the first time.

23. The proper sequence of the events occurring at form load is

_____, _____,

_____, then _____.

24. A form is loaded when the _____ statement or the

_____ method is used.

25. The first event that occurs when the user closes a form is the

_____ event.

26. True or False. The Unload event occurs when the program hides the form.

27. The _____ event lets you determine how the user
closed the form.

28. The _____ and _____
events let you cancel the unloading of a form.

29. The _____ event occurs when you move from the
current form to another form in the same application.

30. The _____ event only occurs after all references to
the form have been destroyed.

5-1   Which of the following methods can be used to validate user input? Check all that apply.

    A. Use option buttons and lists to limit user choices.

    B. Hide controls that the user does not need.

    C. Run the Validate method of the form before saving data.

    D. Create a validation function to check the data.

5-2   Which of the following are benefits of data validation? Check all that apply.

    A. Helps preserve data integrity

    B. Makes data entry faster

    C. Helps avoid runtime errors

    D. Allows forms to be automatically filled out

5-3   Checking data in each field as it is entered is called what?

    A. Form-level validation

    B. Excessive

    C. Field-level validation

    D. Control-level validation

5-4   Which event is triggered when the focus moves to a control that has the CausesValidation property set?

    A. LostFocus

    B. CheckData

    C. Validate

    D. GotFocus

SAMPLE TEST

5-5   What is the default setting of the CausesValidation property?

   A. True

   B. False

   C. Depends on the control

   D. Depends on the type of form being created

5-6   What three things should a form-level validation routine do?

   A. Check the validity of each required field.

   B. Erase the invalid entries.

   C. Notify the user of an error.

   D. Indicate the control that has the error.

5-7   Which properties can be used to limit user access to any control? Check all that apply.

   A. ReadOnly

   B. Visible

   C. Enabled

   D. Disabled

5-8   Which property is used to prevent a user from modifying the data in a text box?

   A. Visible

   B. Enabled

   C. ReadOnly

   D. Locked

5-9   Which events are only fired when the form is first loaded?

   A. Initialize and Load

   B. Load and Paint

   C. Initialize and Resize

   D. Resize and Paint

5-10   What is the first event triggered when a form is unloaded?

   A. Unload

   B. QueryUnload

   C. Terminate

   D. Deactivate

5-11   How can you keep the user from exiting a form by using the Close item on the Control menu or by clicking the Close button?

   A. Place code in the Unload event.

   B. Set a property of the form to hide the button.

   C. This can only be done using a Windows API call.

   D. Place code in the QueryUnload event.

5-12   Which event(s) allow you to determine which key was pressed by the user? Check all correct answers.

   A. Click

   B. KeyPress

   C. KeyAscii

   D. KeyUp

```
S A M P L E   T E S T
```

5-13   When is the Terminate event of a form triggered?

    A. When the user moves to another form or program

    B. When the form is unloaded

    C. Never

    D. When all references to the form are deleted

5-14   Which event is triggered when the user moves to another form?

    A. Unload

    B. Deactivate

    C. Terminate

    D. Load

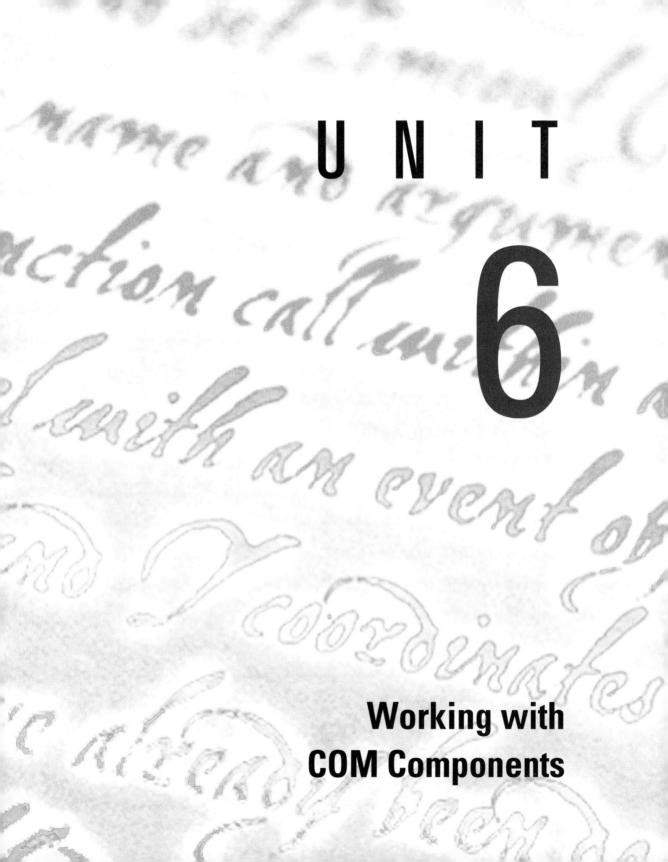

U N I T

6

**Working with
COM Components**

Test Objectives: Creating User Services

- **Add an ActiveX control to the toolbox.**

- **Create a Web page by using the DHTML Page Designer to dynamically change attributes of elements, change content, change styles, and position elements.**

- **Use data binding to display and manipulate data from a data source.**

- **Instantiate and invoke a COM component.**
  - Create a Visual Basic client application that uses a COM component.
  - Create a Visual Basic application that handles events from a COM component.

- **Create callback procedures to enable asynchronous processing between COM components and Visual Basic client applications.**

The Component Object Model (COM) is a specification that was developed by Microsoft to allow different objects to interact with each other. Using COM, your program can work with a variety of objects, such as ActiveX controls, business object servers that enforce business rules, and even some other programs, such as Microsoft Word and Microsoft Excel. In version 6 (and some earlier versions) of Visual Basic, you can even write your own COM components. In earlier versions of Visual Basic, these components were known as OLE or ActiveX components.

This unit shows you how to use COM components in your programs. The unit also shows you how to create dynamic Web pages using the Dynamic Hypertext Markup Language (DHTML) Page Designer. DHTML pages, along with ActiveX controls, are examples of COM components that have a visual interface. Unit 8, "Creating COM Components" shows you how to create different types of COM components.

Add an ActiveX Control to the Toolbox

You can use the controls in the Visual Basic toolbox to create the user interface of a program. You create the interface by placing instances of controls on the form and assigning code to the events of the controls. You are probably also aware that you are not limited to the controls that are shown when you first start Visual Basic. Microsoft includes a number of other controls with Visual Basic and there are a large number of third-party controls available to handle tasks that are not covered by Microsoft controls.

However, in order to use some of these other controls, you must add the controls to the toolbox before you can use them in a program. You add controls to the toolbox using the Components dialog box shown in Figure 6.1. You can access this dialog box by choosing the Components item from the Project menu.

You can also bring up the Components dialog box by right-clicking the toolbox and choosing the Components item from the pop-up menu.

FIGURE 6.1

Selecting controls for your program

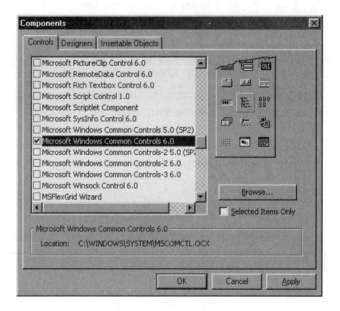

The Controls page of the Components dialog box lists all the controls currently available to you on your computer. To add a control to your project, check the box next to the control in the dialog box. To remove a control, simply clear the check box next to the control. When you click the Apply button of the Components dialog box or exit the dialog box by clicking the OK button, the selected controls are added to the bottom of the toolbox, as shown in Figure 6.2.

You cannot remove a control from a project if it is already in use on a form.

Not all controls are contained in files that are accessible from the Components dialog box. Some controls are embedded in ActiveX servers—either DLL or EXE servers. To use these controls, you must add a reference to the

FIGURE 6.2

Controls added to the
toolbox

server to your project. You do this by opening the References dialog box for
the project, as shown in Figure 6.3. You can access the References dialog box
by choosing the References item from the Project menu. To add a reference
to your project, check the box next to the reference description, just as you
did for a control.

FIGURE 6.3

Adding controls by
adding a reference

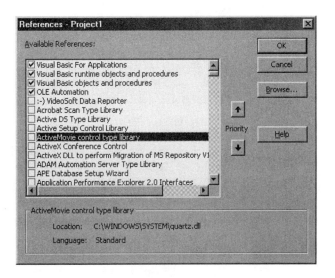

If the DLL or EXE server you are looking for is not shown in the References dialog box, you can click the Browse button of the dialog box to select the file from the Open dialog box.

Create a Web Page by Using the DHTML Page Designer to Dynamically Change Attributes of Elements, Change Content, Change Styles, and Position Elements

These days, nearly every major company and a lot of small companies and individuals have their own Web sites. The latest trend in Web sites is to provide dynamic content for your site. This keeps the site fresh and provides the user with a more engaging experience.

One way to create dynamic Web content is through the use of Dynamic Hypertext Markup Language (DHTML). DHTML enables you to provide dynamic content on Web pages, based on user actions and requests. Visual Basic provides you with a way to quickly and easily create DHTML documents.

With the DHTML Page Designer, you can create interactive Web pages using tools and code similar to the controls and code you use to create a form-based application. After you create the pages, you compile the application and place it on a server where users can access it. At present, only Internet Explorer 4 (or higher) Web browser can use the DHTML pages created in Visual Basic.

To start the process of creating a DHTML application, you need to open a new project and select the DHTML Application option from the Project dialog box, as shown in Figure 6.4. This creates a new project and starts you out with a single Page Designer and Code module. You can add other pages to the project by selecting the Add DHTML Page item from the Project menu.

After the project is created, you open the page by double-clicking it in the Project window of Visual Basic. The Page Designer shows a hierarchical view of the elements of the page, along with the actual appearance of the page. This is illustrated in Figure 6.5. Notice in the figure that you have a toolbox to the left of the development environment. This toolbox is very similar to the standard toolbox and provides you with the tools you need to add elements to your DHTML page.

FIGURE 6.4

Starting a DHTML
project

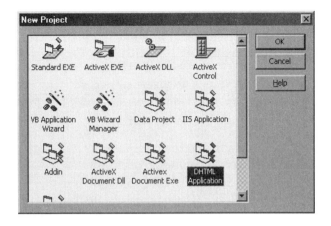

FIGURE 6.5

Designing a page

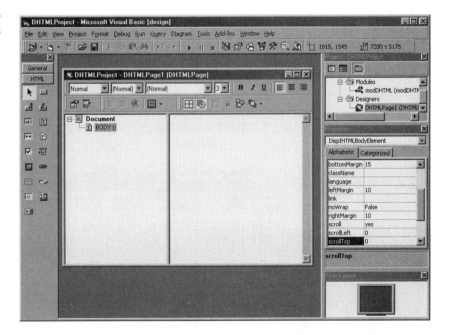

As you add elements to the DHTML page, you will set the properties of
the elements, just as you would set the properties of the controls on a form
of a standard application. One of the key properties of each element is the ID
property. This property is used to identify the element in code, in a manner

similar to the Name property of a standard control. For example, the following code illustrates how to retrieve a person's name from a text box on the page and print it out as a paragraph of the page:

```
Dim sName As String
sName = txtUser.Value
paTest1.innerText = "Hello, " & sName
paTest2.innerText = ""
```

In this code, you see the notation with which all Visual Basic programmers are familiar. Notice also that some of the properties you use are different from the ones used in similar standard controls. For the text box, you retrieve the user input from the Value property instead of the Text property. As you work with the DHTML pages, notice also that the control events have different names from their standard control counterparts. For example, the event that is fired when a user clicks a command button on a DHTML page is the OnClick event. For a standard command button, it would be the Click event.

After you have finished setting up the interface of the program and writing the code, you can test the program by clicking the Run button on the Visual Basic toolbar. Your application will be displayed in a Web browser, as shown in Figure 6.6. As you are running the application, you can debug it using standard Visual Basic debugging tools.

F I G U R E 6.6
Running a DHTML project

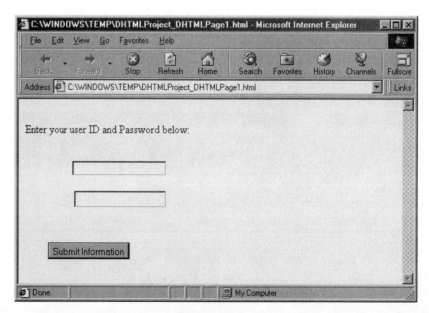

Once you get used to the differences in property, method, and event names, you will find that programming a DHTML page is as easy as programming a standard application. Much of your Visual Basic knowledge can be used in creating these pages. All in all, the DHTML pages provide an easy way for you to create a Web application

Use Data Binding to Display and Manipulate Data from a Data Source

One of the uses of ActiveX controls (one type of COM component) is to build database applications. There are two ways to build a database application:

- Use the methods of ActiveX data objects (ADO) or another database model and set control values with program code.
- Use the ADO data control (ADODC) and the data binding capabilities of the controls to display and manipulate the data.

Many of the standard controls in Visual Basic have data binding capabilities. This means that a particular property of the control can be bound to a data source. This property is then used to display the contents of a particular field of a recordset. Also, if the recordset and the control are properly configured, the control can be used to modify the data in the recordset. Table 6.1 shows the standard controls that can be bound to a data source and the property that is used to display the contents of the recordset.

T A B L E 6.1 Standard Controls That Can Be Bound to a Data Source	Control Name	Property
	PictureBox	Picture
	Label	Caption
	TextBox	Text
	CheckBox	Value

TABLE 6.1 (cont.)	**Control Name**	**Property**
Standard Controls That Can Be Bound to a Data Source	ComboBox	Text
	ListBox	List
	Image	Picture
	OLEControl	N/A

For each of the controls listed above, and for all other data-bound controls, the link between the control and the data in a database is provided by the ADO data control or another data control. The particular data control to which a control is bound is specified by the DataSource property of the control. When setting up the bound control, you set the DataSource property to the Name of a data control on the form. You can only use data controls that are on the same form as the bound control.

Most bound controls allow you to use data controls based on Data Access Objects (DAO) and Remote Data Objects (RDO) as well as ADO data controls.

After you have specified the DataSource property, you specify the particular field of the recordset using the DataField property. The DataField property is set to the name of a field in the recordset defined by the data control. The value of this field is what is displayed by the bound control. When you are in the design environment, the DataField property shows you a list of all the fields available from the selected data control. You can select the field from the list to complete the setup of the bound control.

If you are using DAO or RDO data controls, you can only set the value of the DataSource property from the design environment. It cannot be set from code. You can, however, change the setting of the DataField property with code.

Using the data control and bound controls, you can create a wide variety of data-display and data-entry programs. A typical program is shown in Figure 6.7.

FIGURE 6.7

Displaying data with
bound controls

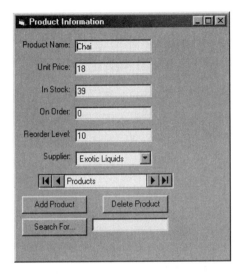

If the data control is set up to allow the editing of data, you can also use the bound controls to modify the information in a database. To change the data, the user simply modifies the contents of the control, e.g., the Text property of a text box. Then, when the user moves to another record or exits the form, the changes are automatically saved to the database.

Unit 10, "Creating Database Applications," describes how to set up a data control for various types of applications.

Instantiate and Invoke a COM Component

ActiveX controls and DHTML pages are examples of COM components that have a visual interface. However, a number of the components that you use are created and used only in the code of your application. These components are provided by ActiveX servers. These servers can be created by you or by other programmers in your organization to enforce business rules or to handle particular calculation functions. The servers can also be other applications, such as Microsoft Word or Excel, that expose objects to your program. No matter where the objects are located, you use the same techniques to create and manipulate the objects.

Using COM Components

In general, to use a COM component in your program, you need to perform the following tasks:

- Set a reference to the proper object library for the task.
- Create an object of the proper type.
- Use the methods and properties of the object to accomplish the task.
- Destroy the object.

Declaring an Object Variable

The first step in using a COM component is making it available to your project. To do this, you must set a reference to the object using the References dialog box of the project. To set up a reference to a component, choose the References item in the Project menu and select the COM component in the dialog box. If the component is not listed, you can click the Browse button to look through the .DLL, .TLB, and .EXE files available to your computer and find the particular component.

Next, create an object variable to hold an instance of the component. There are two steps in creating an instance of a COM component:

1. Declare an object variable for the component.

2. Instantiate the object.

You can declare the variable in one of two ways. You can declare a variable to hold a specific type of object, such as a business rule class, or you can create a generic object variable that can work with any object. This situation is somewhat analogous to using a specific data type or the Variant data type for other variables. Declaring a specific object type is known as early binding, while declaring a generic object variable is known as late binding.

Comparing Early Binding and Late Binding

Whether you use early or late binding for an object variable depends on the task you are performing. For most applications, it is better to use early binding for the following reasons:

- Objects are created faster because the specific object type is known.

- Information about the properties and methods of the object are known at design time, which enables Visual Basic's tools (Auto List Members and Auto QuickInfo) to provide you with information about the properties and methods of the object.

Early binding occurs when you specify the object type in the declaration statement for the object variable, as shown in the following statements:

```
Dim oUser As cUser
Dim oRset As cRset
```

The only real advantage to late binding is that it gives you the flexibility of defining the object type while the program is running. When you need to use late binding, you declare a variable as simply Object and then use the CreateObject function to assign an object to the variable. Only when the object is assigned to the variable is the type of the object known. The following code shows an example of late binding:

```
Dim oWord2 As Object
Set oWord2 = CreateObject("Word.Application")
```

Instantiating the Object

After you declare an object variable, you need to use the variable in your program code before the object is really instantiated. There are three methods for instantiating an object in a program.

The first method of creating an instance of an object is to use the New keyword in the declaration statement of the object variable. The New keyword tells Visual Basic that a new instance of the specified object is to be created. This instance is not created when the declaration statement is executed.

Rather, the instance is created when the object variable is first used, either in setting a property or calling a method. The following code illustrates the use of the New keyword:

```
'An object variable is defined here. The object
' is not created here.
Dim oRset As New cRset
'The object is actually created here.
oRset.Open MainDB, sSQL, 2
```

The second method of creating an instance of an object is to use the Set command. This command assigns an object to an object variable. You can use the Set command to assign an existing object to a variable, or you can use the Set command with the New keyword to create a new instance of an object.

The Set command creates an instance of an object when the command is executed. The following code shows how the Set command is used to assign existing objects and to create new objects:

```
'Object variables are defined here
Dim oRset As Recordset
Dim oRset2 As cRset
'An existing object is assigned to a variable
Set oRset = adcProducts.Recordset
'A new object is created and assigned to a variable
Set oRset2 = New cRset
```

The final method of creating an instance of an object is with the Create-Object function. This function is typically used to create a specific object type with a generic object variable. That is, you typically use this function only when the object type is unknown at design time. When using the CreateObject function, the object variable is declared as simply Object. The object is then created with the Set command and the CreateObject function. The following code shows the use of the CreateObject function:

```
'Declare an object variable
Dim oSpread As Object
'Create an Excel object
Set oSpread = CreateObject("Excel.Sheet")
```

Using the COM Component in Code

After you have created the COM component using the above methods, you can work with the properties and methods of the component just as you would with one of the controls on a form. To access a property or method of the component, you specify the variable containing the instance of the component and the name of the property or method. The following code shows an example of using the methods of a COM component:

```
With oOrderSet
    sOrderSQL = "Select * From Orders Where OrderID=" & _
lOrderID
    .OpenRSet MainDB, sOrderSQL, 2
    If Not .OpenOK Then Exit Sub
    SizeFields Me, oOrderSet
    If bNewRecord Then
        .ClearRecord
    Else
        If .RecCount > 0 Then .FetchRecord
    End If
End With
```

Destroying a COM Component

Creating an instance of a COM component uses memory and other system resources in your program. Therefore, you don't want the instance of the component to be around longer than is necessary. An instance of a component is supposed to be destroyed when the object variable goes out of scope or when your program exits. However, you can specifically destroy an instance of a component by setting the object variable to Nothing, as follows:

```
Set oOrderSet = Nothing
```

Handling Events from a COM Component

In addition to having properties to hold and manipulate information and methods to perform tasks, many COM components also have events as part of their public interface. These events work like the events of a control.

When the component receives a certain Windows message or when a certain condition is met, the event is fired. As with control events, you can write code to respond to the events that are part of the COM component.

To handle events from a COM component, you need to perform two tasks:

1. Notify your program that the component has events that you will be using.

2. Write code for the specific events to which you want your code to respond.

To notify your code that the component has events you want to access, change the declaration that you use for the object variable. To handle events, the declaration must include the WithEvents keyword as shown in the following code:

```
Dim WithEvents oEmployee As cEmployee
```

If you do not include the WithEvents keyword in the declaration, your code cannot respond to the events of the component, even if the component raises events.

To learn how to create events in your own COM components, see Unit 8: "Creating COM Components."

Create Callback Procedures to Enable Asynchronous Processing between COM Components and Visual Basic Client Applications

In the normal operation of a program, the tasks performed by a component are run as the component is called. Once control has been passed to the component, processing in the main program is suspended until the processing in the component is completed. This is known as synchronous processing. However, if a component is going to be running a long process, you may wish to perform other tasks in the program while you are waiting for the component's process to complete. Having multiple processes running at the same time is known as asynchronous processing.

There are two main tasks that must be handled in order for asynchronous processing to work:

- The server application must be able to send a message that a process has completed.

- The client application must be able to receive a message about a completed process and take action on the message.

Using Events for Asynchronous Processing

The simplest way to handle this sending and receiving of messages is through the use of events. If you are creating both the server and client applications, you have control over the events that are raised by the server and can set up the client application to respond to the events.

To set up a server for asynchronous operation, you declare an event using a statement such as the following:

```
Public Event RetrievalComplete(ByVal lNumRecords As Long)
```

This declaration specifies the name of the event and the type of parameter that is passed to the client program. To then trigger the event, use the RaiseEvent statement and specify the value of the parameter to be passed to the client program. The RaiseEvent statement is shown in the following code line:

```
RaiseEvent RetrievalComplete(oRset.RecCount)
```

On the client side, you simply write code in the RetrievalComplete event of the instance of the component. This code is run when the event is triggered from the server.

 Asynchronous callbacks can only be used with Out-of-Process servers (ActiveX EXE).

Add an ActiveX Control to the Toolbox

1. The _____ dialog box provides a list of controls that you can select to use in your program.

2. True or False. All ActiveX controls are contained in OCX files.

Create a Web Page by Using the DHTML Page Designer to Dynamically Change Attributes of Elements, Change Content, Change Styles, and Position Elements

3. DHTML stands for _____.

4. You start the creation of a Web page by creating a new _____ project in Visual Basic.

5. True or False. You can only create one page in a DHTML project.

6. The event fired when a button is clicked in a DHTML page is the _____ event.

7. You retrieve information from a text box on a page using the _____ property.

8. True or False. DHTML controls and standard controls are interchangeable on a DHTML page.

9. When you run a DHTML project from the development environment, the pages are displayed in a _____.

Use Data Binding to Display and Manipulate Data from a Data Source

10. True or False. Bound controls only work with the ADO data control.

11. The _____ property links a bound control to the recordset defined by a data control.

12. The _____ specifies the field in the recordset to be shown by the control.

13. True or False. You can view and modify information in a database using the bound controls.

14. True or False. You can set all the data binding properties of a bound control from code.

15. To work with database information in a text box, you use the _____ property.

16. True or False. When data is changed in a bound control, it is automatically saved as the change is made.

STUDY QUESTIONS

Instantiate and Invoke a COM Component

17. True or False. ActiveX controls are the only components that you can use in your program.

18. COM components contained in an ActiveX server often do not have a

_____.

Create a Visual Basic Client Application That Uses a COM Component

19. To use a COM component in your program you must first set a

_____ to the component.

20. You must declare an _____ to provide a reference for the instance of a COM component.

21. Declaring the specific type of component that you are creating is called

_____.

22. True or False. A COM component is instantiated as soon as it is declared.

23. The _____ command assigns a COM component to an object variable.

24. The _____ function can be used to instantiate a COM component.

25. If you are unsure of the type of object to be used, you should use
_____ binding.

26. True or False. Using the New keyword in a declaration statement automatically creates an instance of an object.

27. To destroy an object, you set the object variable to
_____.

28. True or False. Objects are automatically destroyed when the object variable goes out of scope.

Create a Visual Basic Application That Handles Events from a COM Component

29. The _____ keyword is used to tell your program that you want to respond to the events of a component.

30. The _____ method is used by the component to cause an event to be fired.

31. True or False. Your program can only respond to a single event in a COM component.

32. To take action when an event from a COM component is fired, you must
_____.

Create Callback Procedures to Enable Asynchronous Processing Between COM Components and Visual Basic Client Applications

33.   A component can use the _____ method to trigger an event that notifies the client application of the completion of a task.

34.   True or False. All components use events to enable asynchronous processing.

6-1 Which of the following statements will create an object variable? Check all that apply.

    A. `Dim oUser As Object`

    B. `Dim oUser As String`

    C. `Dim oUser As COMComponent`

    D. `Dim oUser As cUser`

6-2 Which keyword in a declaration statement specifies that an object will respond to events?

    A. RecognizeEvents.

    B. WithEvents.

    C. No special keyword is required.

    D. UsesEvents.

6-3 Which event is triggered when you click a button on a DHTML page?

    A. Click

    B. MouseDown

    C. OnClick

    D. MouseClick

6-4 Which of the following statements about DHTML pages is False?

    A. You can create multiple pages per application.

    B. You can modify the contents of paragraphs on the Web page.

    C. Information in a text box is stored in the Value property.

    D. DHTML applications can be run as stand-alone programs.

6-5   Which two properties must be set to enable a bound control to display information from a database?

   A. DataField and DataSource

   B. DataField and Recordset

   C. DataControl and Field

   D. DataSource and DataBound

6-6   Which property or properties of the bound control can be set from code?

   A. DataSource only.

   B. DataField only.

   C. Both DataSource and DataField can be set from code.

   D. Neither can be set from code.

6-7   What condition must be met to allow a bound control to be used for data editing?

   A. Bound controls can always edit data.

   B. The recordset must be set up to allow editing.

   C. The AllowUpdate property of the data control must be set to True.

   D. The AllowUpdate property of the bound control must be set to True.

6-8   When is the changed data in a bound control saved?

   A. As soon as you change the information

   B. When the LostFocus event of the control is fired

   C. When you click the Save button on the data control

   D. When you move to another record in the recordset

6-9   Which of the following is an advantage of early binding? Check all that apply.

   A. Objects are created faster.

   B. You can change the type of object in code.

   C. Information about the properties and methods of the object are available in the design environment.

   D. There are no advantages.

6-10   Which of the following statements destroys an instance of an object?

   A. `Drop oUser`

   B. `Delete oUser`

   C. `Set oUser = Nothing`

   D. `Set oUser = ""`

U N I T

7

**Implementing Help
and Handling Errors**

Test Objectives: Creating User Services

- **Implement online user assistance in a desktop application.**

  - Set appropriate properties to enable user assistance. Help properties include HelpFile, HelpContextID, and WhatsThisHelp.

  - Create HTML Help for an application.

  - Implement messages from a server component to a user interface.

- **Implement error handling for the user interface in desktop applications.**

  - Identify and trap runtime errors.

  - Handle inline errors.

Exam objectives are subject to change at any time without prior notice and at Microsoft's sole discretion. Please visit Microsoft's Training & Certification Web site (www.microsoft.com/Train_Cert) for the most current exam objectives listing.

reating the user interface with forms and controls and writing code is only part of the process of creating an application. Two other important aspects of programming are providing help to the user and handling errors. No matter how well you design the user interface of your program, there are some tasks that will not be obvious to the user. For these tasks, a good help system will reduce user confusion and can cut down on the amount of technical support you must provide for your application.

While help is important, without proper error handling, your program can give unexpected results. In a worst-case scenario, it can crash. Neither of these results is acceptable to the end user. This unit shows you how to create help systems for your application and how to handle errors.

Implement Online User Assistance in a Desktop Application

If you have worked with any commercial Windows applications (including Visual Basic), you are probably familiar with the online help of the application. The most common form of help comes in the form of help files that are accessible by pressing F1 or choosing items on the Help menu. This type of help is in the process of evolving. Most applications written before mid-1998 use the familiar Windows Help (WinHelp) screens shown in Figure 7.1. These help systems typically provide a table of contents and an index in addition to the actual help in the topics.

Many newer applications, particularly those from Microsoft, are now moving to HTML Help. This type of help system displays the help topics in the form of HTML pages that are viewed in a browser-like interface, as shown in Figure 7.2.

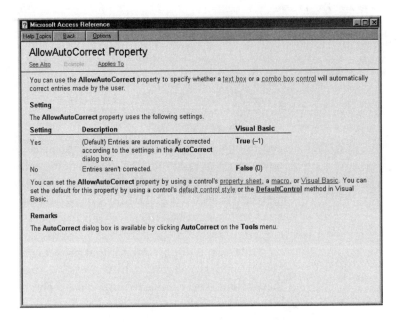

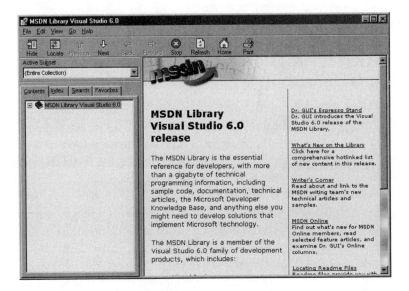

By default, the help system integrated with the applications that you create in Visual Basic is the Windows Help system. However, Visual Basic also gives you the tools to create HTML Help if you desire. In this unit, we cover both types of help systems.

In addition to the help available in either a Windows Help or HTML Help system, there are other tools that you can use to provide help to users of your applications. Here are some of these tools:

Tool tips   Describe buttons or other controls.

WhatsThisHelp   Allows the user to get help for a specific button or control.

Message boxes   Or custom dialog boxes provide the user with timely messages about the program or current tasks.

Enabling Help in Your Application

The first step to setting up a help system for your application is to create the help file itself. As with many other tasks, Visual Basic provides you with tools to assist you in the creation of help files. The tool for creating help files is the Help Workshop. This program is not automatically installed with Visual Basic but is available in the \Common\Tools folder of the Visual Basic CD as HCW.EXE. The Help Workshop, shown in Figure 7.3, assists you with the following tasks:

- Organizing the topics of your help file

- Creating the help project file and contents file

- Compiling and testing the help file

Setting the HelpFile Property

After you create the help file, you need to set several properties in your application in order to make the help file available to your users. The first property that you must set is the HelpFile property of the application. This property identifies the particular help file that will be used for the application. The easiest way to set this property is through the Project Properties dialog box. This dialog box, shown in Figure 7.4, is accessible by choosing the Properties item from the Project menu.

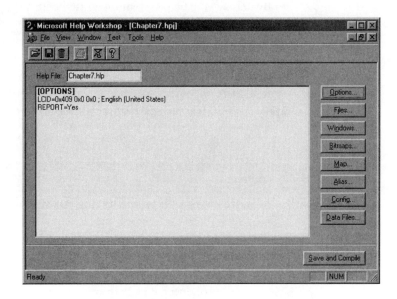

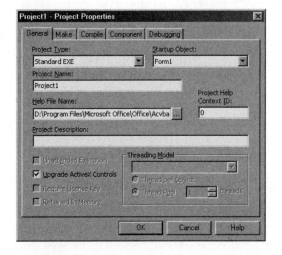

When you are on the General page of the Project Properties dialog box, you can enter the name of the help file or select it using an Open dialog box by clicking the Browse button. Once you have set the name of the help file, you can exit the dialog box and the link to your help file is complete.

In Figure 7.4, notice that the Project Properties dialog box specifies the full path to the help file when you choose the file from an Open dialog box. The full path may work fine on your machine but can cause problems for your users if they do not use the same directory structure.

A better method to set the HelpFile property for your program is to place code at the start of your program. All Visual Basic programs support the App object, which enables you to set and retrieve information about the currently running program. The specific property that identifies the help file for your application is the HelpFile property. Using the App object, you can specify the help file in a line of code such as the following:

```
App.HelpFile = App.Path & "\Test.hlp"
```

Specifying the HelpContextID

Making the link to the help file is just one step in implementing help in your program. In order to create context-sensitive help, you also need to link forms and controls to particular topics in the help file. As you create a help file, each topic is identified by a numeric tag. This numeric tag is associated with a particular form or control through the HelpContextID of the control or form. You can set the HelpContextID in the design environment by set-ting the property in the Properties window for the form or control. You can also set the HelpContextID using an assignment statement in your code.

Once you have set the HelpContextID of your forms and controls, your link to the help system is complete. When the user presses the F1 key for a control, the help system performs the following steps:

1. It checks the control for a HelpContextID and uses the value to find a help topic in the help file.

2. If the control has no HelpContextID value, the help system checks the HelpContextID of the control's container, such as a frame or form. If it finds a HelpContextID value, the help system searches for the cor-responding topic in the help file.

3. If no HelpContextID is found, the help system displays the Index page of the help file.

WARNING If you specify a HelpContextID that does not exist in your help file, the user encounters an error.

Displaying Help from Code

In addition to allowing the user to press the F1 key to get help, many programs also provide a Help menu that allows the user to see the contents of the help file or to look up topics using the Index page. When you create a Help menu, you must place code in the Click events of the menu items to display the help files. To handle the display of help topics, you need to use the Common Dialog control. This is one of the optional controls that you can add to your toolbox and then to a Visual Basic form. After you add the Common Dialog control to your form, you must perform the following tasks to be able to display help:

- Set the HelpFile property of the control.

- Set the HelpCommand property of the control.

- Invoke the ShowHelp method of the control.

The HelpFile property of the Common Dialog works the same as the HelpFile property of the App object described above. You specify the path and name of a help file to create the link between the control and the help file. The HelpCommand property determines the type of help that will be displayed. The possible settings for the HelpCommand property are shown in Table 7.1.

T A B L E 7.2 Settings for the Help- Command Property	**Help Action**	**Common Dialog Constant**
	Execute a Help macro.	cdlHelpCommand
	Display the Contents page of the help system.	cdlHelpContents
	Display a specific topic. (You must also set the HelpContext property.)	cdlHelpContext

T A B L E 7.2 *(cont.)*	**Help Action**	**Common Dialog Constant**
Settings for the Help-Command Property	Display a topic in a pop-up Help window.	cdlHelpContextPopup
	Display help for a particular keyword.	cdlHelpKey
	Display help for a keyword starting with a specific letter.	cdlHelpPartialKey

The following code shows how the Common Dialog is used to display a particular topic in a help file:

```
With cdlHelp
    .HelpFile = App.Path & "\Members.hlp"
    .HelpCommand = cdlHelpContext
    .HelpContext = 110
    .ShowHelp
End With
```

Using WhatsThisHelp

In addition to providing help by pressing the F1 key, you can provide help for some forms through the use of the WhatsThisHelp button. This button is a question mark that is displayed in the upper right-hand corner of some forms, as shown in Figure 7.5.

F I G U R E   7.5

Placing a WhatsThis-Help button on a form

When the user clicks the button, the cursor turns into a question mark. Then, when the user clicks on a control, the help file is displayed with help information for the control. In order to enable WhatsThisHelp, you have to perform the following tasks:

- Set the ControlBox property of the form to True (the default setting).

- Set the BorderStyle property of the form to Fixed Single or Sizable and set the MinButton and MaxButton properties to False; or set the BorderStyle of the form to Fixed Dialog.

- Set the WhatsThisHelp property of the form to True to enable the WhatsThisHelp function.

- Set the WhatsThisButton property of the form to True to display the button.

- Set the WhatsThisHelpID properties of controls to the numeric ID of a topic in the help file.

Creating HTML Help

WinHelp is one method of providing online help for your application. The other method is to use the new HTML Help. The tasks involved in creating HTML Help are similar to those for creating WinHelp files. Specifically, to create HTML Help, you need to carry out three tasks:

- Create an HTML project file to manage the help file project.

- Create HTML files for each of the topics in the help file.

- Compile the HTML files into a single help file.

To assist you in handling these tasks, Microsoft provides the HTML Help Workshop. This is one of the additional tools on the Visual Basic CD. As with the Help Workshop, you have to install the HTML Help Workshop separately; it is not part of the standard installation. The HTML Help Workshop is shown in Figure 7.6.

After you create and compile the help file with the HTML Help Workshop, you have to link the help file to your project. You can set the HelpFile property to either a WinHelp file (with an .HLP extension) or an HTML Help file (with a .CHM extension). As stated above, you can set the HelpFile property of an application from the Project Properties dialog box or by setting the HelpFile property of the App object in code.

FIGURE 7.6

Creating HTML Help

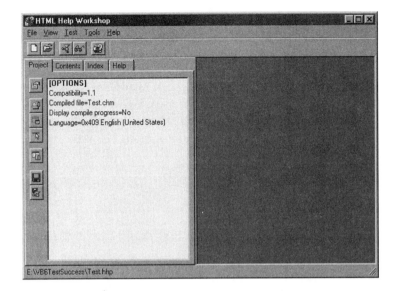

Sending Messages from a Server Component

When you are creating COM components and packaging them in a server, you may need to provide messages from the component to the end user. One method is to use the MsgBox function. However, if the component server resides on a different machine from the client application, the message may be displayed on the server and can cause the server to hang while it waits for someone to acknowledge the message. Therefore, you need a method to inform the client application that something has occurred and that a message needs to be displayed. There are two methods that you can use to perform this task:

- Create an event in the component and raise the event.

- Use the Err object and raise an error.

For the first method, you need to create an event procedure in the component, then use the RaiseEvent method to fire the event. The client application then needs to have code to respond to the event. Also, the object variable containing the instance of the component needs to have been created using the WithEvents keyword.

You can learn more about creating and handling events in COM components in Unit 6, "Working with COM Components," and Unit 8, "Creating COM Components."

The second method of passing information from a server component to a client application is through the Err object. The Err object contains information about any error that occurs in your program. Usually, this object is used to notify you of a Visual Basic error. However, using the Raise method of the Err object, you can specify your own error number and description. If the client application's code includes error handling (which all applications should include), the error you raise from the server component can be used to display a message to the user and, optionally, to refer the user to a help topic for further information. The Raise method of the Err object uses the following syntax:

```
Err.Raise number, source, description, helpfile, _
helpcontext
```

The arguments of the method are as follows:

Number   Specifies the error number. You should add the number that you specify to the constant vbObjectError to ensure that your error number does not conflict with any of Visual Basic's internal error numbers.

Source   Specifies the name of the object or application that raised the error.

Description   Specifies text that describes the error. This is where you would place the message that is to be displayed to the user.

Helpfile   Specifies the path and name of a help file containing more information about the error.

Helpcontext   Specifies the particular context ID of the help topic related to the error.

Implement Error Handling for the User Interface in Desktop Applications

Errors are a normal occurrence in every program. As you create your programs, you can use a variety of techniques to try to avoid errors. For example, you can disable or hide controls that the user should not use in a particular instance. You can also use lists, check boxes, and option buttons to limit a user's choices to only valid entries. Finally, you can write code to validate the user's input before you try to process it.

A number of these techniques are covered in Unit 5, "Writing Code for Your Application."

However, you can only do so much to prevent a user from causing errors. There are some errors that you cannot prevent, such as a user forgetting to put a disk in a drive before copying a file or trying to copy a file to a full disk. Since you cannot prevent these errors ahead of time, you have to have code in place to handle the errors as they occur.

Identifying and Trapping Runtime Errors

Visual Basic does not have built-in error-handling capabilities to take care of errors automatically. Instead, Visual Basic provides you with the capability to identify errors, then to handle them with your own code. There are two key pieces to identifying and trapping errors: the Err object and the On Error and Resume statements.

Determining Which Error Occurred

The Err object is the mechanism by which Visual Basic identifies to your program that an error occurred. The Err object provides you with information about the type of error that occurred and, to some extent, where the error occurred. This information is provided through the properties of the Err object. The key properties of the Err object are as follows:

Number Identifies the numerical ID of the error that occurred. This number can identify Visual Basic internal errors or errors that occurred in third-party controls or custom components. You can also create error numbers for errors in your server components using the Raise method of the Err object.

Source Identifies the location where the error occurred. If the error occurred in a standard module or form of your program, the Source property returns the name of your project. If the error occurs in a component from an ActiveX server, the Source property returns the name of the component's class or object.

Description   Provides a text description of the error that occurred. This is most often used when displaying information to the user or logging the error to a database or error log.

HelpFile   Provides the name of a help file that contains more information about the error. This is an optional parameter when an error is raised manually and is only available if properly coded by the creator of the component that caused the error.

HelpContextID   Provides the topic ID in the help file specified in the HelpFile property.

LastDLLError   Identifies the error that caused the failure of a DLL call in your program.

For most error-handling tasks, you will use the Number property or the LastDLLError property of the Err object.

Given the number of the error that occurred, how do you determine exactly what the error is and how it should be handled? The more you work with Visual Basic, the sooner you will become familiar with specific error numbers. For the ones you don't know, Visual Basic lists all its errors in the help files. The error list contains a description of the error and its probable causes. To avoid getting an error such as "Division by Zero," you would handle it by just checking the value of your variables before the division occurs. For other errors, the handling is a little more complex. An example of the error list for Visual Basic is shown in Figure 7.7.

FIGURE 7.7

Error descriptions in the help file

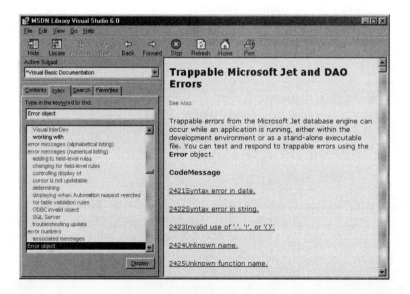

Trapping and Handling Runtime Errors

You need to have code in place to trap and then handle most types of errors. You need to place error-handling code in almost every procedure in your program, as Visual Basic does not have a global error-handling capability. If a specific procedure does not have error handling, any error that occurs is passed back up the procedure call stack until an error-handling routine is found. If no error handler is found by the time the program reaches the top-level procedure, the error is displayed to the user and the program terminates.

The first statement that you use in error handling is the On Error statement. This statement tells your program what to do in the event of an error. There are three basic forms of the On Error statement:

On Error GoTo [line label]   Tells Visual Basic to branch to the line label (or line number) specified in the command, whenever an error occurs. This line number or label corresponds to the beginning of the error-handling routine in the procedure. The On Error statement in this form causes your program to deal with errors immediately as they occur.

On Error Resume Next   Tells Visual Basic to move to the next line in the code if an error occurs. If the error is in the current procedure, the next line of code is executed. If the error occurs in a Sub procedure called from the current procedure, execution continues on the next statement after the procedure call. This form of the On Error statement is used with inline error processing or when you want to ignore any errors that might occur.

On Error GoTo 0   Tells Visual Basic to disable the error handlers in the current procedure. If an error occurs, the error is passed up the call stack to determine if an error handler can be found. If there are no error handlers, a Visual Basic runtime error is generated and your program terminates. Typically, you only use this statement to allow higher-level procedures to handle the errors.

The On Error GoTo [line label] statement is the one most commonly used in error handling. The statement forces your program to branch to a particular line in the current procedure when the error occurs. The line that you specify is the first line of the error-handling routine. In the error-handling routine, you typically use a Select Case statement to take action depending on the error number. After you have identified the error, your program can take action to correct the error or to display a message to the user. You can also use the error-handling routine to log errors to a database or log file.

After your program has corrected the error or notified the user that an error has occurred, you need a way to continue the execution of the program. For this task you use one of the three forms of the Resume statement described below:

Resume Causes your program to retry the statement that caused the error. If the statement is a subprocedure call, the call is repeated and the subprocedure is run from the beginning.

Resume Next Causes your program to continue execution on the line following the one where the error occurred. If the error occurred in a subprocedure, the line following the procedure call is the next one executed.

Resume [line label] Causes your program to branch to the line label specified in the Resume statement. The program attempts to continue execution at that point. The label must be in the same procedure as the Resume [line label] statement. Using the Resume [line label] statement enables you to redirect the execution of a program if an error occurs. You use this statement to branch around statements that would cause additional errors after the first one has occurred.

In addition to the Resume statements, you can use the Exit Sub or Exit Function statements to get out of the procedure where the error occurs. This action is often warranted if the error would prevent the proper execution of the remainder of the procedure. The following code shows a complete error-handling routine that you would find in a typical program:

```
Private Function ChngSubArch() As Boolean
Dim iTriesCnt As Integer, bUpdateOK As Boolean, iErrReturn _
    As Integer

On Error GoTo CaptureErr6

ChngSubArch = True
iTriesCnt = 0
bUpdateOK = True
'Code to handle the task of the function

Exit Function
```

```
CaptureErr6:
Select Case Err.Number
    Case 3046, 3158, 3186, 3187, 3188, 3189, 3218, 3260
        'Record is locked by another user
        iTriesCnt = iTriesCnt + 1
         'Automatically retry 10 times then check with user
        If iTriesCnt > 10 Then
            iErrReturn = MsgBox("Retry operation",vbYesNo)
            If iErrReturn = vbYes Then
                iTriesCnt = 0
                Resume
            Else
                bUpdateOK = False
                Resume Next
            End If
        End If
    Case 3197
        'Record was changed by another user
    Case Else
        'Log error to database or text file
        bUpdateOK = False
        Resume Next
End Select
End Function
```

One final note about creating an error handler. As you can see in the code above, you need to place an Exit Sub or Exit Function statement ahead of the line where the error handler starts. This is to keep the error processing statements from being executed when no error has occurred.

Handling Inline Errors

One of the forms of the On Error statement was the On Error Resume Next statement. This statement causes your program to try to continue execution on the line following the statement that caused the error. You can use this statement to cause your program to ignore errors. You may want to use this statement for cases where the error will not affect the execution of the rest of the procedure. For example, if you are trying to delete a file, an error occurs if the file does not exist. However, since your objective was to eliminate the file, this error is of no consequence. Therefore, using the On Error Resume Next statement to ignore the error makes sense.

The other use of the On Error Resume Next statement is to handle inline processing of errors. In this situation, you would check the properties of the Err object immediately after a statement has executed that could cause an error. One of the most common uses of this type of error processing is to check for errors that occurred during a DLL call. The following code illustrates the use of this type of error processing:

```
Private Sub cmdSave_Click()
On Error Resume Next
SaveRecord
If Err.Number > 0 Then
    MsgBox "The save operation could not be completed."
    Err.Clear
    Exit Sub
End If
'Additional processing
End Sub
```

As you can see from the code, inline error-handling routines always start with a statement that checks the Number property of the Err object. If the property is greater than zero, an error has occurred. Finally, the error-handling routine typically ends by clearing the Err object properties using the Clear method, which removes the current error from within the Err object and enables the application to properly trap for any new errors that might occur.

Set Appropriate Properties to Enable User Assistance

1. You set the HelpFile property in the design environment using the
_____ dialog box.

2. The HelpFile property of the _____object lets you
create a link to a help file using program code.

3. WinHelp files have the file extension of _____.

4. The _____ property of a control links the control
to a specific help topic.

5. The _____ key is the default key for obtaining help.

6. If there is no help topic identified for a control, the system looks for a topic associated with
_____.

7. True or False. Specifying a help topic that does not exist will result in an error.

8. The _____ assists you in organizing and compiling
WinHelp files.

9. The _____ page of the help file is displayed if no topics are identified for controls or forms.

10. The _____ property of the Common Dialog control specifies the file to use for help displayed by the control.

11. The _____ property of the Common Dialog control determines the type of help that is displayed.

12. To display a particular help topic using the Common Dialog control, you must specify the _____ property in addition to setting the correct value of the HelpCommand property.

13. You call the _____ method of the Common Dialog to display the help files.

14. To display WhatsThisHelp, your form should have a BorderStyle setting of _____.

15. The _____ property of a form determines whether WhatsThisHelp is enabled for the form.

16. True or False. WhatsThisHelp will work with a Sizable form if the MinButton and MaxButton properties are set to False.

17. Setting the _____ property of a form will display the WhatsThisHelp button of a properly configured form.

18. To specify the topic shown in WhatsThisHelp, you need to set the _____ property of a control.

Create HTML Help for an Application

19.   The _____ is a tool to help you create HTML Help.

20.   HTML Help files have an extension of _____.

21.   True or False. You need to create a separate HTML file for each topic of HTML Help.

Implement Messages from a Server Component to a User Interface

22.   You can trigger an event from a server component using the _____ method.

23.   One method of passing messages from a server component to a client application is to use the _____ method of the _____ object to trigger an error from the component.

24.   The _____ property of the Err object tells the client program which component caused the error.

25.   True or False. You can specify an error number that is the same as one of Visual Basic's internal numbers.

26.   To pass help information about an error, you need to set the _____ and _____ properties of the Err object.

27.   True or False. Triggering an error automatically displays a message to the user.

Implement Error Handling for the User Interface in Desktop Applications

28. To determine which error occurred in your program, you need to check the
_____ property of the Err object.

29. The _____ property of the Err object is used to
handle errors that occur in a DLL call.

Identify and Trap Runtime Errors

30. True or False. You must place error-handling code in every procedure of your program.

31. To ignore an error and try to execute the next statement in a procedure, you use the
_____ statement.

32. To disable error handling, use the _____ statement.

33. True or False. If you do not have error handling enabled and an error occurs, your program
will terminate.

34. After you have handled an error, you use the _____
statement to retry the operation that caused the error.

35. To continue operation of the procedure on the line following the error line, you would use
the _____ statement.

36. You should use the _____ statement prior to the start of the error-handling routine to prevent the error-handling code from being run when no error has occurred.

37. To branch to another part of your procedure after an error has occurred, use the _____ statement.

38. True or False. You must use a Select Case statement to handle errors in an error handler.

39. True or False. If you are logging errors to a database or log file, you would typically include the _____ and _____ properties of the Err object.

Handle Inline Errors

40. To enable inline error handling, you need to place the _____ statement at the beginning of the procedure.

41. To determine if an error has occurred, you check the _____ property of the Err object for a value that is _____ .

42. To set up the Err object for the next error, you use the _____ method to reset the properties.

43. True or False. Inline error processing is the only way to handle errors returned by DLL calls.

44. True or False. You should place an inline error handler as close as possible to the line that can cause the error.

SAMPLE TEST

7-1   Which of the following statements is used to ignore errors in a procedure?

    A. `On Error GoTo [line label]`

    B. `On Error Resume Next`

    C. `On Error GoTo 0`

    D. `Error Off`

7-2   Which statement would you use to branch to a particular line in a procedure after handling an error?

    A. `GoTo [line]`

    B. `Resume Next`

    C. `Resume [line label]`

    D. `Resume`

7-3   Which property of the Err object tells you what error occurred in a DLL call?

    A. Number

    B. LastDLLError

    C. Description

    D. Source

7-4   Which of the following statements would be used to assign a help file to an application?

    A. `App.Help = "Test.hlp"`

    B. `Set Help = "Test.hlp"`

    C. `App.HelpFile = "Test.hlp"`

    D. `Project.HelpFile = "Test.hlp"`

S A M P L E   T E S T

7-5   What happens if there is no HelpContextID setting for a control?

    A. The help topic for the control's container is shown.

    B. An error occurs.

    C. The Index page of help is shown.

    D. No help is displayed.

7-6   What happens if an invalid HelpContextID is set for a control?

    A. The help topic for the control's container is shown.

    B. An error occurs.

    C. The Index page of help is shown.

    D. No help is displayed.

7-7   Which of the following code segments would display a particular topic in a help file?

    A.
```
cdlHelp.HelpFile = "Test.hlp"
cdlHelp.HelpCommand = cdlHelpContents
cdlHelp.ShowHelp
```
    B.
```
cdlHelp.HelpFile = "Test.hlp"
cdlHelp.HelpCommand = cdlHelpKey
cdlHelp.HelpContext = 120
cdlHelp.ShowHelp
```
    C.
```
cdlHelp.HelpFile = "Test.hlp"
cdlHelp.HelpCommand = cdlHelpContext
cdlHelp.HelpContext = 120
cdlHelp.ShowHelp
```

D.

```
cdlHelp.HelpFile = "Test.hlp"
cdlHelp.HelpCommand = cdlHelpContext
cdlHelp.HelpContext = "Printing"
cdlHelp.ShowHelp
```

7-8   Which properties of a form must be set to allow WhatsThisHelp?

    A. WhatsThisHelp and WhatsThisHelpID

    B. WhatsThisButton and WhatsThisHelpID

    C. WhatsThisHelp and WhatsThisButton

    D. WhatsThisHelp and HelpContextID

7-9   WinHelp files have what file extension?

    A. .WIN

    B. .HLP

    C. .CHM

    D. .HTM

7-10   HTML Help files have what file extension?

    A. .WIN

    B. .HLP

    C. .CHM

    D. .HTM

7-11   Why should you precede error-handling code with an Exit Sub statement?

    A. To make it easy to get out of the procedure after handling the error.

    B. To avoid running the error-handling code if no error occurred.

    C. You should not place this statement ahead of the error handler.

    D. To disable the error handler.

7-12   Which of the following are valid statements for continuing operation after an error has been encountered? Check all that apply.

    A. Resume

    B. Resume Next

    C. Resume [line label]

    D. Continue

7-13   Which of the following statements are valid On Error statements? Check all that apply.

    A. On Error Resume Next

    B. On Error Retry

    C. On Error GoTo 0

    D. On Error ProcessErr

7-14   What happens if your program encounters an error and the routine has no error handler?

    A. The program displays a message and retries the operation.

    B. The program terminates.

    C. The program attempts to find an error handler in a higher-level procedure.

    D. The program exits the procedure without displaying a message.

U N I T

8

Creating COM Components

Test Objectives: Creating and Managing COM Components

- **Create a COM component that implements business rules or logic. Components include DLLs, ActiveX controls, and active documents.**

- **Create ActiveX controls.**
  - Create an ActiveX control that exposes properties.
  - Use control events to save and load persistent properties.
  - Test and debug an ActiveX control.
  - Create and enable property pages for an ActiveX control.
  - Enable the data binding capabilities of an ActiveX control.
  - Create an ActiveX control that is a data source.

- **Create an active document.**
  - Use code within an active document to interact with a container application.
  - Navigate to other active documents.

 Exam objectives are subject to change at any time without prior notice and at Microsoft's sole discretion. Please visit Microsoft's Training & Certification Web site (www.microsoft.com/Train_Cert) for the most current exam objectives listing.

V isual Basic has always been an excellent tool for creating programs quickly. The Integrated Development Environment (IDE) makes it easy to design the user interface by creating instances of controls and placing them on the forms. The IDE also makes it easy to debug your programs, since it allows you to watch the values of variables and to step through your program line by line.

When Visual Basic was first introduced, the primary focus was creating stand-alone applications for the desktop of a single user. You did not have to worry too much about network access or access to the Internet. However, as the computing landscape has changed, Visual Basic has changed to help you meet the challenges of today's programs.

Many programs today must be capable of implementing the business rules of a company, providing access to corporate as well as desktop data, and providing links to data to be displayed on the Internet or on company intranets. Programs also have to be good at making use of reusable program components. This simplifies the management of projects involving programming teams and helps make program maintenance easier. Microsoft's answer to many of these needs is the Component Object Model (COM). Not only can Visual Basic make use of COM objects created by Microsoft and third-party vendors, Visual Basic enables you to create your own COM components. These components can be used in your programs or in any program that supports COM objects.

Create a COM Component That Implements Business Rules or Logic. Components Include DLLs, ActiveX Controls, and Active Documents

While a complete discussion of COM objects is well beyond the scope of this book, this unit looks at the creation of three types of COM objects:

- ActiveX servers that are used to implement business rules

- ActiveX controls that enable you to create reusable controls with new or enhanced features

- ActiveX documents that make it easy to create programs for use on a company intranet or on Internet sites

Creating ActiveX Servers for Implementing Business Rules

ActiveX servers provide a way for a company to create a set of functions once and have these functions available to a variety of programs. Placing the functions in a server allows business rules or data-access methods to be created once and used many times. This makes program maintenance easier and can result in greater data integrity by ensuring that rules are consistently enforced. ActiveX servers are one of the keys to multi-tier client/server applications. There are two types of ActiveX servers that you can create with Visual Basic:

In-Process server Is contained in a DLL file. An In-Process server typically runs faster than an Out-of-Process server because the code runs in the same address space as the calling application. One of the disadvantages of an in-process server is that it is less fault tolerant. Since it runs in the same address space as the client application, a fatal error in the DLL will also bring down the application using the DLL.

Out-of-Process server   Is contained in an EXE file. An Out-of-Process server is a stand-alone application that can be run on a server to take advantage of the server's speed. The key disadvantage of an Out-of-Process server is that the server components run in a separate address space from the calling application and the inter-application communication can slow performance.

Creating either type of ActiveX server requires the same basic steps:

1. Start the appropriate type of project.

2. Build the classes that define the objects of the server.

3. Set up the Object Model of the server.

4. Create any supporting routines needed by the server.

5. Test the server.

6. Compile the server and make it available for use.

To begin creating the server, open either an ActiveX EXE or ActiveX DLL project. When you open one of these projects, Visual Basic creates a single class module for you and typically opens the code window. At this point, you need to add code to the class and then to add additional class modules and standard modules to the project to handle the tasks you wish to perform. If you are creating an ActiveX EXE server, you may also want to add a BAS module and a Sub Main procedure to allow the program to be started in stand-alone mode.

After you have finished setting up all the class modules and standard modules of the server, you need to compile the server to make it available for others to use.

Create ActiveX Controls

With ActiveX controls, you can create a user interface component with your own custom methods, events, and properties. The great thing about doing this in Visual Basic is that all your standard programming techniques can be used to create the component. You create properties by writing

Property procedures using standard code. Methods are created by writing Sub and Function procedures and exposing them through a public interface. You create events using the Event procedure declaration.

Setting Up the Properties of a Control

To make the programming easier, you can use the standard components from the Visual Basic toolbox to make up the interface of your new control. Using Visual Basic's wizards, you can easily incorporate the properties, methods, and events of these standard controls into your control. Finally, you can use the IDE to debug your control, just as you would debug a standard program created with Visual Basic.

You can also use some third-party controls in your ActiveX controls, but you should carefully read your license agreements to determine whether you are able to distribute these controls in this manner.

There are three basic categories of controls that you can create with Visual Basic:

An extension of an existing control   You take a standard control and add capabilities to it. For example, you might create a text box that only accepts numeric input or a list box that is capable of sorting items in descending order.

A new control created from constituent controls   You use several standard controls working together to create a control for a specific task. You may wish to create a command button array for recordset navigation or a single control that handles all the tasks associated with a two-column pick list.

A user drawn control   You create the entire interface of the new control with drawing methods and the Print method. This is the most difficult method of creating a control. An example of this type of control would be a round command button.

Getting Started with Control Creation

The simplest way to create an ActiveX control is to use standard controls to create the components of the new control. This technique applies whether you are simply extending the capabilities of one of Visual Basic's built-in controls or creating an entirely new control. This is the technique that is discussed in this unit.

To get started with any control creation project, you need to open an ActiveX Control project from the New Project dialog box, as shown in Figure 8.1. The UserControl form that is created by Visual Basic looks very similar to a form that you would use for a standard programming project. The UserControl form is shown in Figure 8.2.

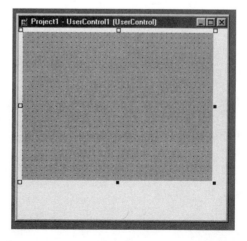

The UserControl form is not only similar to the standard form in appearance. The UserControl form shares many of the same properties that are present in a standard form. In addition, you use the UserControl form as a container for all the components of your ActiveX control, just as a form is a container for the various controls used in your application. While many properties are similar between the UserControl form and the standard form, two properties of the UserControl form deserve special mention:

BackStyle   Determines whether the form behind the control is visible through the blank areas of the UserControl form. This is the same as the BackStyle property of a Label control. For most controls you create, set this property to Transparent (0), especially if you are creating a control from multiple constituent controls. (You can also leave this property setting up to the developer who is using your control by exposing it through a public property procedure.)

ToolboxBitmap   Determines the image that is displayed for your control in the toolbox of anyone who is using the control. If you do not specify a value for this property, the control is shown in the toolbox with the default image, meaning that there is nothing to distinguish your control from any other using the default value. The bitmaps used for this property must be 16 × 15 pixels, and icon files are not usable.

Adding Controls to the UserControl Object

After you set any of the necessary properties for the UserControl itself, you are ready to start adding constituent controls. To begin adding these controls, draw them on the UserControl object just as you would draw them on a form. For example, if you wanted to create a toolbar that could be used for recordset navigation on your data-entry forms, you could draw a series of command buttons on the UserControl. One possible appearance of this toolbar is shown in Figure 8.3.

As you can see in Figure 8.3, the UserControl form was resized after the constituent controls were added so that the UserControl form exactly fits the outer boundaries of the constituent controls. It is a good idea to make sure that there is no excess space surrounding the constituent controls of your ActiveX control. This way, when a user draws an instance of your control on a form, the boundaries of the visible components are also the boundaries of the control itself.

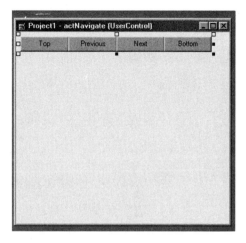

As a developer works with instances of your control, they will probably not
draw the control on the form to exactly the same size or proportion that you
used in creating the control. To ensure that the control always looks good on
a form, you have to be able to handle the changing size of the control.

When a developer draws an instance of your control, the Resize event of
the UserControl object is fired. You can place code in this event to change the
size and position of the constituent controls in response to the control being
resized. You can also place code in the event to ensure that the control does
not exceed a certain minimum or maximum size. The following code shows
how to resize the command buttons in the toolbar shown in Figure 8.3.
Notice that the code does not allow the control to be below a minimum size.

```
Private Sub UserControl_Resize()
Dim I As Integer, iBtnWidth As Integer
'Check for minimum height and width
If UserControl.Height < 375 Then UserControl.Height = 375
If UserControl.Width < 4815 Then UserControl.Width = 4815
'Set the size of the consituent buttons
iBtnWidth = Int(UserControl.Width / 4)
For I = 0 To 3
    cmdNav(I).Height = UserControl.Height
    cmdNav(I).Width = iBtnWidth
    If I = 0 Then
```

```
            cmdNav(I).Left = 0
      Else
            cmdNav(I).Left = cmdNav(I - 1).Left + iBtnWidth
      End If
   Next I
   End Sub
```

Figure 8.4 shows several instances of the control drawn on a form. Notice how the constituent controls were sized to fit the size of the control.

FIGURE 8.4

Using the toolbar in
a form

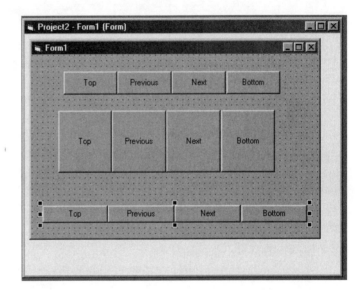

Creating the Programming Interface for the Control

In the programming interface of the standard controls in Visual Basic, you handle the appearance and the behavior of a control through its properties and accomplish tasks with the control through its methods and events. The controls that you create also need to have properties, methods, and events so that the developers using your control (including you) can work with the control. The programming elements of your ActiveX controls can be broken out into two broad categories:

Custom properties, methods, and events   These are the elements you create through code in Property, Sub, Function, and Event procedures.

Properties, methods, and events of constituent controls   These are built into the controls you used to create the user interface, but they need to be assigned to elements accessible by the user of your control.

Creating Custom Properties, Methods, and Events   If you are familiar with the creation of these elements in class modules, you already know how to create custom elements for a control. You create Properties of a control using public property procedures. You use a Property Let procedure to enable the user to set the value of a property and a Property Get procedure to enable the user to retrieve the value of a property. If you are passing an object reference to your control (for instance, a recordset for a database application) you replace the Property Let procedure with a Property Set procedure. The easiest way to create the procedures is with the Add Procedure dialog box. This dialog box, shown in Figure 8.5, is accessible by choosing the Add Procedure item from Visual Basic's Tools menu.

FIGURE 8.5

Using the Add Procedure dialog box to create a property

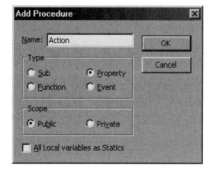

In the dialog box, you specify the name of the property and choose the Property option of the dialog box. For a property procedure, you should also be sure that the Scope option is set to Public. This allows others to work with the property. After entering this information and clicking the OK button, the dialog box creates both a Property Let and a Property Get procedure for the new property. The property procedures created by the dialog box contain only the header information for the property. You need to add code to the procedure to have them set and retrieve values.

For a more thorough discussion of the creation of properties, see the *MCSD: Visual Basic 6 Desktop Applications Study Guide* (Sybex, 1999) by this author.

While the Add Procedure dialog box handles the basics of property procedure creation, there are several tasks that you may need to handle yourself, depending on how the properties will be used:

- Specify the data type of the Property Get function. The default type is Variant.

- Specify the data type of the variable passed to the Property Let procedure. This data type should match the one set for the Property Get function.

- If you want to create a read-only property, include only a Property Get procedure.

- If you are working with an object, change the Property Let procedure to a Property Set procedure.

After creating the properties, you also need to create any custom methods that are required by the control. A method is simply a Sub or a Function procedure that is declared as Public to allow it to be accessed from outside the control. You can create a method by typing **Public Sub** and the procedure name directly into the code window of the control. When you press Enter, Visual Basic completes the header for the method and places an End Sub statement below the header. (If you are creating a function, replace the Sub keyword with the Function keyword and specify the type of data to be returned.) You can also create a method using the Add Procedure dialog box. For a method, enter the name of the procedure, indicate if it is a Sub or Function procedure and specify the Scope option as Public.

The final elements you need to create for the control are the custom events. Again, you can use the Add Procedure dialog box to create the Event procedure declaration. You also have to add code elsewhere in your control to fire the event. The following steps show you how to create an event for your control:

1. Use the Add Procedure dialog box to create the Event declaration.

2. Add to the declaration statement the names of the arguments that will be passed by the event to a program using the control. These arguments will show up in the header for the event procedure in code.

3. Use the RaiseEvent statement to trigger the event and to pass information to the calling program.

Working with the Elements of Constituent Controls   After you have created the custom elements for your control, you also need to assign some of the elements of the constituent controls to elements that are accessible by users of your control. The elements include many of the standard properties, methods, and events of the constituent controls, such as Font, Move, Click, etc. While this seems to be a daunting task, Visual Basic makes it easy with a wizard.

The Control Interface wizard is one of the add-ins that comes with Visual Basic. To use the wizard, you must first add it to the list of add-ins using the Add-In Manager. You can then select the wizard from the Add-Ins menu. After the wizard displays its initial startup screen, you can click the Next button to start the process of assigning elements of the constituent controls to public elements of your ActiveX control. Figure 8.6 shows you the second page of the wizard, where the work of creating public elements starts.

F I G U R E   8.6

Using the Control Interface wizard

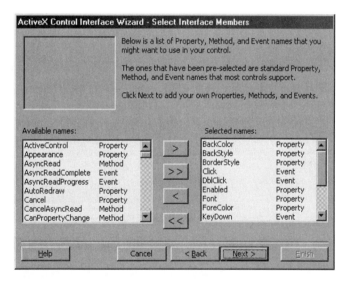

The Control Interface wizard takes you through the following steps to enable you to create a public interface from the properties, methods, and events of the constituent controls. Each step corresponds to a screen in the wizard.

1. Select the members of the constituent controls that you want to include as part of the public interface. The screen shows you a list of the available members and the members that you have selected to be made public.

2. Create new custom elements for the control. The screen shows you a list of all the elements you have already created and provides a means to create additional elements using an Add Procedure dialog box.

3. Assign properties and methods. From the list of elements that you have assigned to be public, you can select an element and link it to a property or method of a constituent control. For example, you might choose to assign a public Font property to the Font properties of each of the controls, to allow the user to change the font for all the constituent controls at once. The assignment of public elements to constituent controls is called mapping.

4. Set the attributes of the properties, methods, and events of your control. This final page of the wizard, shown below, enables you to specify whether a property is read-only and to specify the arguments for a method or event procedure.

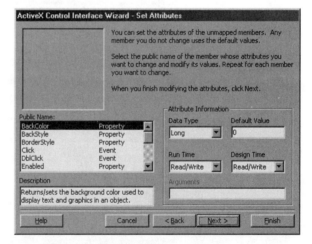

The list below describes the attributes that can be set for each of the elements of your control:

Properties   You can specify the data type, default value, design-time accessibility, and runtime accessibility of a property. The accessibility options determine whether the property is read/write, read-only, write-only, or not available.

Methods   You can specify the data type of the return value. If you specify a data type, a Function procedure is created; otherwise a Sub procedure is created. You can also specify the arguments of the procedure.

Events   You can specify the arguments for the event. The arguments determine the information that will be passed to the calling program.

Upon completion of the steps in the wizard, the wizard creates all the necessary code to implement the public members of the control and to map properties, methods, and events from the public members to the constituent controls. You simply need to add any necessary code for the custom members that you defined. Figure 8.7 shows an example of the code created by the Control Interface wizard.

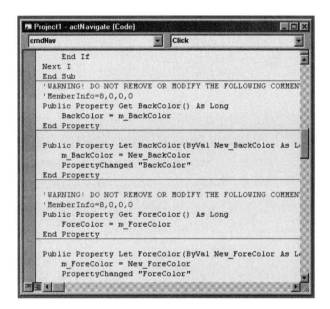

Saving Persistent Property Information for Your Control

When you work with a standard control in a program, you know that the changes you make to the properties of the control will be retained when you save your project. Then, when you reopen the project, the settings will be exactly as you left them when you saved. Unfortunately, this is not the case for controls that you create. Unless you take specific action to save the settings a user might change, the property settings for your control will be lost between programming sessions.

The upside of this problem is that Visual Basic does include tools for saving this information, and these tools can be implemented with minimal effort. Saving property information is handled through an object called the PropertyBag. This object serves as a repository for any property information that you wish to store and retrieve. The PropertyBag works with two events and one method of the UserControl object:

PropertyChanged   This method lets you notify your control that a property has been changed and needs to be written to the PropertyBag.

WriteProperties   This event is used to save the property information when the user saves the project.

ReadProperties   This event is used to retrieve the information in the PropertyBag.

Follow these steps to save and retrieve information from the PropertyBag about the properties of your control:

1. Place a PropertyChanged method in each Property Let procedure of your control. You need to specify the name of the property that was changed as shown in the following code:

```
PropertyChanged "BackStyle"
```

2. In the WriteProperties event, use the WriteProperty method of the PropertyBag to store the values of the properties for your control.

3. In the ReadProperties event, use the ReadProperty method of the PropertyBag to retrieve the values of the properties for your control. The following code shows a sample pair of WriteProperties and Read-Properties event procedures:

```
Private Sub UserControl_WriteProperties(PropBag As _
    PropertyBag)
  PropBag.WriteProperty "BackColor", _
    UserControl.BackColor, &H8000000F
  PropBag.WriteProperty "BackStyle", _
    UserControl.BackStyle, 0 _
  PropBag.WriteProperty "BorderStyle", _
    UserControl.BorderStyle, 0
  PropBag.WriteProperty "ForeColor", _
    UserControl.ForeColor, &H80000012
End Sub
```

```
Private Sub UserControl_ReadProperties(PropBag As _
    PropertyBag)
  UserControl.BackColor = _
    PropBag.ReadProperty("BackColor", &H8000000F)
  UserControl.BackStyle = _
    PropBag.ReadProperty("BackStyle", 0)
  UserControl.BorderStyle = _
    PropBag.ReadProperty("BorderStyle", 0)
  UserControl.ForeColor = _
    PropBag.ReadProperty("ForeColor", &H80000012)
End Sub
```

If you use the Control Interface wizard to create the public interface of your control, most of the code for saving and retrieving properties is written for you. You only need to handle this task manually for properties that were not created through the Control Interface wizard.

Testing and Debugging Your Control

After you have completed the interface design and the programming interface for your ActiveX control, the only remaining task is to test the control. You test a control by using a project group in Visual Basic. The project group allows you to have the control project and a test project open at the same time, making it easy to step through the code in your control and determine any errors that might occur. The following steps give you the basics of testing your ActiveX control:

1. Add a standard project to your development environment to create a project group.

2. Close the UserControl window of your control project. If the User-Control (form) window is open, Visual Basic assumes that you are still working on the design of the control and will not allow you to create an instance of the control in another form.

3. Create an instance of the control on your test form. Then you can test the properties of the control and write code to test its methods.

As you are setting the properties of the control in the design environment and as you use the methods of the control while your program is running, Visual Basic is running the code for the control. Since you are working in the development environment, you can debug your control using all of Visual Basic's debugging tools. You can set breakpoints in the code of your control and watch the values of properties and other variables in the code. When the code of the control is paused, you can use the Immediate window to display or set the value of a variable or to execute commands. The ability to use these debugging tools makes it easy to track down and eliminate errors in your controls.

You can learn more about Visual Basic's debugging tools in Unit 11, "Debugging Your Application."

Creating Property Pages for a Control

When you only have one or two properties for a control, it is very easy to handle these from the Properties window. However, as controls get more sophisticated and their interfaces become more complex, it is difficult to know which properties are important and how to best set these properties. This is where using Property Pages become advantageous.

In keeping with current programming practice, you should create property pages for your controls as well. This not only makes it easier for a user to manage your control, but it adds a more professional appearance to your control. Fortunately, Visual Basic provides a great tool for creating and managing property pages. The Property Page wizard enables you to easily set up the pages of the Property Pages dialog box for your control and to specify which properties will appear on each page. The wizard, shown in Figure 8.8, leads you through the task of creating the pages.

FIGURE 8.8

Using the Property Page wizard

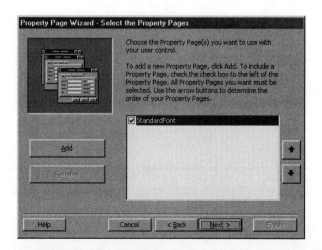

The Property Page wizard walks you through each of the following steps. There is a page of the wizard for each of these steps.

1. On the first page of the wizard, you create the pages that you want in your property pages. The wizard automatically creates two pages for you: the StandardColor and StandardFont pages. You can remove these pages if desired by clearing the check box next to the page name in the dialog box. The dialog box also has an Add button that lets you create new pages for your property pages.

2. The next page lets you assign any of the public properties of your control to a property page. In the dialog box, select the tab that represents the page where you want the properties to go. Then, select the properties to be placed on the page and use the arrow buttons to move the properties from the selection list to the desired page.

You cannot add new properties to the StandardColor or StandardFont pages, nor can you remove the properties assigned to these pages. These defaults are set by the wizard and cannot be changed. You can only assign properties to the pages you create.

3. Click the Finish button and you are done. When a user looks at the Properties window for your control, they will see a custom property. Clicking the button next to the custom property will bring up the property pages. An example of the property pages for a custom control is shown below.

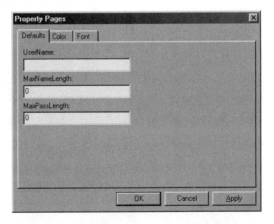

Enabling Data Binding for a Control

Many of Visual Basic's standard controls and a large number of third-party controls enable you to work directly with data from a database. These controls can be bound to a data source and allow you to directly view and edit information in the database. In version 6 of Visual Basic, you can now work directly with data from your custom ActiveX controls. You can set up your control to be bound to a data source, or you can set up a control to be a data source.

By setting a few key properties, you can set up your control to be data bound. When the control is bound to a data source, your control behaves just like the bound controls that are intrinsic to Visual Basic. In other words, your control can directly view and edit information from a database. To set up your control for data binding, follow these steps:

1. Set the DataBindingBehavior property of the control to 1 - vbSimple-Bound. This indicates that the control can be bound to a data source.

2. Open the code window for your UserControl object.

3. Select the Procedure Attributes item from the Tools menu, then click the Advanced button in the dialog box. This will bring up a dialog box where you can set the properties of the control that will be data bound. The data binding dialog box is shown in Figure 8.9.

FIGURE 8.9

Setting data binding behavior

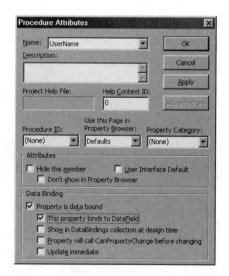

4. Select the property that will be the default data-bound property for the control in the Name drop-down list. Check the Property Is Data Bound check box in the dialog box to indicate that the property can be bound to a data source. Then check the box marked This Property Binds To DataField. This indicates that the property is the default data-bound property for the control.

5. If you choose to bind other properties to a data source, you can select the property name in the Name drop-down list and check the Property Is Data Bound box. These other properties become part of the Data-Bindings collection for your control.

Creating a Data Source

In addition to allowing you to bind a control to a data source, Visual Basic allows you to set up an ActiveX control as a data source. An ActiveX control that is set up as a data source must use the ActiveX Data Objects 2 in order to access the database.

You can learn more about ADO in Unit 10, "Creating Database Applications."

To create a data source control, you must carry out the following steps:

1. Set the DataSourceBehavior property of the control to
   1 - vbDataSource.

2. Write code to set up a recordset that the control will access. The following code shows an example of this:

```
Private rsAuthors As Recordset
Private cnMain As Connection

Private Sub UserControl_GetDataMember(DataMember As _
String, Data As Object)
    Set Data = rsAuthors
End Sub

Private Sub UserControl_Initialize()
    Dim sConnStr As String
```

```
      sConnStr = "Provider=Microsoft.Jet.OLEDB.3.51;"
      sConnStr = sConnStr & _
         "Persist Security Info=False;"
      sConnStr = sConnStr & _
         "Data Source=C:\data\Biblio.mdb"
      Set cnMain = New Connection
      cnMain.Open sConnStr
      Set rsAuthors = New Recordset
      rsAuthors.Open "Select * From Authors", cnMain, _
         adOpenKeyset
   End Sub
```

Create an Active Document

ActiveX documents are another of the COM components that you can create with Visual Basic. ActiveX documents provide a way for you to leverage your Visual Basic programming knowledge to create Web-based applications. The ActiveX document is a container on which you can place controls just as you would for a Visual Basic form. Then, using Visual Basic code, you can write procedures behind the document to perform tasks. This makes creating ActiveX documents an extension of standard Visual Basic programming. The great thing about ActiveX documents is that, once you are done, you have a complete application that can be run from a Web browser.

To start creating an ActiveX document, choose the ActiveX Document EXE option from the New Project dialog box. When you choose this option, Visual Basic places a UserDocument object in the development environment, as shown in Figure 8.10. The UserDocument is similar to a form with no borders and is very similar to the UserControl object that you use to create ActiveX controls.

After you start the new project, you can start adding controls to the User-Document to create the user interface for the ActiveX document. After you finish the user interface, open the code window to add program code to perform the necessary tasks for the application.

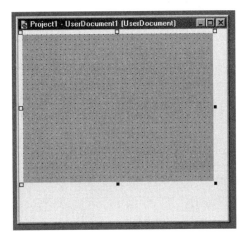

After you have completed the coding for the application, you need to test the
application. Again, the Visual Basic development environment makes testing
and debugging your application relatively easy. When you run an ActiveX document from the development environment, Visual Basic automatically starts
Internet Explorer and opens the document in the browser. As you work
through the application in the browser, the document is still active in Visual
Basic. This allows you to set breakpoints, watch the values of variables, and
make modifications to the document when you encounter an error. Figure 8.11
shows a sample ActiveX document running in Internet Explorer.

Interacting with a Container

As stated earlier, an ActiveX document is similar to an ActiveX control. One of the similarities is the ability of both the UserDocument object and the UserControl object to store data between sessions. As with the UserControl, the UserDocument object uses the PropertyBag object to store data.

To store information from a UserDocument, use the WriteProperty method of the PropertyBag. To retrieve information, you use the ReadProperty method. For these methods, you specify the name of the property and the default value. Additionally, the WriteProperty method accepts as an argument the value to be stored for the property. The default value is necessary, particularly for the ReadProperty method, in the event that a property's entry cannot be found in the PropertyBag.

The methods of the PropertyBag are used in code in the ReadProperties and WriteProperties events of the UserDocument. The ReadProperties event is fired when the document is opened. The WriteProperties event is fired when the document is closed but only if a flag has been set to indicate that a property has been changed. The flag is set using the PropertyChanged function of the UserDocument. You will use the PropertyChanged function any time a value changes that you want to store, typically when the user changes the contents of a text box or other control. The following code shows a typical use of these methods.

```
Private Sub txtDates_Change()
PropertyChanged
End Sub


Private Sub txtDestination_Change()
PropertyChanged
End Sub


Private Sub txtName_Change()
PropertyChanged
End Sub


Private Sub txtPurpose_Change()
PropertyChanged
End Sub
```

```
Private Sub UserDocument_ReadProperties(PropBag As _
PropertyBag)
txtName.Text = PropBag.ReadProperty("Name", "")
txtDestination.Text = PropBag.ReadProperty("Destination", _
"")
txtDates.Text = PropBag.ReadProperty("Dates", Format _
(Date, "Short Date"))
txtPurpose.Text = PropBag.ReadProperty("Purpose", "")
End Sub

Private Sub UserDocument_WriteProperties(PropBag As _
PropertyBag)
PropBag.WriteProperty "Name", txtName.Text, ""
PropBag.WriteProperty "Destination", txtDestination.Text, ""
PropBag.WriteProperty "Dates", txtDates.Text, ""
PropBag.WriteProperty "Purpose", txtPurpose.Text, ""
End Sub
```

Navigating in an ActiveX Document Application

Like programs that you create with standard forms, ActiveX document applications are not limited to a single document. You can create multiple documents in the project and move back and forth between the documents. The key to moving between documents is the HyperLink object of the User-Document. This object allows you to specify a particular document or to move forward or backward in the History list. There are three methods of the HyperLink object:

NavigateTo   Tells the container to move to a specific file or URL specified as an argument of the method.

GoForward   Tells the container to move to the next item in the History list.

GoBack   Tells the container to move to the previous item in the History list.

The NavigateTo method is the only one that requires you to specify a file name or URL. The other two methods work with the History list. The following code shows how these methods are used in a program:

```
Private Sub cmdTimes_Click()
Dim sName as String
sName = txtName.Text
Hyperlink.NavigateTo App.Path & "\Times.vbd"
End Sub

Private Sub cmdReturn_Click()
Hyperlink.GoBack
End Sub

Private Sub cmdNext_Click()
Hyperlink.GoForward
End Sub
```

Create a COM Component That Implements Business Rules or Logic

1. An _____ ActiveX server runs in the same address space as the calling application.

2. An _____ ActiveX server can be run as a stand-alone application on a server computer.

3. True or False. Business rules can only be stored in a stand-alone ActiveX server.

4. _____ modules make up the main components of a server.

5. ActiveX servers are compiled to either _____ or _____ files.

6. True or False. ActiveX servers can only be used in client/server applications.

Create an ActiveX Control That Exposes Properties

7. The procedure that allows the user to set a property value is a _____ procedure.

8. Assigning an object reference to a property is accomplished with a _____ procedure.

9. True or False. A Property Get procedure can be used to return objects or standard data types.

10. The _____ property of the UserControl object determines whether the form shows through the spaces between constituent controls.

11. For a property to be accessible to the users, its scope must be set as _____.

12. A method for an ActiveX control is created with a _____ or _____ procedure.

13. To create a read-only property, you include a _____ procedure but not a _____ procedure.

14. The _____ method is used to notify the calling program of an event.

15. True or False. The properties of constituent controls cannot automatically be set by the user of an ActiveX control.

16. The _____ makes it easy for you to manage the properties and methods of an ActiveX control.

17. True or False. Code written using the Control Interface wizard does not need to be modified to complete your control.

Use Control Events to Save and Load Persistent Properties

18. The object that is used to save property settings of an ActiveX control is the

_____.

19. True or False. Saving settings for properties does not work with multiple instances of an ActiveX control.

20. The _____ event of the UserControl is used to store properties.

21. True or False. To set the flag indicating that a property needs to be saved, you must specify the property name.

22. The _____ event of the UserControl is triggered when the control is opened and is used to retrieve property settings.

23. You notify the control that a property needs to be saved by using the

_____ method.

24. The PropertyChanged notification provided by the PropertyChanged method is usually placed in the _____ procedure.

25. For the ReadProperty method, you need to specify both _____ and _____.

26. To save a property, you need to use the _____ of the
_____ object.

27. The event that is used to save property values is fired when you
_____ your project and when the
_____ flag is set.

Test and Debug an ActiveX Control

28. True or False. You can set breakpoints and watch the value of variables in your ActiveX control when you are testing.

29. Adding a test project creates a project _____.

30. Before you can test your ActiveX control, you must close the
_____ window.

31. You need to place code in the _____ of the User-Control to handle the sizing of constituent controls as an instance of the control is drawn on the form.

Create and Enable Property Pages for an ActiveX Control

32. The _____ is used to create property pages for your control.

33. True or False. You can add properties to the StandardColor and StandardFont pages of the property pages.

34. Property pages are accessible by clicking the button next to the _____ property in the Properties window.

Enable the Data Binding Capabilities of an ActiveX Control

35. The _____ property indicates that your control can be bound to a data source.

36. True or False. You can only bind one property to a data control.

37. The default data-bound property is bound to the _____ of the control.

38. You set the field(s) to be bound to a data source using the _____ of the _____ dialog box.

39. The DataBindings collection contains a list of _____.

Create an ActiveX Control That Is a Data Source

40. True or False. You can create a data source control using Data Access Objects.

41. The _____ determines whether a control can be used as a data source.

42. True or False. A data source that you create can only be bound to ActiveX controls that you create, not to standard data-bound controls.

43. True or False. You can use any ADO recordset as the source for a data source control.

Use Code within an Active Document to Interact with a Container Application

44. You can save the values of information entered by the user with the _____ object.

45. You indicate that information needs to be stored by running the _____ method.

46. Settings are retrieved from storage during the _____ event.

Navigate to Other Active Documents

47. True or False. You can only call other ActiveX documents from an ActiveX document.

48. The _____ object is what allows you to move between documents in an ActiveX document application.

49. The _____ method is used to move to a specific document.

50. The _____ and _____ methods are used to move back and forth in the History list.

8-1 How do you create a read-only property in an ActiveX control?

    A. Create a Property Get procedure without a Property Let procedure.

    B. Create a Property Let procedure without a Property Get procedure.

    C. Set the Locked property of the control.

    D. Set the Scope option of the Property Get procedure to Private.

8-2 What statement is used to trigger an event in your ActiveX control?

    A. LoadEvent

    B. RaiseEvent

    C. FireEvent

    D. Trigger

8-3 Which property statement is required to set an object reference in a property?

    A. Property Get

    B. Property Let

    C. Property Set

    D. Property Read

8-4 Which of the following procedures can be used to create a method in a control? Check all that apply.

    A. Sub procedure

    B. Event procedure

    C. Property procedure

    D. Function procedure

SAMPLE TEST

8-5   What does the Control Interface wizard do for you? Check all that apply.

    A. Designs the visual interface of your control

    B. Helps you create properties, methods, and events for your control

    C. Lets you assign properties of the control to properties of the constituent controls

    D. Handles the code for storing property changes

8-6   How are the property pages of a control accessed? Check all that apply.

    A. Click the button next to the Custom property in the Properties window.

    B. Double-click the control.

    C. Choose the Property Pages item from the Tools menu

    D. Right-click the control and select Properties.

8-7   Which events are used to store and retrieve developer settings for your control?

    A. WriteProperties and Retrieve

    B. WriteProperties and ReadProperties

    C. Save and Load

    D. Save and Read

8-8   How do you indicate that a property needs to be saved?

    A. Raise the Save event.

    B. Use the PropertyChanged method.

    C. It is handled automatically.

    D. Place a button on the control for the user to click.

8-9   What method is used to retrieve developer settings for your control?

    A. The Read method of the UserControl object

    B. The Retrieve method of the PropertyBag object

    C. The ReadProperty method of the PropertyBag object

    D. The ReadProperty method of the UserControl object

8-10   Which property is used to determine whether a control can be data bound?

    A. DataSourceBehavior

    B. AllowBinding

    C. DataField

    D. DataBindingBehavior

8-11   Which property of your control works with the default bound property?

    A. DataSource

    B. BoundField

    C. DataField

    D. Value

8-12   Which property is used to determine whether a control can be a data source?

    A. DataSourceBehavior

    B. AllowBinding

    C. DataField

    D. DataBindingBehavior

8-13   If you have multiple bound properties, where are the non-default properties stored?

    A. The fields collection

    B. The PropertyBag

    C. The DataBindings collection

    D. The property pages

8-14   Which of the following is true of In-Process servers? Check all that apply.

    A. An ActiveX DLL is an In-Process server.

    B. They are faster than Out-of-Process servers.

    C. They can run as a stand-alone application.

    D. They run in the same process space as the client.

8-15   Which of the following is an advantage of an Out-of-Process server? Check all that apply.

    A. It can run as a stand-alone application.

    B. There are more multithreading options than for an In-Process server.

    C. It can handle more objects in a single project than an In-Process server.

    D. It is faster than an In-Process server.

8-16   What is the primary object used in creating ActiveX documents?

    A. UserControl

    B. Form

    C. UserDocument

    D. Class Module

```
SAMPLE TEST
```

8-17 How do you store information from an ActiveX document so it is available when the document is reloaded?

    A. Write the information to a file.

    B. Use the methods of the PropertyBag object.

    C. It cannot be done.

    D. Specify the initial settings in the HyperLink object.

8-18 How do you display one document from another?

    A. Use the Show method of the document.

    B. Use the NavigateTo method of the HyperLink object.

    C. Use the Display method of the document.

    D. Use the Navigate method of the UserDocument object.

8-19 Which of the following are methods of the HyperLink object? Check all that apply.

    A. NavigateTo

    B. Search

    C. GoForward

    D. GoBack

8-20 Using the NavigateTo method, which of the following can be accessed? Check all that apply.

    A. Another ActiveX document

    B. An HTML file on your local drive

    C. A standard form in the application

    D. A Web site

U N I T

9

Managing COM Components

Test Objectives: Creating and Managing COM Components

- **Debug a COM client written in Visual Basic.**

- **Compile a project with class modules into a COM component.**
  - Implement an object model within a COM component.
  - Set properties to control the instancing of a class within a COM component.

- **Use Visual Component Manager to manage components.**

- **Register and unregister a COM component.**

 Exam objectives are subject to change at any time without prior notice and at Microsoft's sole discretion. Please visit Microsoft's Training & Certification Web site (www.microsoft.com/Train_Cert) for the most current exam objectives listing.

In Unit 8, "Creating COM Components," you saw how to create ActiveX controls and ActiveX documents. These are two types of COM components that you can create for use in your Visual Basic programs and for use in other programs that can use COM components. You also saw that you can create COM components for handling business rules and functions and that these components are usually contained in ActiveX DLL or EXE servers. The basis of these components are class modules. The creation of class modules was covered in Unit 1, "Designing Your Applications." This unit builds on the topics that were presented in Units 1 and 8. Here, we review how to manage all the components that you create and how to make those components available to other applications.

Debug a COM Client Written in Visual Basic

A COM client application is a standard executable that uses COM components from one or more sources. These components can be in the following form:

- ActiveX controls in OCX files

- ActiveX Component servers that you create

- ActiveX Component servers created by others, including Word, Excel, Project, etc.

Starting a Project

To begin creating a COM client application, you open a new Standard EXE project in Visual Basic. After you have opened the project, you need to add references to the COM components that you wish to include in your application. If the components are ActiveX controls, you can add them to your project through the Components dialog box shown in Figure 9.1. You can access the Components dialog box by choosing the Components item from the Project menu or by pressing Ctrl+T.

For components in an ActiveX server, you must add the reference to the server through the References dialog box. This dialog box, shown in Figure 9.2, shows a list of all registered DLL and EXE servers available to your program. You can access the References dialog box by choosing the References item from the Project menu.

After you have added all the necessary controls and references to your project, you can start writing code for the application. To use the ActiveX controls, you place instances of a control on the form and use code to set its properties and invoke its methods. To use a COM component from an ActiveX server, use a declaration statement to create an instance of the component in code, then use the object variable to reference the properties and methods of the component.

FIGURE 9.2

Adding references to a
project

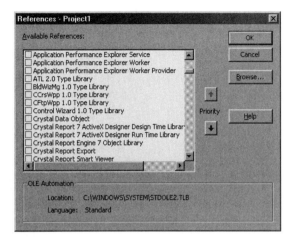

 Creating an instance of a COM component and using it in code is covered in Unit 6, "Working with COM Components."

Avoiding Problems with COM Components

As you are creating COM client applications, one of the best ways to handle errors is to avoid them in the first place. Visual Basic can provide you with help about components in the form of the Auto List Members and Auto Quick Info features. These features are enabled by default and can be found using the Options dialog box shown in Figure 9.3. To open the Options dialog box, select the Options item from the Tools menu.

Auto List Members provides you with a drop-down list of all the properties and methods associated with an object. When you type the dot (.) after the name of a control or the variable for a component, you can start typing the name of the property or method you want to access. The Auto List Members finds the first occurrence that matches the letters that you have typed. When you find the item you want, you can press Tab, the spacebar, or Enter to accept the choice. Visual Basic then finishes typing the name of the property or method for you. Using this feature helps you avoid typing the name of an element incorrectly or specifying an element that does not exist. These are two common errors in code. Auto List Members is shown in Figure 9.4.

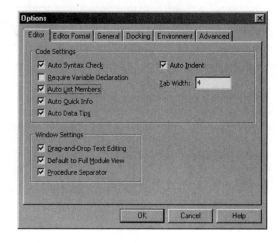

FIGURE 9.3

Setting the options for your project

FIGURE 9.4

Using Auto List Members

For COM components, Auto List Members and Auto Quick Info only work if you have declared a specific type of component in the variable declaration.

Auto Quick Info is another feature that helps you avoid errors. As you specify the method of a component, Auto Quick Info displays information about the parameters that are required for the method call. This feature shows you the type of data to pass and which parameters are optional. The information is displayed in the form of a tool tip, as shown in Figure 9.5.

FIGURE 9.5

Using Auto Quick Info

 Another feature that saves keystrokes is the code completion shortcut. As you type the name of a variable or object, you can press the Ctrl+Spacebar key combination to complete the name. This is very useful when you use long variable names.

Finding and Killing Bugs

After you have written the code for your application, run the program to find any bugs. How you locate and deal with the bugs depends on the type of COM components you are working with. If you are working with ActiveX controls or ActiveX servers that were created by someone else, you will need to get the error number and find information about the error in the help file of the component. Other errors that occur may be the result of not creating the reference to the proper server or not properly setting the object variable in code.

If the COM component is a control or server that you wrote, you can use a project group to view the code for both the client and the component. This makes it easier to determine whether an error is in the client application or in the component itself. You can find out more about project groups in Unit 11, "Debugging Your Application."

Finally, if you are creating components within your application through the use of class modules, you can find the bugs in the classes using the standard debugging tools described in Unit 11. You should, however, ensure that you have the break option set to break on errors in class modules. With this option set, your program pauses at the line in a class module that causes the error. If the option is not set, your code will pause at the line that makes the call to a property or method of the class. The break options are shown in Figure 9.6. These options are part of the Options dialog box found under the Tools menu.

FIGURE 9.6

Setting the break options

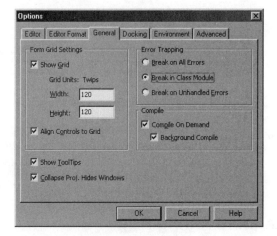

Compile a Project with Class Modules into a COM Component

When you are creating an ActiveX server to provide COM components, you start with an ActiveX DLL or ActiveX EXE project. The actual components that the server provides are created with class modules. In the class modules, you create the properties, methods, and events that make up the public interface of the component. Creating class modules is covered in Unit 1.

Implementing an Object Model within a COM Component

Within a COM component, not every class has the same importance to the component, nor does every component occupy the same level in the object hierarchy. In many cases, one class is used to manage a group of other class objects. This group of objects is known as a collection. The ranking of classes and their relation to each other is formalized in the object model of the component. The object model defines the relationship between multiple objects within a component.

As an example of an object model, consider an application designed for tracking employees in a company. The top-level object of the model would be the company. The company would then consist of multiple departments, and each department would have multiple employees. You can readily see how these objects are related. The company object would manage the collection of department objects and possibly customer objects. Each department object would have a collection of employee objects.

The object model of the company component is created as you create the properties and methods of the classes used to define the objects. One tool that is very useful in creating classes and setting up the object hierarchies that make up the object model is the Class Builder utility. The Class Builder utility is a Visual Basic add-in that lets you easily add collections to a class and automatically creates the Add and Remove methods needed for managing the collection. The Class Builder utility also makes it easy for you to create a new class based on an existing class. This enables you to create a type of object inheritance in your components. The Class Builder utility is shown in Figure 9.7.

FIGURE 9.7

Using the Class
Builder utility

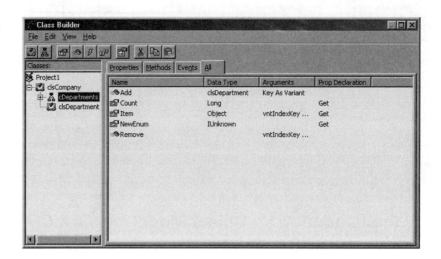

Controlling the Instancing of a Class within a COM Component

When you are creating components in a server, you must specify how each component can be used by applications that access the server. For each of the classes in a server, you should specify the Instancing property to determine how the class can be used. The following list specifies the different settings of the Instancing property:

Private   The class can be used only within the server. It is not available to client applications.

PublicNotCreatable   This defines a class that can be used by client applications but only if it has already been created by the server. Client applications cannot create an instance of the class using the New keyword or the CreateObject function.

SingleUse   Other applications can create and use objects of the class. However, each time a client application creates an object from the class, a new instance of the class is started by the server.

GlobalSingleUse   Similar to SingleUse, but an application does not have to specifically create the object to use its methods and properties. The methods and properties are treated as global functions.

MultiUse   Similar to SingleUse, but the server creates only a single instance of your class, no matter how many clients create objects from the class. All objects from the class are generated from the single instance.

GlobalMultiUse   Similar to MultiUse except that the methods and properties are treated as global functions, which means that applications do not have to specifically create an instance of the class.

Depending on the type of server you are creating, all these options may not be available to you. An ActiveX EXE server can use any of the settings of the Instancing property; however, the ActiveX DLL server cannot use the SingleUse or the GlobalSingleUse settings. Fortunately, Visual Basic provides you with only the choices that are available for your type of project.

The other property that determines the behavior of a component is the Persistable property. This property determines whether the object created from the class can persist data between one instance of the object and another. There are only two settings of the Persistable property:

- Not persistable (the default setting)

- Persistable

Persisting the properties of an object is similar to persisting information about an ActiveX control. You saw how to use the PropertyBag to persist data in an ActiveX control in Unit 8.

Use Visual Component Manager to Manage Components

As you create more classes and ActiveX controls, you need a method to organize and manage the components. In Visual Basic 6, Microsoft has included the Visual Component Manager. This tool provides a way to store your components and to catalog them with information about each component. Organizing your components makes it easier to find the component you need for a particular project.

The Visual Component Manager, shown in Figure 9.8, usually loads automatically when you start Visual Basic. If the manager does not load, you should start it from the Add-Ins Manager. Once the Visual Component Manager is loaded, you can access it by clicking its button in the toolbar or by choosing the Visual Component Manager item on the View menu.

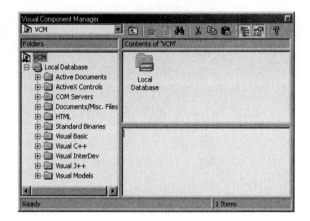

Adding Components

The first step to using the Visual Component Manager (VCM) is to add components to the repository. The first time you open the VCM, there are no components in the repository. If you click the Local Database icon in the left panel of the VCM, you will be asked if you would like to include Visual Basic's templates in the manager. If you answer Yes, this is an easy way to get some components into the manager and to set up the folder structure for the VCM. You can add folders to the database and delete folders in a manner similar to using Windows Explorer.

To add one of your own components to the VCM, follow these steps:

1. Open the VCM.

2. Select or create the folder where you want to store the component.

3. Click the Publish New Component button on the VCM's toolbar to bring up the Publish wizard. On the first page of the wizard, shown below, enter the name of the component and the file where it is stored.

You can also specify the type of component and what type of information the component includes.

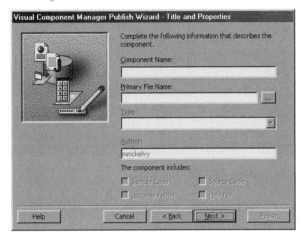

4. On the next page of the wizard, shown below, you can specify a description of the component and a series of keywords that will make it easy to find the component when you want to include it in other projects.

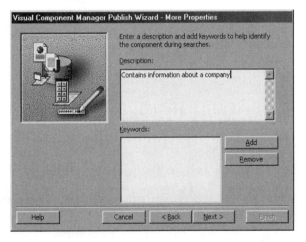

5. The final page of the wizard lets you specify any additional files that are required for the proper operation of the component. Clicking the Finish button adds the component to the repository.

Retrieving a Component

When you are starting a new project, you may need to retrieve components that you have previously created. This is where the power of the VCM really comes into play. To add an existing component to a new project follow these steps:

1. Open the Visual Component Manager.

2. Locate the component(s) you need for the project. You can click the Search button to bring up the Find Items dialog box, shown below. This dialog box lets you look for the name of a component or for key-words that are listed for the component.

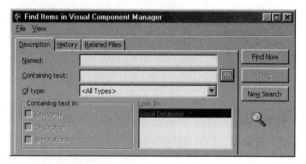

3. After finding the component, double-click the icon representing the component to add it to your project.

Register and Unregister a COM Component

After you have created a COM component, you must register it before it can be used. This must occur whether the component is on your development machine or on a client machine. On your development machine, the component is registered as it is compiled. There are several methods of registering a COM component on a client machine:

- Run the component (if it is capable of being run by itself). This action automatically registers the component.

- Use the REGSVR32.EXE program to register the component. With this method, you specify the path and the name of the component as a command line argument of the REGSVR32.EXE program.

- Use a setup program to register the component as your program is being installed on another computer. Setup programs are discussed in Unit 12, "Preparing Your Application for Distribution."

There will come a time when a component is no longer needed and you want to remove the information about the control from the system registry. How you unregister a component depends on the type of component. If the component is an EXE server, you can run the .EXE with the UnRegserver parameter as illustrated in the following line of code:

```
Payroll.exe /UnRegserver
```

If you are working with a DLL server, you need to use the Regsvr32 utility and specify the /U parameter. This is shown in the following code:

```
Regsvr32.exe /u C:\Automation\Payroll.dll
```

STUDY QUESTIONS

Debug a COM Client Written in Visual Basic

1. To use an ActiveX control in a program, you must first add it to the

_____.

2. The _____ dialog box lets you include COM components in your project.

3. True or False. To create a COM client application, you must use a special type of Visual Basic project.

4. _____ gives you a list of methods and properties for a component.

5. To see what parameters are required for a component method, you should have the _____ feature turned on.

6. True or False. You can debug the compiled code of ActiveX controls or server components that have been written by others.

7. A _____ can be used to debug components that you have written and the client application that is using the components.

8. To see errors that occur in a class module, you must have the _____ option turned on.

9. True or False. For Auto List Members to work, you must specify the component type in the declaration statement.

Implement an Object Model within a COM Component

10. True or False. All classes or objects in a server have the same ranking.

11. _____ hold a group of instances of another object.

12. The _____ defines the relationship between multiple objects in a component.

13. The _____ add-in makes it easy to set up object hierarchies that make up an object model.

14. True or False. Only classes created with the Class Builder utility are included in the object model.

15. True or False. The Class Builder utility will allow you to create a class based on another class.

Set Properties to Control the Instancing of a Class within a COM Component

16. The _____ property is used to control how a class from a server can be used.

17. To create a class that can only be used within the server, set the Instancing property to _____.

18. A new instance of a class is started for each object created from the class if the Instancing property is set to _____ or _____.

19. True or False. Both ActiveX DLL and ActiveX EXE servers can use the same settings of the Instancing property.

20. True or False. When the Instancing property is set to MultiUse, only a single instance of the class is started for objects created from the class.

21. The _____ property determines whether you can persist data between instances of an object.

Use Visual Component Manager to Manage Components

22. The _____ helps you organize the components you use to create applications.

23. True or False. The Visual Component Manager only allows you to work with components that you create.

24. The two key pieces of information needed for storing a component in the VCM are _____ and _____.

25. You can use _____ to make it easier to find a component for a new project.

26. True or False. The VCM provides you with a wizard to help you publish a component.

27. To find a component easily, click the _____ button on the VCM toolbar.

28. To add a component to your project, _____ the icon representing the component.

29. True or False. Only ActiveX controls can be added to the VCM.

Register and Unregister a COM Component

30. The _____ utility can be used to register or unregister a component.

31. True or False. You can register an EXE server by running the program.

32. For a client machine, you should register the component as part of the _____ process.

33. The _____ parameter tells the registration utility to unregister the component.

34. For an EXE server, you can unregister the server by running it with the _____ command line switch.

SAMPLE TEST

9-1   Which of the following provide COM components that you can use in a client application? Check all that apply.

    A. ActiveX Control OCX files

    B. Other standard programs that you create

    C. ActiveX Servers

    D. Code contained in BAS modules

9-2   What do you have to do before you can use a COM object in your program?

    A. Declare a variable as an object variable.

    B. Set a reference to the server or control.

    C. No special action is required.

    D. Start your project as an ActiveX client project.

9-3   Which of the following settings of the Instancing property apply only to Out-of-Process servers? Check all that apply.

    A. Private

    B. SingleUse

    C. MultiUse

    D. PublicNotCreatable

SAMPLE TEST

9-4   Which property of a component lets you keep data from one instance to another?

   A. Instancing

   B. Persistable

   C. KeepData

   D. Persistent

9-5   What is the Object Model for a component?

   A. The help file that describes the component

   B. A definition of the relationship between classes in the component

   C. A diagram of the component

   D. A listing of the properties of the component

9-6   Which Visual Basic features can help you avoid errors when working with COM components? Check all that apply.

   A. Auto List Members

   B. Auto Data Tips

   C. Auto Quick Info

   D. Auto Indent

S A M P L E   T E S T

9-7   Which setting of the Instancing property starts a new instance of the server object for each created object?

    A. Private

    B. PublicNotCreatable

    C. MultiUse

    D. SingleUse

9-8   The Class Builder utility add-in helps you do which of the following? Check all that apply.

    A. Create collections for holding multiple instances of a class.

    B. Create the properties, methods, and events of a class.

    C. Write the documentation for a component.

    D. Create a class based on an existing class.

9-9   If you want a class to only be used within the server, which setting of the Instancing property would you choose?

    A. Private

    B. PublicNotCreatable

    C. MultiUse

    D. SingleUse

9-10 What does the Instancing property do?

A. Sets the number of objects that can be created from the class

B. Determines whether the class inherited properties from another class

C. Specifies how other programs can use the class in an ActiveX server

D. Specifies how other programs can use the class in a standard program

9-11 What is the purpose of the Visual Component Manager?

A. To show you samples of a component

B. To verify the correctness of code in components

C. To organize your components to make them easier to reuse

D. To register all the components on your computer

9-12 Which of the following must you specify when adding a component to the Visual Component Manager? Check all that apply.

A. Name

B. Keywords for identifying the component

C. Which applications use the component

D. File containing the component

9-13 Which of the following are ways to register a component? Check all that apply.

A. Copy the component to your project directory.

B. Run the component if it is an EXE server.

C. Use the Regsvr32 utility.

D. Create a setup program to handle the registration.

9-14   Which parameter is used when running an Out-of-Process server to cause it to unregister itself?

    A. /u

    B. /UnRegserver

    C. /Discard

    D. You cannot unregister a server with a command line argument.

U N I T
10

**Creating Database
Applications**

Test Objectives: Creating Data Services

- Access and manipulate a data source by using ADO and the ADO Data control.

 Exam objectives are subject to change at any time without prior notice and at Microsoft's sole discretion. Please visit Microsoft's Training & Certification Web site (www.microsoft.com/Train_Cert) for the most current exam objectives listing.

One of the most common programming tasks today is creating programs that view and manipulate data in a database. Database programs are used for managing inventory, tracking customer orders and sales, tracking employee information, and a host of other tasks. While the demand for database programming has increased, so has the number of options for handling database information. Programmers can now choose between a variety of desktop- and server-based database systems. Also, an increasing number of programs need to access data from multiple data sources.

Access and Manipulate a Data Source by Using ADO and the ADO Data Control

Recent versions of Visual Basic have made database access increasingly easy. In version 6 of Visual Basic, Microsoft has introduced a new set of methods and tools for creating database applications. The new techniques are based on a technology known as ActiveX Data Objects or ADO. ADO allows the developer to use a single set of tools for accessing information on a user's hard drive and on the corporate database server. Previously, multiple tools were required to perform these tasks.

The easiest way to create database applications is through the use of the ADO data control and the bound controls that come with Visual Basic. Using these controls, you can quickly and easily write a program that allows a user to view and edit information in a database. This unit covers how to use the ADO data control and the bound controls to create applications. You will also see how to use ADO methods in code to add the features to your program that are not available with just the ADO data control.

Setting Up the ADO Data Control

Two of the main functions you need to have for any database program are a link to the information in the database and a way to navigate between records in the database. The ADO data control (ADODC) handles these two tasks for you. When you bind controls to the ADODC, the bound controls automatically handle displaying the data while the ADODC handles saving changes to the data. The only key functions that you need to handle with code are adding a new record, deleting an existing record, and finding a particular record in the recordset. Figure 10.1 shows you a typical data-entry screen that you can create with the ADODC and bound controls.

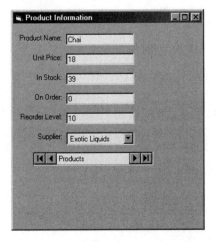

FIGURE 10.1

A sample data-entry screen

The first step to creating a program with the ADODC is to add the control to your toolbox. If you look closely at the toolbox, you will see that there is a data control already there. This is the DAO data control that was used in previous versions of Visual Basic. While the DAO data control is still the default, Microsoft recommends that all new database programming use ADO and the ADODC. To add the ADODC to your toolbox, right-click the toolbox and choose the Components item from the pop-up menu. You can then check the box next to Microsoft ADO Data Control 6 in the Components dialog box. When you click the OK button, the control is added to the toolbox and you are ready to start setting up the control.

Setting the Required Properties of the ADODC

After adding the control to the toolbox, you need to draw an instance of the control on your form. At this point, you only need to set two properties to complete the basic setup of the ADODC:

ConnectionString   Specifies the type and location of the database that you are trying to access. In addition, if you are working with a secured database, the ConnectionString also specifies the security information, such as user ID and password.

RecordSource   Specifies the particular fields and records that you want to work with. The RecordSource property can contain the name of a table, the name of a stored procedure or query, or a valid Structured Query Language (SQL) statement.

The ConnectionString property is the one that you need to set first. Without a proper connection to a database, you cannot specify a valid value for the RecordSource property. The best way to set the ConnectionString property is through the ConnectionString Builder dialog box accessible from the ADODC property pages. To create a connection to a Microsoft Access database, follow these steps:

1. Open the property pages for the ADODC by right-clicking on the control.

2. Select the Use Connection String option and click the Build button.

3. From the dialog box shown below, select the data provider. Visual Basic sets up ADO with a number of data providers including ones for Microsoft Access, Microsoft SQL Server, and Oracle. You may also have other providers installed on your machine. The dialog box shows a list of all providers available on your machine. For Access databases, select the Microsoft Jet 3.51 OLE DB Provider.

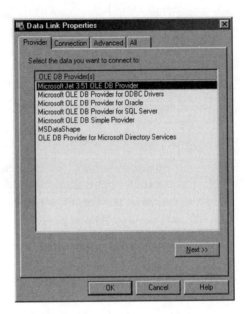

4. Click the Connection tab of the dialog box to specify the actual database that you will be accessing. Fill in the name of the database or select it from the Open dialog box available by clicking the ellipsis button. After specifying the database name, you need to specify a username and password, if the database is secured.

5. Click the OK button of the Data Link Properties dialog box, then the OK button of the property pages to accept the connection information.

After you set the ConnectionString property, you can set the Record-Source property to identify the specific data you want. Again, the easiest way to set the RecordSource is through the property pages. On the RecordSource tab of the property pages, shown in Figure 10.2, you can specify the command type for the RecordSource. The command type tells Visual Basic what type of data source you will be entering. A command type of adCmdUnknown or adCmdText allows you to specify a SQL command in the box marked Command Text. If you choose a command type of adCmdTable, the drop-down list labeled Table Or Stored Procedure Name will be populated with the names of all the available tables in the database. You can then select the desired table from the list. Likewise, if you choose a command type of adCmdStoredProc, the list will be populated with all the available queries or stored procedures available in the database.

F I G U R E   10.2

Setting the Record-
Source property

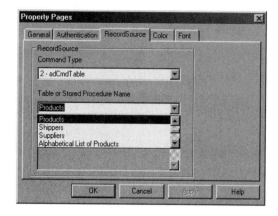

After setting both the ConnectionString and RecordSource properties, you have created the link between the data control and the data that you wish to access. You can then start linking bound controls to the ADODC to create a data-entry screen.

Setting Optional Properties of the ADODC

While the ConnectionString and RecordSource properties are the only properties that you are required to set for the ADODC, there are several other properties that you need to set to get the most out of the ADODC. The first of these key properties is the CursorType property. This property determines how the data control will work with the data specified in the RecordSource property. There are three types of cursors that you can create with the ADODC:

Static cursors   Provide a snapshot of the data at the time the recordset was created. The information in this type of cursor cannot be edited and you cannot add or delete records with a static cursor. Therefore, this type of cursor can only be used when you are viewing data. The static type of cursor is the default that is created with the ADODC.

Dynamic cursors   Provide you with a link to the data with which you can edit records, add new records, and delete existing records. In addition, a dynamic cursor automatically reflects the changes to records that are made by other users in a multiuser environment. This is the most flexible type of cursor.

Keyset cursors   Provide a data link that is similar to a dynamic cursor except that changes made by other users are not automatically reflected in the cursor.

If you are only going to be viewing data, the default static cursor is the fastest one for data navigation and is the best choice. However, if you plan to allow your users to edit data, set the CursorType property to one of the other types defined above.

In addition to the CursorType property, there are three other properties that determine how the ADODC will interact with the data that you have requested:

BOFAction   Determines what the ADODC does when the user moves to the beginning of the file. The options are to set the BOF flag for the cursor or to move to the first record of the cursor.

EOFAction   Determines what the ADODC does when the user moves to the end of the file. The options are to set the EOF flag for the cursor, to move to the last record of the cursor, or to add a new record.

LockType   Determines whether to use optimistic or pessimistic locking. Optimistic locking only locks records when the data updates are being written to the database. Pessimistic locking locks records as soon as the user starts the process of editing the data. The LockType property can also be used to specify that the cursor be accessed as read-only.

Working with Bound Controls

The second piece to creating database applications is to bind controls to the ADODC. These bound controls are the ones that allow you to display and edit the data from a database. Of the standard controls in Visual Basic's toolbox, eight of the controls can be bound to an ADODC:

TextBox   Displays and allows the editing of text information. The information from the database is handled by the Text property of the control.

Label   Displays text information. The information from the database is handled by the Caption property of the control.

ComboBox   Allows the user to select an item from a list or to enter a new item. The Text property of the control is the one bound to a data source.

ListBox   Allows the user to select an item from a list. The List property of the control is bound to a data source.

CheckBox   Allows the user to toggle between On and Off, Yes and No, etc. The Value property is bound to the data source.

PictureBox   Displays pictures that are contained in the database. The Picture property is the bound property.

Image   Displays pictures that are contained in the database. The Picture property is the bound property.

OLE   Is a control that provides links to OLE objects in a database. It has no bound property.

These controls are the ones that you will use most in your development of database applications with the ADODC. For each of these controls, you need to set two properties to bind the control to a data source.

Binding Standard Controls

The first property that you need to set is the DataSource property. This property identifies the data control that contains the recordset that the control will access. The DataSource property can be set to the name of an ADODC, a DAO data control or an RDO (Remote Data Objects) data control. When you set the DataSource property from the Properties window, you are provided with a list of all the data controls (of any type) that are present on the current form. You can select the name of the data control from the drop-down list, as shown in Figure 10.3, or enter the name in the Edit portion of the property.

After you have set the DataSource property, you need to set the DataField property of the control. This property identifies the specific field in the database to which the control is bound. After the DataSource property is set, the DataField property will have a drop-down list containing all the fields defined in the recordset of the data control. You simply pick the name of the field from the list and the process of binding the control is complete.

You can cycle through all the entries in the drop-down lists of the Data-Source and DataField properties by double-clicking on the property name in the Properties window.

F I G U R E   10.3

Setting the Data-
Source property

Other Bound Controls

In addition to the standard controls that can be bound to a data control, many third-party controls can be bound to provide even greater flexibility in the design of your database applications. Microsoft has even provided additional controls with Visual Basic that can be bound to a data control as listed:

DataGrid   Provides a spreadsheet-style interface to enable the display and editing of multiple records at a time.

DataCombo   Provides a way to set up a combo box with a list derived from one data control while the data being manipulated resides in another data control. The user can also enter values that are not in the list.

DataList   Is similar to the DataCombo but it does not allow the user to enter new values.

MSHFlexGrid   Is the hierarchical flex grid control. This provides a spreadsheet-style interface to enable the user to view multiple records in a recordset. This control also provides greater formatting capabilities than the DataGrid.

MaskedEdit   Enables the user to enter data using a template to format the input.

RichTextBox Enables the display and editing of Rich Text Format (RTF) text.

Chart Enables the display of data in the form of graphs.

For each of these controls, you need to set the DataSource property to the name of a data control on your form. The rest of the binding process (specifying individual fields, etc.) is different for each control and is beyond the scope of this book.

Extending the Capabilities of the ADODC

While the ADODC and the bound controls allow you to display and edit information without any additional programming, there are several capabilities that are lacking from a complete database application:

- The ability to add new records

- The ability to delete existing records

- The ability to search for a specific record

These capabilities can be handled through the use of ADO methods, upon which the ADODC is based. To implement each of these capabilities, you use the Recordset object of the ADODC. The Recordset object is a reference to the ADO recordset that is created when you set the ConnectionString and RecordSource properties of the ADODC.

Creating and Deleting Records

While a database application that enables editing of data is useful, sooner or later, you need to add records to the database. To add a new record to the database, you use the AddNew method of the Recordset object. The AddNew method is invoked with the following line of code:

```
adMembers.Recordset.AddNew
```

In this example, adMembers is the name of the ADO data control to which the record is being added.

The AddNew method clears the data buffer of the recordset and prepares it to accept values for the new record. When this method is used with the data control, the bound controls are cleared to allow the entry of the new information. When the user navigates from the new record to another record or adds another new record, the data that was entered for the new records is automatically saved to the database. Once again, you can see that the data control shields you from many of the tasks involved in working with databases.

If you can add records, you probably also need to be able to delete records. Once again, a method of the Recordset object is used to accomplish this task. The Delete method of the Recordset object removes the current record in the recordset. The following line of code illustrates the use of the Delete method:

```
adMembers.Recordset.Delete
```

When you invoke the Delete method, the record is removed from the database. There is no way to recover the record, so care must be used when deleting records. Also, if you delete a record, the data from the record remains in the bound controls until you move to another record. If a user tries to edit this data, an error occurs. Therefore, after you delete a record, you should move the record pointer to another record in the recordset. The following code shows a more complete deletion routine. This routine verifies that the user wants to delete the record, then moves the record pointer after the deletion is performed.

```
Private Sub cmdDelete_Click()
    Dim sMsg As String, iRetValue As Integer
    sMsg = "Do you really want to delete this record?"
    iRetValue = MsgBox(sMsg, vbExclamation + vbYesNo)
    If iRetValue = vbNo Then Exit Sub
    With adMembers.Recordset
        .Delete
        If Not .EOF Then
            .MoveNext
        Else
            .MoveLast
        End If
    End With
End Sub
```

Finding a Record

Finding specific records in a recordset is more complex than adding new records or deleting existing ones. Finding a record involves invoking the Find method of the recordset and specifying the criteria of the record you wish to find. You also need to check the EOF property of the recordset to determine whether the Find method was successful in locating a record.

The basic setup of the Find method consists of calling the method of the recordset and passing it the criteria for which you are searching. The criteria consist of three items:

- The field name to be searched

- The comparison operator, such as >, <, =, Like, or Between

- The value to which the field contents are compared

The field name item is the name of the field as it is listed in the recordset. The power of the Find command lies in the proper use of the comparison operator and the comparison value. Simple comparisons use a single value and an operator such as <, >, or =.

The Like and Between comparison operators are more complex. The Like operator allows you to compare a text field to a text pattern. The Between operator, unlike the other operators, takes two values for comparison. The Between operator is usually used to find records with a value in a specific numeric or date range.

The basic syntax of the Find method is shown in the following code:

```
adMembers.Recordset.Find "FirstName='Mike'"
```

When you are specifying the criteria for the Find method, several rules must be followed:

- The criteria for the Find method must be literal strings or string variables.

- For criteria that are literal strings, the criteria must be enclosed within double quotes.

- The comparison value must be of the same type (text, numeric, date) as the field being searched. Otherwise, an error will occur.

- Text values, including patterns, must be enclosed within quotes (single or double) in the criteria.

- Date values must be enclosed within # signs.

The criteria are the only required parameters of the Find method. However, to increase the flexibility of your searches, you can also specify these optional parameters:

SkipRecords   Specifies the number of records to move from the identified starting point.

SearchDirection   Specifies whether to search forward or backward.

Start   Specifies a bookmark object from which to start the search. This is usually the current record, the first record, or the last record of the recordset.

If these optional parameters are omitted, the search finds the first record that matches the criteria after the current record.

As stated above, you can determine whether the search was successful by checking the EOF property of the Recordset object. If the EOF property is set to True, the search did not find a record that matched the specified criteria. If the property is set to False, a record was found. In a complete search function, you would set a bookmark to the current record, then perform the search. If the search failed, you could return to the record where you started. This is illustrated in the following code:

```
Dim vBookMark As Variant
vBookMark = adMembers.Recordset.Bookmark
adMembers.Recordset.Find "Author>='McK'"
If adMembers.Recordset.EOF Then
    'Record not found
    adMembers.Recordset.Bookmark = vBookMark
End If
```

Access and Manipulate a Data Source by Using ADO and the ADO Data Control

1. ADO is an acronym for _____.

2. The ADO data control provides a link between _____ and _____.

Setting Up the ADO Data Control

3. The only two properties you are required to set for the ADO data control are _____ and _____.

4. True or False. The ADO data control and the DAO data control both use the same property settings to access information in a database.

5. The _____ property of the ADO data control sets the location of the database that you are accessing.

6. True or False. The ADO data control is the default data control in the toolbox.

7. To specify the particular data you need to access, you set the _____ property.

8. The _____ type of cursor does not allow the user to edit information in the database.

9. You can edit data in the _____ and
_____ types of cursor.

10. To allow editing of the data with the ADO data control, you need to change the value of the
_____ property.

11. ADO supports two types of record locking: _____
and _____.

12. To specify the type of record locking, you should set the _____
property.

13. True or False. When you specify the data to be accessed, you are only allowed to specify the
name of a table.

14. If you want to add records automatically when you reach the end of the recordset, you
specify a setting of the _____ property.

Working with Bound Controls

15. Bound controls handle the following functions for a database application:
_____ and _____
data.

16. To work with text or numbers in a data-entry application, you would use either the
_____ or _____
control.

17. The _____ of a standard bound control identifies
the data control that contains the data for the application.

18. To specify the particular field of the recordset to be accessed, you need to set the
_____ property.

19. If you are working with the TextBox control, the information from the database is handled
by the _____ property.

20. True or False. You can only have one data control on any given form.

21. True or False. A standard bound control can only be bound to a single data control at a time.

22. For handling Boolean (True/False) data, the _____
control is the control of choice.

23. True or False. The standard bound controls only work with the ADO data control.

24. The _____ and _____
controls provide a spreadsheet-style interface for working with multiple records at a time.

25. The _____ control can be bound to a data control to provide graphical display of information.

26. Every bound control has a _____ property.

Extending the Capabilities of the ADODC

27. To extend the capabilities of the ADO data control, you must write program code using _____.

28. The _____ object is used when working with extended capabilities of the ADO data control.

29. To add a record to the database, you use the _____ method.

30. When you add a new record using the data control, the values of the bound controls are _____.

31. True or False. The data control automatically saves the information from a new record when you move to another record.

32. The _____ method is used to remove a record from the database.

33. True or False. A deleted record can be recovered easily with another program command.

34. True or False. An error occurs if a user tries to edit a record that has just been deleted.

35. After deleting a record, your code should

_____.

36. To search a recordset, you use the _____ method.

37. The criteria for the search specifies _____,

_____, and _____.

38. The default search looks for the _____ moving in

the _____ direction.

39. The optional _____ parameter of the search lets

you specify the number of records to skip.

40. If you want to search backward through the recordset, you must specify the optional

_____ parameter.

41. In the search criteria, literal strings must be contained within

_____.

42. The _____ property of the recordset can be used to

determine whether the search was successful.

$$\boxed{\text{S A M P L E ~ T E S T}}$$

10-1 To set the location of the database for the ADO data control, you set which property?

    A. DatabaseName

    B. Location

    C. ConnectionString

    D. RecordSource

10-2 Which of the following are valid settings for the RecordSource property? Check all that apply.

    A. The name of a table

    B. The name of another data control

    C. The name of a query or stored procedure

    D. A valid SQL statement

10-3 To use a table for the RecordSource, you should set the CommandType property to what?

    A. adCmdUnknown

    B. adCmdTable

    C. adCmdText

    D. adCmdStoredProc

10-4 Which of the following cursor types allows you to edit the information in the database? Check all that apply.

    A. Static

    B. Forward-only

    C. Dynamic

    D. Keyset

10-5 To make the information in the data control read-only, you would set which property?

  A. ReadOnly

  B. LockType

  C. Locked

  D. NoEdit

10-6 Which property of a bound control determines the data control to which it is bound?

  A. DataField

  B. DataControlName

  C. DataSource

  D. BoundSource

10-7 Which of the following can a bound control be bound to? Check all that apply.

  A. DAO data control

  B. ADO data control

  C. Recordset object

  D. RDO data control

10-8 Which property of a bound control specifies the actual data to be displayed?

  A. DataField

  B. DataControlName

  C. DataSource

  D. BoundSource

10-9 Which of the following is true of saving the data that a user enters?

   A. The data is saved as the user types the information.

   B. The data is saved when the user moves to another record or closes the form.

   C. You must run the Update method to save the data.

   D. Editing of data is not allowed with the data control.

10-10 Which method is used to add a record to the database?

   A. Add

   B. Insert

   C. AddNew

   D. NewRecord

10-11 Which method is used to delete a record from the database?

   A. Delete

   B. Remove

   C. Erase

   D. You cannot delete records using the data control.

10-12 Which of the following is true of deleting a record?

   A. The record can be recovered using a Restore method.

   B. The information is not deleted until the recordset is closed.

   C. The information is deleted immediately and cannot be recovered.

   D. The information is not physically removed from the database.

10-13   Why should you move the record pointer after deleting a record?

    A. You shouldn't move the pointer.

    B. To show that the deletion worked correctly.

    C. To avoid an error if the user tries to edit the deleted record.

    D. To confuse the user.

10-14   Which ADO method is used to find the next record that meets your criteria?

    A. Find

    B. Search

    C. Seek

    D. FindNext

10-15   What information *must* be specified in a search using ADO methods? Check all that apply.

    A. The field to be searched

    B. The search direction

    C. The starting point of the search

    D. The value to searched

10-16   Which property do you check to determine if a search was successful?

    A. RecordFound

    B. NoMatch

    C. EOF

    D. RecordNumber

U N I T

11

Debugging Your Application

Test Objectives: Testing the Solution

- **Given a scenario, select the appropriate compiler options.**

- **Control an application by using conditional compilation.**

- **Set watch expressions during program execution.**

- **Monitor the values of expressions and variables by using the Immediate window.**
  - Use the Immediate window to check or change values.
  - Use the Locals window to check or change values.

- **Implement project groups to support the development and debugging processes.**
  - Debug DLLs in process.
  - Test and debug a control in process.

- **Given a scenario, define the scope of a watch variable.**

fter you finish the interface design and the programming for your application, you are ready to start the task of preparing your application for distribution. The first two tasks in this process are debugging your application and then compiling it. Debugging is the process of finding and eliminating errors in your program. Compiling is the process of making an executable file that can run on other machines, without requiring Visual Basic to be installed on the machine.

Given a Scenario, Select the Appropriate Compiler Options

In the current version of Visual Basic, you can create many different types of components. In addition to standard programs, you can create ActiveX servers (in the form of DLL or EXE files), ActiveX controls, ActiveX documents, and DHTML Web pages. Any of these programs have to be prepared for use by others before you can distribute the program. For most types of programs, this preparation involves compiling the program into an EXE, DLL, or OCX file. The type of file that is created depends on the type of Visual Basic project you used to write the application.

To compile a project, you need to choose the Make item from the File menu of Visual Basic. This will bring up the Make Project dialog box, shown in Figure 11.1. In this dialog box, you choose the filename and location for the executable file that you are creating.

For each type of project that you create, there is a set of default compilation options. For many of your projects, these default options will be acceptable. However, to get the maximum performance out of your program, you may want to set some of these options to values other than their defaults. In the Make Project dialog box there is an Options button. This button brings up the Project Properties dialog box for your project with the Make and Compile pages shown. This is illustrated in Figure 11.2.

FIGURE 11.1

Compiling a project to
an executable file

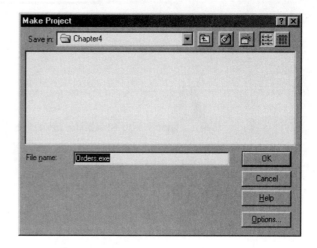

FIGURE 11.2

Setting the compiler
options

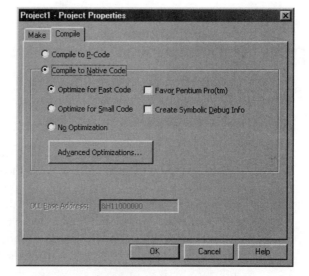

You can also access this dialog box from the Properties item of the
Project menu.

The Make page of the dialog box enables you to set version information for the program and to supply arguments for conditional compilation. (This is discussed in the section, "Control an Application by Using Conditional Compilation.") To set the compiler options, you need to be on the Compile page of the dialog box.

Choosing Native Code or P-Code

Your first major decision in compiling your application is whether to use P-code or native code. P-code is the type of compilation that was used for all Visual Basic programs prior to version 5. To address speed concerns, Microsoft started including the option to compile to native code. Native code compilation is now the default method. However, for some projects, you may want to choose P-code.

The key advantages of compiling to P-code are:

- Faster compilation times
- Smaller executable files

The disadvantages of using P-code are that your application may run a little slower and you cannot take advantage of some of the compiler optimizations that are available with native code compilation.

If you choose to compile to native code, your application will probably run faster and you can take advantage of the compiler optimizations. However, native code compiles more slowly and creates larger executable files.

In making the determination between P-code and native code, you should try both methods and determine the speed and size differences for your particular application. You can then decide whether executable size or speed is more important to you.

Contrary to what many people think, compiling to native code does not eliminate the need to distribute supporting DLL and OCX files with your applications. The executable created with native code compilation is not a true stand-alone executable.

Selecting Native Code Optimization Options

If you choose to compile to P-code, you are finished making choices about your compilation options. If, however, you choose to compile to native code, there are a number of other options that are available to you. The first set of options is shown on the Compile page of the Project Properties dialog box shown in Figure 11.2. These options are summarized below:

Optimize for Fast Code   Instructs the compiler to optimize program loops and other structures to produce the fastest possible code. This is done by looking for program structures that can be replaced by an equivalent faster structure. For example, if the compiler determines that part of an If statement can never be accessed, it can eliminate that part of the statement so it is never evaluated.

Optimize for Small Code   Instructs the compiler to keep the size of the executable file as small as possible. This option causes the compiler to skip optimizations that would speed up the program if they would also increase the size of the executable.

No Optimization   Instructs the compiler to create an executable file without trying to optimize for either size or speed.

You can only select one of the three optimizations options listed above. The other two options on the Compile page, listed below, can be used in conjunction with any of the options selected above:

Favor Pentium Pro(tm)   Instructs the compiler to optimize your program so that it will run faster on Pentium Pro processors. If you know that all the machines used by your target audience have Pentium Pro processors, choose this option. Machines using other processors can still run the program, but performance will be poorer than if you had not selected this option.

Create Symbolic Debug Info   Instructs the compiler to create a separate file (with the extension .PDB) that contains symbolic debugging information. You only need this option if you are using a debugging program other than the one built into Visual Basic.

Working with Advanced Options

There are still more compiler options that you can select, if you want to wring every last ounce of performance out of your program. To access these options, click the Advanced Optimizations button on the Compile page. This brings up the dialog box shown in Figure 11.3.

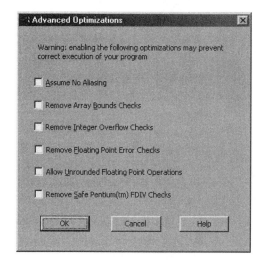

These six options enable you to tweak every bit of speed out of your program. For most of your programs you will not need to use these options. Also, these options should be used with care, as they may adversely affect the performance of your program on some machines and in some circumstances. The six advanced optimization options are as follows:

Assume No Aliasing   Aliasing enables you to use more than one variable name to reference a specific variable location, which typically occurs when you pass arguments to a subroutine by reference. Selecting this option tells the compiler that your program does not use aliasing. Typically, this option should be left off.

Remove Array Bounds Checks   Whenever Visual Basic accesses an element of an array, it checks to make sure that the index it is using is within the bounds of the array. If the index is out of bounds, an error occurs. With this option turned on, Visual Basic does not perform the bounds check and does not generate errors. Removing the bounds checking can cause your program to retrieve a value from an invalid memory location and can result in crashes or strange behavior of your program.

Remove Integer Overflow Checks   This option causes Visual Basic to bypass the normal checks that make sure a value will fit in the data type defined. When the checks are in place, an error occurs if the number you are storing is larger than the capacity of the variable that you created; for example, if the program tries to store a long integer in an integer variable. When this option is on, the checks are removed and no overflow error occurs, but you may get incorrect results from some of your calculations.

Remove Floating Point Error Checks   This option is similar to the checks performed for integers. Visual Basic checks floating point operations to determine whether the value will fit in the declared variable and to verify that there is no division by zero. With this option turned on, these checks are bypassed, eliminating the reporting of overflow errors and division-by-zero errors. If these conditions occur, however, the results of your program may be incorrect.

Allow Unrounded Floating Point Operations   This option keeps the compiler from forcing floating-point operations to be rounded to a particular size.

Remove Safe Pentium FDIV Checks   By default, Visual Basic produces code that is not affected by the Pentium bug that was discovered several years ago. However, checking for the bug does slightly increase the size of your program and slow it down. For most applications, you can safely remove the checking, since Pentium II and Pentium Pro machines are not affected by the bug, and many programs will be unaffected no matter what machine they are run on.

Control an Application by Using Conditional Compilation

When you are compiling your program, determining which options to use is only half the process. For many programs, you need to determine which parts of the program to compile. For a variety of reasons, you may want to compile only certain parts of the program. For example:

- Compile parts of the program containing debugging information only when you are in the development mode.

- Eliminate specific program features for a demonstration version of your program.

- Use the same code base to create multiple versions of your program, such as Standard and Professional versions.

The process of compiling only specific parts of your program is known as conditional compilation. Conditional compilation gives you the ability to tell the Visual Basic compiler to include or to skip certain parts of your code as you are creating the executable for the program.

Marking the Code to Be Compiled

Conditional compilation is based on a variation of the familiar If…Then…Else programming structure. For conditional compilation, you specify the area of code to be compiled with a #If structure. The following code shows an example of this structure:

```
#If bDemoMode Then
    mnuPrint.Enabled = False
#Else
    mnuPrint.Enabled = True
#End If
```

In this example, if the value of the variable bDemoMode is True, the menu option for printing is disabled. If the value is False, the printer menu is enabled, allowing the users to print from the program. A conditional compilation structure can use four statements:

#If   Starts the conditional compilation structure. Statements that follow the If portion of the structure will be compiled if the condition is true.

#ElseIf   Is used to test an additional condition if all preceding conditions are false.

#Else   Is used to indicate the code to be run if all previous conditions are false.

#End If   Indicates the end of the conditional structure.

Using combinations of these statements, you can exercise a great deal of control over the segments of your code that are compiled.

When you compile your code to create an executable, all the forms and modules of your program are compiled. Conditional compilation allows you to specify certain blocks of code within procedures that should be compiled or skipped.

Setting the Conditional Variables

The conditions that you use for conditional compilation are not ordinary variables. Normal variables and constants in a program are evaluated while the program is running. The conditions for the #If statements must be available to Visual Basic during the compilation. Therefore, you must use special techniques to specify the values of variables used in conditional compilations. There are three methods for setting the values of these variables:

- Set the variable in code using the #Const directive.

- Use the Project Properties dialog box.

- Use command line switches.

The first method of setting the value of a variable is to use the #Const directive. To use this method, simply specify the directive, the name of the variable (now a constant), and the value that you want to assign. The following line of code illustrates this method:

```
#Const bDemoMode = True
```

As you can see, this is very similar to the Const directive used to create a constant in your Visual Basic programs. However, there is one key difference. A normal constant can be set in a public module and have its value carried throughout your code. For conditional compilation, the value of a conditional variable set using the #Const directive is only valid for the module in which the directive is used. If you are using the conditional variable in other modules, you have to set the value in each module. Another drawback of using the #Const directive is that you have to change lines in your code to change the value of the variables each time you want to use different compilation options.

The best method for setting the value of conditional variables is through the use of the Project Properties dialog box. The Make tab of the Project Properties box, shown in Figure 11.4, has an edit box where you can set conditional compilation arguments.

FIGURE 11.4

Setting conditional
compilation
arguments

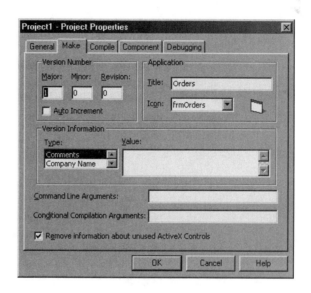

In the dialog box, you set the value of the variables by entering the name of the variable and its value in the Conditional Compilation Arguments box at the bottom of the dialog box. If you need to specify more than one variable, separate the assignment statements with a colon, as shown in the following line:

```
bDemoMode=True:bDebugMode=False:iVersion=2
```

The final method of setting the conditional compilation arguments is through the use of command line switches. These switches are used when Visual Basic is started to set certain parameters of the program. The compilation arguments are set with the /d command line switch. The arguments and their values follow the /d switch. As with the arguments in the Project Properties dialog box, multiple arguments are separated by colons. The following command line could be used to start Visual Basic and to set the compilation constants:

```
vb6.exe /make Membership.vbp /d
bDemoMode=True:bDebugMode=False:iVersion=2
```

Set Watch Expressions During Program Execution

One of the many benefits of programming in Visual Basic is the ease with which you can debug your programs. Visual Basic provides you with a set of tools that allow you to trace and correct errors in your programs while running in the development environment. These tools allow you to find an error, to correct it, and to continue running your program.

To help you with debugging your program, Visual Basic pauses the execution of the program whenever an error occurs and highlights the program line that caused the error. This lets you determine the exact type of error and its location, making it easier for you to determine how to correct the error. Visual Basic highlights an error with a highlight bar on the offending line, as shown in Figure 11.5.

FIGURE 11.5

Highlighting an error

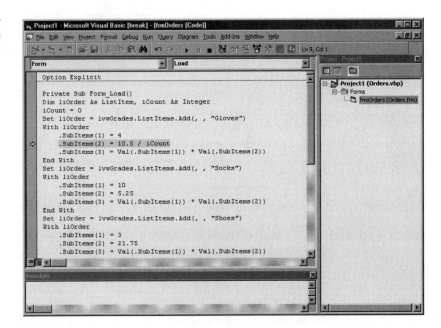

The typical behavior for Visual Basic is to pause, or break, on any errors that are not handled by your program. You can, however, change this behavior by setting the error-trapping option for your project. There are three options for breaking on errors:

Break on All Errors   Causes Visual Basic to pause on any error, whether or not it is handled by an error handler in your code.

Break in Class Module   Causes Visual Basic to pause on errors that are not handled by an error handler. This break will occur whether the error is in the main part of the program or in a class module. Using this setting is the only way to discover where specific errors occur in a class module.

Break on Unhandled Errors   Causes Visual Basic to pause on errors that are not handled by an error handler in your code. The difference between this option and the Break in Class Module option is that the Break on Unhandled Errors option only shows the line of code that references a class if an error occurs in the class.

You set the error-trapping option from the General tab of the Options dialog box, shown in Figure 11.6. You access this dialog box by choosing the Options item from the Tools menu.

FIGURE 11.6

Setting error-handling options

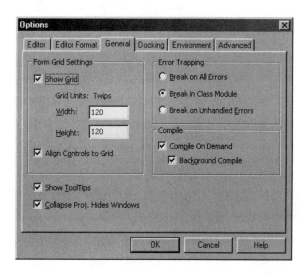

Setting Watches for Your Variables

Visual Basic pauses when an error occurs to show you what the error is and where it occurred. However, Visual Basic cannot tell you why the error occurred. To determine why an error occurred, you have to do some detective work. To aid you in this investigation, Visual Basic has a series of tools to help you determine the values of variables and to determine other information about your program that could have led to the error.

The Watch window is one of these tools. The Watch window lets you determine the value of any variable or expression in your code. Each variable or expression that you are observing is called a watch. For each watch that you create, the Watch window, shown in Figure 11.7, displays the following items:

- The name of the variable or the text of the expression being checked

- The current value of the expression

- The module and procedure where the expression is being evaluated

- The type of data represented by the expression

F I G U R E 11.7

Tracking information about expressions

Each watch in the Watch window is an expression or variable that you tell Visual Basic to track. To add a variable or expression to the Watch window, you choose the Add Watch item from the Debug menu. This brings up the Add Watch dialog box, as shown in Figure 11.8.

F I G U R E   11.8

Creating a watch

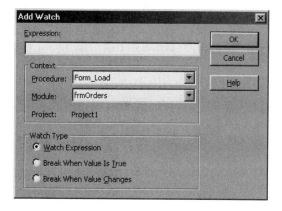

You can also access the dialog box by right-clicking in the Watch window and choosing the Add Watch item from the pop-up menu. Once the dialog box is displayed, you need to specify the following information:

- An expression or the name of a variable that you wish to track.

- The procedure(s) and module(s) where you want to track the value of the expression. You can specify a single procedure and module or have Visual Basic track the value of the expression throughout your program.

- The action to take for the watch, also known as the watch type. You can choose to take one of three actions with a watch:

Watch Expression   Displays the value of the expression and takes no other action.

Break When Value Is True   Pauses the program when the value of the expression or variable is True. This watch can be used only for a logical expression or a Boolean variable.

Break When Value Changes   Pauses the execution of the program when the value of the expression changes.

After you have set this information, Visual Basic monitors the values of your expressions as your program is run. As you are running your program, you can modify the watches that are shown in the Watch window. Whenever your program is paused, you can add new watches, delete existing watches, or modify the behavior of an existing watch. To edit or delete a watch, highlight the watch in the Watch window and right-click the mouse to show the pop-up menu. Editing a watch uses the same dialog box that you used to create a watch, as shown in Figure 11.8.

The Watch window is useful not only for monitoring the information in your program. If you have a watch set to a single variable, you can modify the value of the variable while your program is paused by highlighting the value in the Watch window and changing it to a new value. This feature is very helpful if you have determined that an improper value of a variable has caused the error and you want to determine if a proper value will allow the program to continue without further problems.

Monitoring Variables with Other Tools

The Watch window is not the only tool for observing the value of variables and expressions. Two other tools allow you to quickly determine the value of a variable or expression without having previously set a watch.

The first of these tools is the Quick Watch window. To use this window, highlight a variable or expression in your code and choose the Quick Watch item from the Debug menu. The Quick Watch window shows you the expression that you selected, the context of the expression, and its current value. The Quick Watch window also gives you the option of adding the expression to the Watch window so that you can observe the value as your program continues to run. The Quick Watch window is shown in Figure 11.9.

FIGURE 11.9

Using the Quick Watch window

The other tool is the Auto Data Tips tool. You turn this tool on using the Options dialog box located under the Tools menu. When the tool is on, you can determine the value of a variable by resting the mouse over the variable in the code window. The value then appears in a tool tip, as shown in Figure 11.10.

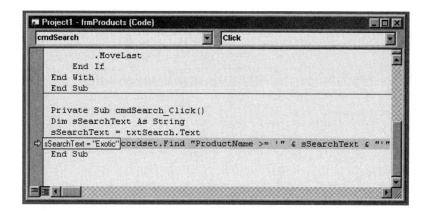

Monitor the Values of Expressions and Variables by Using the Immediate Window

You saw in the last section that there were several ways to observe the values of variables and expressions. You could use the Watch window, the Quick Watch window, and the Auto Data Tips to observe the value of a variable. With the Watch window, you could also change the value of a single variable. While being able to observe a variable and change its value is a powerful debugging tool, there are things the Watch window cannot do. For example, you cannot run a command in the Watch window. For these other debugging tasks, Visual Basic provides you with two other tools: the Immediate window and the Locals window.

Monitoring Values in the Immediate Window

The Immediate window provides you with a method to execute code commands while your program is paused. You can use these commands to do these tasks:

- Determine the contents of a variable or property.

- Set the value of a variable or property.

- Create or destroy objects.

- Open or close recordsets.

- Carry out any other task that can be executed with a single command.

To run a command in the Immediate window, type the command and press Enter. The code will be run and the results, if any, will be displayed.

To monitor the value of a variable or expression, you type a question mark in the Immediate window followed by the expression or variable name to be evaluated. This is shown in the following code segment:

```
? sSrchSQL
```

The results of the command, the value of the variable, are shown in the Immediate window directly below the command. This is illustrated in Figure 11.11.

FIGURE 11.11

Monitoring a value in the Immediate window

To change the value of a variable or property, you use an assignment statement, just as you would in your program code. For example, to set the value of the sSrchSQL variable shown above, you would use the following code:

```
sSrchSQL = "Select * From Members Where MemID=125"
```

You can also run any other single-line statement in the Immediate window.

If you know that you will be checking the value of a particular variable over and over in a program, you might want to place code in your program that outputs the value of the variable or expression. You can do this with the Print method of the Debug object. The results of the `Debug.Print` are displayed in the Immediate window. To use this method, just place the method call and the variable or expression to be evaluated in your program code, as illustrated by the following statement:

```
Debug.Print sSrchSQL
```

Using the Locals Window

The Locals window is another tool you can use to monitor the value of variables. Like the Watch window, the Locals window enables you to determine the value of a variable or, if necessary, to change the value of the variable. The main differences between the Locals window and the Watch window are as follows:

- The Locals window shows you all the variables in a particular procedure; the Watch window only shows those variables for which you have set a watch.

- The Watch window can show you the value of variables outside the current procedure; the Locals window cannot.

- The Watch window can show you the value of an expression; the Locals window cannot.

- The Locals window shows you the current property values for the current form and all its controls in addition to the values of variables.

The Locals window presents the variable and property information in a hierarchical tree view (much like the TreeView control) that you can expand or collapse as much as you want. To use the Locals window, you need to be in the code window for a procedure, then choose the Locals item from Visual Basic's View menu. This will display the variables for the current procedure, as shown in Figure 11.12.

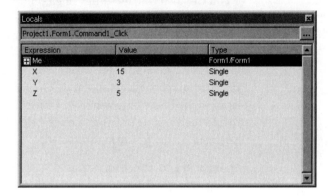

Implement Project Groups to Support the Development and Debugging Processes

Since Visual Basic gives you the capability to create servers, ActiveX controls, and other components, it also gives you a way to easily debug all these components. Prior to version 5 of Visual Basic, the only way to debug a server was to start the server in one instance of Visual Basic, then create a test application in another instance of Visual Basic. You then had to switch back and forth between the instances to watch the calls to the server and how the server handled the tasks.

Visual Basic 6 makes this process much easier. In Visual Basic 6, you can create a program group that contains both your server and the client application that you will use to test the server. Using the project group, you can step directly from the statement in the client program that calls the server to the statement in the server component that executes the task. This makes it much easier to follow the progress of the code through both the client and the server.

To create a project group, you choose the Add Project item from the File menu. This brings up the Add Project dialog box, shown in Figure 11.13. From the dialog box, you can choose a new project or open an existing project. Once you have opened the second project, a project group will be created for you. The project group and its component projects will be shown in the Projects window, as shown in Figure 11.14.

F I G U R E   11.13

F I G U R E   11.13

Adding a project to the desktop

F I G U R E   11.14

A project group

Once you have created a project group, you need to determine which of the projects in the group should be the first one to start. You then set that project as the startup project by right-clicking on the project and choosing the Set as Start Up item from the pop-up menu, as shown in Figure 11.15.

F I G U R E   11.15

Choosing the startup
project of a group

Debugging DLLs in Process

To debug a DLL in process, you need to create a project group and run the
client application as defined in these steps:

1. Create the DLL server application.

2. Add a new project to create a project group.

3. Write code in the new project to access components from the DLL
   server.

4. Set the client project as the startup project.

5. Set watches and breakpoints in both your client and server projects as
   needed.

6. Start the client program by clicking the Run button.

When you click the Run button or press F5, the client application runs
and displays the startup form for the application. As you run the client program, code statements in your program will create objects from the server.
This causes the server to load and run as needed. Using watches and breakpoints, you can monitor the execution of both the client and the server to
look for errors and their causes.

Debugging a Control

Testing and debugging a control is very similar to testing and debugging a DLL. There is one key difference. When you create a control, part of the code for the control is running as you create instances of the control on your test form. This means that some of the debugging of the control is done while you are in design mode. To test and debug a control, follow these steps:

1. Create the control.

2. Close the user interface window for the control.

3. Add a project to the desktop to create a project group. The control you are creating is automatically added to the toolbox of the new project.

4. Add an instance of the control to the new project and test items such as resizing or changing the properties of the control. This allows you to determine if your property procedures are working correctly.

5. After writing code to test the methods of the control, start the test application and run the tasks that will use the methods of the control.

As with debugging a DLL, you can set watches and breakpoints in both the test application and the control. This lets you monitor all the processes involved in using the control.

Given a Scenario, Define the Scope of a Watch Variable

You can specify the context of the watch variable, which is similar to the scope of a variable but with a key difference. The context setting of a variable tells you only where the watch expression will be evaluated. It does not affect the usage scope of a variable. For example, you can create a global variable in your program but, if you set a watch for the variable with a context of a single procedure, the Watch window displays the value of the variable only while that procedure is running. All other times, the watch is out of scope. A watch can also be out of scope if you are trying to watch a local variable and you are outside of the procedure in which the variable was defined.

STUDY QUESTIONS

Given a Scenario, Select the Appropriate Compiler Options

1. True or False. It makes no difference whether you compile to native code or P-code.

2. Compiling to _____ produces a faster executable.

3. Compiling to _____ produces a smaller executable and results in faster compile times.

4. True or False. Optimizing for faster code can produce larger executable files.

5. The _____ option keeps you from getting integer overflow errors but may cause incorrect results in your program.

6. True or False. You need to create symbolic debug information if you are using Visual Basic's internal debugging tools.

7. _____ is the best optimization to pick if you are concerned about executable file size.

8. True or False. Compiling to native code means that you do not have to distribute runtime libraries with your program.

9. If all of your target machines are Pentium II or Pentium Pro, you can use the _____ and _____ compiler options.

10. True or False. All Visual Basic programs are compiled to an EXE file.

Control an Application by Using Conditional Compilation

11. The _____ statement starts a conditional compilation structure.

12. True or False. You use standard variables as conditions for conditional compilation.

13. To specify a second condition in a conditional compilation structure, you use the _____ statement.

14. The statements after the #Else conditional statement are compiled when

_____.

15. You use the _____ statement to define a conditional variable in code.

16. If you want to use a conditional variable throughout your program, you must set its value in the _____ dialog box or as a

_____.

17. True or False. A good use of conditional compilation is to include debugging information while you are developing but to remove it for your production executable.

Set Watch Expressions During Program Execution

18. To set up a watch, you must specify the _____ or _____ to be evaluated.

19. The context of a watch determines which _____ and _____ the watch will be evaluated in.

20. True or False. You can change the value of a variable in the Watch window.

21. True or False. A watch can be set up to pause your program when its value changes.

22. The _____ lets you view the value of a variable by resting the mouse over the variable in your program code.

23. True or False. You cannot change a watch after you have started running your program.

Monitor the Values of Expressions and Variables by Using the Immediate Window

24. To check the value of a variable in the Immediate window, place a _____ in front of the variable name.

25. True or False. You can run any type of single-line code statement in the Immediate window.

26.   To display information in the Immediate window from your code, you use the
_____ method of the _____
object.

27.   True or False. The values of watched expressions are automatically shown in the Immediate
window.

28.   To change the value of a variable, you use _____.

29.   The Locals window shows you all the variables in _____.

30.   In addition to variables, the Locals window shows you the
_____.

31.   True or False. You cannot change the value of a variable in the Locals window.

32.   The information in the Locals window is organized in a
_____ structure.

33.   True or False. The Locals window and the Watch window provide exactly the same information.

Implement Project Groups to Support the Development and Debugging Processes

34.   A project group contains _____.

35. To determine which project is run by Visual Basic, you must set the

_____.

36. True or False. A server is started automatically as its components are accessed.

37. True or False. You can set watches and breakpoints in both the client and server projects of a project group.

38. True or False. Debugging a server with a project group requires you to have two instances of Visual Basic running.

39. The _____ of a control can be debugged while you are still in the design environment.

40. _____ of a control can only be debugged while a test program is running.

41. To allow a control to be used in a test project, you must

_____.

42. True or False. The control you are creating is automatically added to the toolbox of the new project you add to the project group.

43. To determine the value of a variable in a control, you need to set up

_____.

Given a Scenario, Define the Scope of a Watch Variable

44.   True or False. The scope of a variable and the scope of a watch are the same.

45.   The scope of a watch is determined by _____.

46.   The scope of a variable is determined by _____ and

_____.

47.   True or False. A watch variable is out of scope if you are outside the procedure for which the watch was defined.

11-1 Which of these tools displays the value of a variable? Check all that apply.

    A. Immediate window

    B. Auto Data Tips

    C. Call stack

    D. Auto Quick Info

11-2 Which tool lets you edit the value of a variable? Check all that apply.

    A. Watch window

    B. Auto Data Tips

    C. Quick Watch

    D. Locals window

11-3 Which of following are displayed in the Locals window? Check all that apply.

    A. The value of variables in the current procedure

    B. The value of all variables in the program

    C. The names of all forms in the program

    D. The properties of the current form

11-4 Which compiler options would be a benefit for a program to be run on a Pentium Pro machine? Check all that apply.

    A. Create Symbolic Debug Info

    B. Remove Safe Pentium FDIV Checks

    C. Favor Pentium Pro

    D. Create Symbolic Debug Information

SAMPLE TEST

11-5   Which of following are advantages of compiling to P-code? Check all that apply.

    A. Smaller executable size

    B. Faster program execution

    C. Eliminates the need for runtime libraries

    D. Faster compile times

11-6   Which of following are advantages of compiling to native code? Check all that apply.

    A. Smaller executable size

    B. Faster program execution

    C. Eliminates the need for runtime libraries

    D. Faster compile times

11-7   If you are concerned about program size, which compiler option would you check?

    A. Optimize for Fast Code

    B. No Optimization

    C. Optimize for Small Code

    D. Favor Pentium Pro

11-8   Which of the following statements would you use to specify a condition for conditional compilation? Check all that apply.

    A. #Else

    B. #ElseIf

    C. #Select Case

    D. #If

11-9   How do you set the value of a conditional variable? Check all that apply.

    A. Use an assignment statement.

    B. Use the #Const statement.

    C. The compiler will prompt you for values.

    D. Set the argument in the Project Properties dialog box.

11-10   When is the program code of a User Control running and able to be tested? Check all that apply.

    A. When a project containing the control is running

    B. When the control is being added to another project and the properties are being set

    C. When the control is being built

    D. During compilation of the control

11-11   How do you debug a DLL?

    A. Run multiple instances of Visual Basic: one for the server and one for the client application.

    B. Use a project group.

    C. Use a third-party debugger.

    D. There are no special requirements for debugging a DLL.

11-12   Which Visual Basic object allows you to print to the Immediate window?

    A. App

    B. Form

    C. Debug

    D. Err

11-13 What must be specified when you create a watch? Check all that apply.

    A. The name of the variable

    B. The name of your program

    C. The context of the watch

    D. The value to set for the variable

11-14 Which of the following actions are valid for a watch? Check all that apply.

    A. Display the value of the variable.

    B. Set the variable to a predefined value.

    C. Pause when the value of the variable is changed.

    D. Pause when the variable is created or destroyed.

U N I T

12

Preparing Your Application for Distribution

Test Objectives: Deploying an Application

- Use the Package and Deployment wizard to create a setup program that installs a desktop application, registers the COM components, and allows for uninstall.

- Plan and implement floppy disk-based deployment or compact disc-based deployment for a desktop application.

- Plan and implement Web-based deployment for a desktop application.

- Plan and implement network-based deployment for a desktop application.

Test Objectives: Maintaining and Supporting an Application

- Fix errors, and take measures to prevent future errors.

- Deploy application updates for desktop applications.

Exam objectives are subject to change at any time without prior notice and at Microsoft's sole discretion. Please visit Microsoft's Training & Certification Web site (www.microsoft.com/Train_Cert) for the most current exam objectives listing.

While the majority of the work in creating an application is the coding, completing the application is not the final step in the life of a program. Unless you are only going to use the program on your own machine, you need a way to distribute the application by way of a setup program.

Use the Package and Deployment Wizard to Create a Setup Program That Installs a Desktop Application, Registers the COM Components, and Allows for Uninstall

While the creation of a setup program is much easier than the design and implementation of the program itself, it does require some planning and some decisions. For example, you need to decide whether the application is to be distributed via floppy disks or CDs or across a network. For many programs, you may even want users to be able to download your program and the latest support files over the Internet. Other issues you need to address are whether to have a single installation type or multiple types, such as Typical, Custom, or Portable. You also need to determine whether all files for the program must be copied to the user's hard drive or whether some can remain on the installation CD.

After planning the way the setup program operates, you need to create the setup program itself. The program should be easy to use and should provide the user with choices about how to install your application. If your installation routine is hard to use or does not allow the user flexibility in the installation options, they may get frustrated and not use the application at all. Remember, the setup routine is the first thing a user sees when working with your program.

To help you with the task of creating a good setup program for your application, Visual Basic includes the Package and Deployment wizard, shown in Figure 12.1.

FIGURE 12.1

Using the Package and Deployment wizard

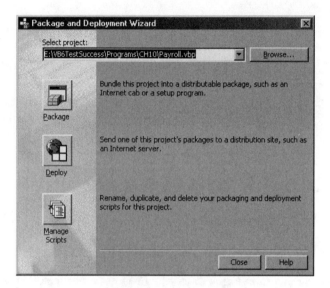

The Package and Deployment wizard helps you with the following tasks related to distributing your application:

- Compiling your program, if necessary. Typically, your application is already compiled, since that is a part of testing the program.

- Determining the files that must be distributed with the program. These files include the VB runtime libraries, any other required .DLL files, and any files required by your program, such as help files and databases.

- Compressing the files that are included on the distribution disks to minimize the number of disks needed for a standard installation or to minimize download time for an Internet installation.

- Creating a setup program for copying files to the user's machine and uncompressing the files.

- Creating the disks or download files that will be used to distribute the program.

The final step of creating a setup program is testing it. This is something that the Package and Deployment wizard cannot help you with. However, you should thoroughly test the setup program on as many machines as you reasonably can. Also, make sure that you test on machines other than your development machine to ensure that all necessary files are included in the setup.

Plan and Implement Floppy Disk-Based Deployment or Compact Disc-Based Deployment for a Desktop Application

The most common form of installation program is the disk-based installation. With this type of installation, your application and all the necessary components and support files are contained on one or more floppy disks or CDs. The files that are required by your application are determined by the controls and references (usually .DLL files) that you used to create the program. In turn, each of these controls and references may depend on other files in order to perform their tasks. Information about the dependencies of many controls and DLLs are contained in .DEP files. In addition, the primary file used for determining the dependencies of controls is the VB6Dep.ini file. This file defines the dependencies for Visual Basic's controls and objects, such as ADO or DAO.

Fortunately, most of the work of determining file dependencies is handled for you by the Package and Deployment wizard. The wizard scans your project to determine what components you have used in your application, then searches the appropriate files to determine the dependency of the components. From these dependencies, the wizard builds a list of files that should be included on your distribution disks.

For a disk-based installation program, you use two pieces of the Package and Deployment wizard. First, you use the packaging function to determine the file dependencies and to create the .CAB files that will contain all the necessary files for your application. Then you use the deployment function to create the setup program and to create the actual distribution disks.

Packaging the Components of Your Application

To start creating the setup program for your disk-based installation, you need to start the Package and Deployment wizard. You can start the program directly from the Windows Start menu. By default, the wizard is installed in the same program group as Visual Basic or Visual Studio.

You can also attach the Package and Deployment wizard to the Add-Ins menu of Visual Basic using the Add-In Manager.

After starting the wizard, you need to choose the project file corresponding to your application. You can then click the Package button to begin the packaging process. The wizard examines your project and determines what files need to be included with the application. The wizard also checks to make sure that the source code files are not newer than the executable file for your application. If the source code files are newer, the wizard offers to recompile the application for you. After examining the project, the wizard asks you to choose the type of package to create, using the screen shown in Figure 12.2.

FIGURE 12.2

Selecting the package type

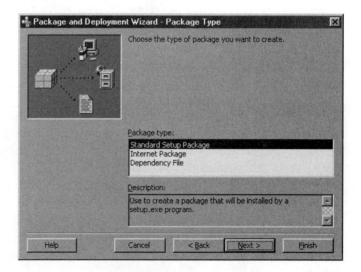

To complete the packaging of a disk-based installation, you need to perform the following steps:

1. Choose the Standard Setup Package option and click the Next button in the wizard.

2. Choose where you want the package to be created. This location is simply where the packaging files are to be stored. This is not the final location of your distribution disks. The default is the same location as your project file. However, it is advisable to place the package files in a different directory to avoid clutter. After choosing the location, click the Next button.

3. Next, you are shown the files that the wizard has determined need to be included with your application. At this point, you can add files to the Included Files list. The files you add may include database files, .INI files, documentation, or ReadMe.txt files. This screen of the wizard is shown below.

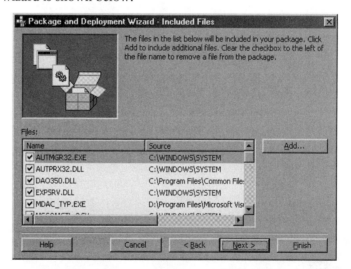

4. Next, you determine the number of .CAB files that the wizard will create. If you are distributing the application on a CD, you will probably choose a single file. For floppy disk installations, you need to choose multiple .CAB files and specify the maximum size of the file (usually the capacity of the disk). The .CAB files are the repository for

all the files needed by your application. The Cab Options screen is shown below.

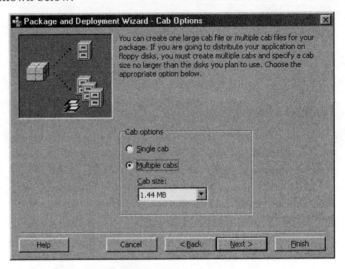

5. The last screens of the Package portion of the Package and Deployment wizard let you specify other details of the installation, such as:

- The title to be shown by the setup program

- The location of Start menu items

- The installation location of individual files

- Whether particular files can be shared among multiple applications

- A name for the package script

A script can be used to recall a particular set of packaging options for an application. This makes it easier for you to recreate the setup package if you need to make and distribute corrections to your program.

6. After you have selected all the necessary options, click the Finish button to create the setup package. At this point, the wizard creates the .CAB files for your program and returns you to the main screen of the Package and Deployment wizard, shown in Figure 12.1. You then need to use the Deploy function of the wizard to create the actual distribution disks.

Deploying to Disks

The second phase of creating an installation routine is the deployment of the package to the media that is available to the end user. Typically, this is in the form of floppy disks or CDs. However, the Package and Deployment wizard is capable of handling distribution over a network or across the Internet.

For a disk-based installation, you need to copy the setup program itself and any .CAB files that were created for the package to the appropriate disks. To handle this task, follow these steps:

1. Start the Package and Deployment wizard, if it is not already running.

2. Click the Deploy button on the main screen of the wizard.

3. On the first screen, choose the package to deploy. If you have just created a package, it is the default selection. Otherwise, you have to select the package from the list. Click the Next button.

4. The Deployment Method screen, shown below, lets you choose whether to deploy to floppy disks (if you created multiple .CAB files), to a folder (used for CD or network distribution), or to the Web.

   - For CD distribution, choose the Folder option. You can then copy the files from the chosen folder to the CD at a later time.

   - If you are deploying via floppy disks, choose the Floppy Disks option.

After you have made your selection, click the Next button.

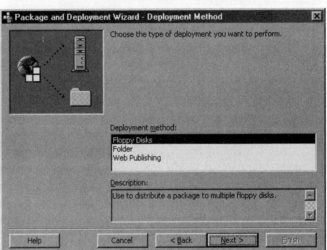

5. On the next screen, choose the folder where the files for a CD-based deployment will be copied. If you are creating a floppy disk-based deployment, you choose the drive location of the disks. Clicking the Next button takes you to the final screen of the wizard.

6. On the final screen, you can give a name to the deployment script for this installation. Like the script name for the Package process, this script allows you to recall the information used in the deployment. Again, this makes it easier to recreate the installation package for distributing updates to your program.

Depending on the type of application you are packaging, you may encounter other screens in the Package and Deployment wizard. For example, if you are working with a database application, you need to select the database drivers to include in the setup.

Plan and Implement Web-Based Deployment for a Desktop Application

Another method of installation that you can create with the Package and Deployment wizard is a Web-based installation. Using Web-based installation enables you to distribute your applications over the Internet. This type of distribution is becoming increasingly popular for several reasons:

- There are no disks for you to mail to users, saving you the cost of both the disks and the postage.

- The end user does not have to handle multiple disks, as is the case for a floppy disk installation.

- Users can always get the latest version of the program.

- Users can always download updates to the component files that are used by your program.

The process of creating a Web-based installation program is not very different from creating a disk- or network-based installation program. To create a Web-based installation program, follow these steps:

1. Create a package for your application just as you would for a disk- or network-based installation, as described previously in the section, "Packaging the Components of your Application." With a Web-based application, you should create multiple .CAB files to enable users to download smaller files. This lessens the chance that the file transfer will be interrupted in the middle of a file.

2. Start the deployment portion of the wizard by clicking the Deploy icon and select the package to be deployed.

3. Select Web Publishing as the deployment method.

4. Select the files from the package that you want to deploy. The file list (illustrated below) includes the `setup.exe` file, a `SETUP.LST` file, and

the .CAB files for the package. You can choose to include any or all of the files to be deployed. After choosing the files, click the Next button.

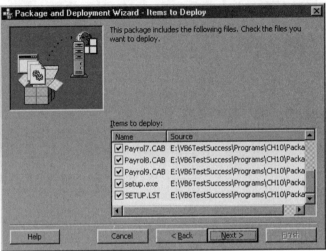

5. The Additional Items to Deploy screen enables you to specify additional items that need to be deployed along with your package files. These items might include graphics files or Web pages that are related to the application.

6. After selecting all the files to be deployed, specify the URL where the files will be placed and choose the Web Publishing protocol. You can choose either HTTP Posting or FTP Transfer.

7. Click the Finish button to publish the files. Typically, when you start to publish the files, you need to specify your user ID and password for the server to which you are sending files. The wizard then logs onto the Internet and attempts to post the files to the location you specified.

After the files have been successfully transferred to the Internet, you need to create a Web page that makes it easy for users to download all the files associated with the installation routine.

Plan and Implement Network-Based Deployment for a Desktop Application

Creating a network-based installation is very similar to creating a disk-based installation. The difference is that the setup files are copied to a central location that is accessible to everyone who needs to install the software, instead of being placed on disks. Users can then install the program directly from the network drive.

Network-based installation is very appealing for companies that are installing a program to a number of machines. Some of the advantages of network installations are as follows:

- Disks are not needed for the installation, enabling any user to install the application at any time.

- A Management Information Systems (MIS) group can remotely install the application on all the required client machines using server scripts.

- Using network security permissions, the installation of the program can be limited to only those users who need the application.

Packaging an application for network installation is the same as for disk-based installations. The difference between creating a network-based installation and a disk-based installation is in the deployment section of the wizard. The following steps show how to handle the deployment of a network-based installation:

1. Start the deployment portion of the wizard and select the package that you wish to deploy over the network. Then, click the Next button.

2. On the Deployment Method screen, select the Folder method. Then, click the Next button.

3. On the Folder screen of the wizard, click the Network button. This brings up a dialog box that allows you to select the folder on the network server where you wish to have the setup files copied. After you select a folder and return to the Folder page of the wizard, click the Next button.

4. On the final page of the wizard, you can specify a name for the deployment script and click the Finish button to handle copying the files.

The rest of the discussion in this unit addresses the test objectives associated with the objective heading "Maintaining and Supporting an Application."

The life cycle of a program does not end when the program is distributed. Over the life of their use, most programs will require fixes to bugs and most will have enhancements added. The design of your program will have an impact on how easy it is to handle the maintenance of the program. This section discusses the mechanics of maintaining a program.

Fix Errors, and Take Measures to Prevent Future Errors

After you have distributed your application, you are ready to sit back and reap the rewards of your hard work. However, a program is seldom 100% correct when the first version goes out the door. No matter how well you test the program, it is virtually impossible to find every bug, especially those that are caused by user actions for which you didn't plan.

To handle this, you need to have a plan in place for allowing users to report errors so that you can make the appropriate corrections. Many companies use a Web site to allow users to report the errors. However, the error reporting is only as good as the user's ability to ferret out the error information. To make it easy for the user to help you determine where errors occur you should have your program perform two tasks:

- Display meaningful error messages.

- Log the errors to a file.

Meaningful error messages give the user better information about what occurred in the program to cause the error and allows them to provide you with a more comprehensive report. However, the best information about errors comes from an error log that you create for your program. The error log can contain information about the error, including the following:

- The form or module where the error occurred

- The particular procedure where the error occurred

- The error number

- The error description

- The date and time of the error

- The user ID of the person using the program

- Your program's version number

It is important to log the user ID and version number. Many errors by a single user may indicate a need for increased training in addition to error correction. Often a user may have an older version with errors that you have already corrected.

To facilitate error logging, you can create a public procedure that handles the writing of the error information to a file. Call this procedure from every error-handling routine in your program. With the log created, you can have the user send you the log file or an error report that will help you quickly locate the errors they have found.

To correct the errors, you need to perform program debugging just as you did before the program was released. Debugging techniques are covered in Unit 11, "Debugging Your Application."

Deploy Application Updates for Desktop Applications

After the initial distribution of your program, you may need to distribute updates to the program. This can occur for a variety of reasons including these:

- To correct reported errors
- To add new features

Whatever the reason, you need to create new installation routines for your updated program. If you used the Package and Deployment wizard to create your initial installation, you were prompted to create scripts for the different parts of the installation. If you saved these scripts, creating the new installation program for the application update is easy. Follow these steps:

1. Start the Package and Deployment wizard and select the project for your application.

2. Click the Package button in the wizard.

3. Select the packaging script from the previous installation and click the Next button. Then follow the prompts to finish the packaging.

4. After the packaging is complete, click the Deploy button of the wizard and follow the steps outlined in the previous sections for your installation type.

One other consideration in creating updates to your program is making sure that a separate version number is created for each update that you distribute. This helps you to know whether users are working with the most current version of your program. You can set the version number of your program on the Make page of the Project Properties dialog box shown in Figure 12.3. You can set the Major, Minor, and Revision version numbers for the program. You can also choose to have Visual Basic automatically increment the Revision number each time you run the Make Project command for the application.

FIGURE 12.3

Setting version
numbers

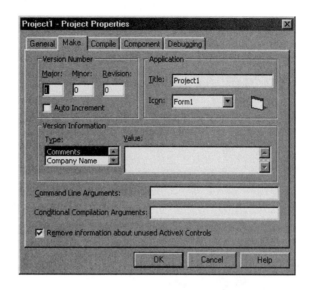

If you need to use the version number in your program, for error reporting or another task, the version information is stored in the Major, Minor, and Revision properties of the App object.

Use the Package and Deployment Wizard to Create a Setup Program That Installs a Desktop Application, Registers the COM Components, and Allows for Uninstall

1. The Package and Deployment wizard can help you with all aspects of creating a setup program except _____.

2. The files needed for your application are compressed into _____ files.

3. Information about required files for many Visual Basic controls and DLLs is contained in the _____ file.

4. Information about the dependencies of other controls is contained in _____ files.

5. True or False. You must manually add all the files that your application is dependent upon.

Plan and Implement Floppy Disk-Based Deployment or Compact Disc-Based Deployment for a Desktop Application

6. True or False. The Package and Deployment wizard prompts you to recompile your program if your source code files are newer than your executable file.

7. For disk-based installation, you should choose the _____ Setup Package option.

8. For _____ installations, you should have multiple .CAB files created.

9. True or False. You can specify where on a user's machine specific files should be copied.

10. True or False. You can name the packaging script for reuse.

11. To deploy a floppy disk-based installation, you need to specify the _____ as the location for the installation.

Plan and Implement Web-Based Deployment for a Desktop Application

12. True or False. Web-based installations can save you money.

13. Web-based installation ensures that users always get _____.

14. True or False. The initial packaging for a Web-based installation is the same as for a disk-based installation.

15. In the deployment function of the wizard, you should select _____ as the deployment method.

16. The deployment location for a Web-based installation is the _____.

17. You can choose between _____ and
_____ as the Web Publishing Protocol.

Plan and Implement Network-Based Deployment for a Desktop Application

18. One advantage of network-based installation is that
_____ are not needed.

19. True or False. Network-based installation allows an administrator to remotely install applications.

20. The deployment method for a network-based installation is the
_____ method.

21. The main difference between network- and disk-based installations is the
_____ of the setup files.

Fix Errors, and Take Measures to Prevent Future Errors

22. For maintaining your program, you need to provide users with a way to
_____.

23. An _____ allows you to store information about errors that occur in the program.

24. True or False. Using the error log is better than depending on users' descriptions of errors.

Deploy Application Updates for Desktop Applications

25. True or False. An update installation can use the same packaging and deployment options as the original installation.

26. A _____ makes it easier to create update installation packages.

27. When you update a program, you should change its _____.

28. The AutoIncrement feature increments the _____ version number.

29. To retrieve version number information in a program, you use properties of the _____ object.

12-1 How would you create disks for installing your program from floppy disks?

    A. Copy the necessary files to multiple floppies using Windows Explorer.

    B. Use the Package and Deployment wizard to create multiple .CAB files that will fit on floppies; then deploy the files to floppies.

    C. Floppies should not be used with new programs.

    D. Use the Package and Deployment wizard to create a single .CAB file and the setup program; then copy the files to floppies.

12-2 Which type of file contains dependency information for a component? Check all that apply.

    A. .CAB files

    B. .DEP files

    C. .DLL files

    D. VB6Dep.ini

12-3 In creating a .CAB file, the Package and Deployment wizard does which of the following?

    A. Places exact copies of your distribution files in the .CAB file

    B. Compresses files to save space and stores the compressed files

    C. Places in the .CAB file references to Web pages where the distribution files can be found

    D. None of the above

12-4   What Internet information do you need to specify to facilitate a Web-based installation? Check all that apply.

    A. The name of the Web page the users will access to download the files

    B. The URL of the server you will be publishing the files to

    C. The transfer protocol to use for publishing the files

    D. The IP address of your Web site

12-5   Why would you need to distribute a program update? Check all that apply.

    A. To provide error corrections

    B. To get more money

    C. To distribute enhancements

    D. None of the above

12-6   Which version property is automatically updated by the AutoIncrement setting?

    A. Revision

    B. Version

    C. Major

    D. Minor

12-7   Version information is stored as properties of which object?

    A. Form

    B. Program

    C. App

    D. None of the above

12-8 Which types of files are not automatically added to your installation package by the Package and Deployment wizard? Check all that apply.

    A. The program executable

    B. Database files

    C. Private .INI files

    D. Required DLLs and custom controls

U N I T
13

Final Review

Final Review

The previous 12 units covered the basics of the information that you need to pass the Visual Basic Desktop Applications certification exam. All the objectives that are listed on the Microsoft Web site are covered in this book. At this point, you are ready to test your knowledge of Visual Basic as a whole. This unit presents you with a series of questions similar to those you will encounter on the actual exam. The real exam will have about 50–55 questions with a 90-minute time limit. Currently you have to score about 71.5 percent or better to pass. The 55 questions in this unit are representative of what you will see on the exam.

1   The following code is used to declare a procedure in a class. Where can the procedure be used?

```
Friend Sub EncryptString(ByVal strInput As String)
```

    A. Only in the class itself.

    B. Anywhere in your application.

    C. Anywhere within the server in which the class is contained.

    D. This is not a valid declaration.

FINAL REVIEW

2   A data-access component has the property settings shown in the following figure. What type of data-access component is this?

A. Data consumer only

B. Data source only

C. Both a data consumer and data source

D. None of the above

3   What must you do to edit a project that is controlled by Visual SourceSafe? Check all that apply.

A. Check in the project.

B. Log into Visual SourceSafe.

C. Check out the project.

D. Archive the project.

4   What does the following code do for the menu item? Check all that apply.

```
fillNew.Caption = "&Create a Database"
```

A. Disables the item

B. Places a checkmark in front of the item

C. Changes the text shown to the user

D. Sets the hotkey for the item to C

5   What does the following figure indicate about the selected menu item?

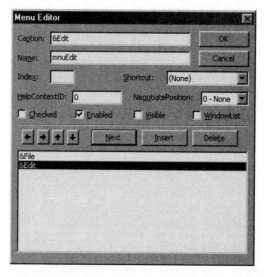

A. The item is disabled.

B. The item is not visible to the user.

C. A checkmark will appear next to the item.

D. The item's shortcut key is Ctrl+X.

FINAL REVIEW

6 Which of the following statements are true of pop-up menus? Check all that apply.

A. A pop-up menu can have multiple levels.

B. A pop-up menu can also be displayed as part of the main menu.

C. The pop-up menu is automatically invoked by clicking the right mouse button.

D. You can have multiple pop-up menus on a form.

7 Working with the following code, when is the pop-up menu invoked?

```
Private Sub Form_MouseDown(Button As Integer, Shift As _
Integer, X As Single, Y As Single)
If Button = vbRightButton Then
    Me.PopupMenu mnuFormat
End If
End Sub
```

A. When any mouse button is clicked

B. When the left mouse button is clicked

C. When the right mouse button is clicked

D. Never

8 Which of the following code samples is the correct way to add an item to a menu?

A. `mnuFile.Items.Add filNew`

B. `frmMain.Menus.Add edtUndo`

C. `frmMain.Controls.Add mnuHelp`

D. `Load filRecent(1)`

9 Which property of a menu item array tells you the highest index number in the array?

    A. Count

    B. LastItem

    C. UBound

    D. LBound

10 Which code segment will reposition a control within its container? Check all that apply.

    A. `txtMember.Move 100, 50`

    B. `txtMember.Width = 1000`

    C. `txtMember.Visible = False`

    D. `txtMember.Left = 100`
       `txtMember.Top = 50`

11 Which control provides a repository for images for use by other controls?

    A. Image

    B. PictureBox

    C. ImageList

    D. PicClip

12 Which style of toolbar button allows you to toggle the button between the up and down position to indicate the status of an option?

    A. tbrDefault

    B. tbrCheck

    C. tbrButtonGroup

    D. tbrDropDown

13   Which properties of a Node object must be set to relate it to another node? Check all that apply.

    A. Relative

    B. Text

    C. Key

    D. Relationship

14   Which view of the ListView control would be used with the following code?

```
Set liOrder = lvwGrades.ListItems.Add(, , "Gloves")
With liOrder
    .SubItems(1) = 4
    .SubItems(2) = 10.5
    .SubItems(3) = Val(.SubItems(1)) * Val(.SubItems(2))
End With
```

    A. Icon view

    B. Report view

    C. Small Icon view

    D. List view

15   Which object is used to define the columns of a ListView control?

    A. ListItem

    B. ColumnHeader

    C. Column

    D. SubItem

```
┌─────────────────────────────┐
│     F I N A L   R E V I E W  │
└─────────────────────────────┘
```

16 Which of the following are true about adding a control to a control array at runtime? Check all that apply.

    A. You must set the Visible property of the control to make it accessible to the user.

    B. The control array must already exist.

    C. The Index value must be the next sequential number after the upper bound of the array.

    D. The Index of the new control must be unique.

17 Which of the following statements is True?

    A. You can remove an element of a control array that was created in design mode.

    B. You can only remove control array elements that are added at runtime.

    C. You can remove all but the first element of a control array.

    D. You cannot remove control array elements.

18 Which of the following code segments would be used to change the Font of all text boxes on a form?

    A.

```
For Each TextBox In Controls
    TextBox.Font.Name = "Times New Roman"
Next TextBox
```

    B.

```
Dim ctlFont As Control
For Each ctlFont In Controls
    ctlFont.Font.Name = "Times New Roman"
Next ctlFont
```

FINAL REVIEW

C.

```
Dim ctlFont As Control
For Each ctlFont In Controls
    If TypeOf ctlFont Is TextBox Then
        ctlFont.Font.Name = "Times New Roman"
    End If
Next ctlFont
```

D.

```
TextBoxesFont.Font.Name = "Times New Roman"
```

19 Which of the following code segments can be used to process all the open forms in a program? Check all that apply.

A.

```
For I = 0 To Forms.Count
    Debug.Print Forms(I).Name
Next I
```

B.

```
For All Forms
    Debug.Print Form.Name
Next Control
```

C.

```
For Each chgForm In Forms
    Debug.Print chgForm.Name
Next chgControl
```

D.

```
For I = 0 To Forms.UBound
    Debug.Print Forms.Item(I).Name
Next I
```

20 Field-level validation checks data for validity at what point in time?

    A. Immediately as the data is changed

    B. When the data is saved to a database

    C. As the user exits the field

    D. When the user clicks the Validation button

21 To implement field-level validation, which event would you write code for?

    A. LostFocus

    B. Change

    C. Validate

    D. GotFocus

22 Which event is fired each time the form gains focus?

    A. Initialize

    B. Load

    C. Activate

    D. LostFocus

23 Which form event enables you to determine how the user closed the form?

    A. Unload

    B. QueryUnload

    C. Terminate

    D. Deactivate

24   Which of the following statements is true about unloading a form? Check all that apply.

    A. The QueryUnload event is triggered before the Unload event.

    B. The Terminate event is triggered as the form is unloaded.

    C. The Terminate event is triggered when all references to the form are deleted.

    D. The Unload event is not triggered if there is code in the QueryUnload event.

25   Which of the following declaration statements will allow an object to respond to events?

    A. `Dim oUSer As cUser`

    B. `Dim WithEvents oUSer As cUser`

    C. `Dim WithEvents oUSer As New cUser`

    D. `Dim oUSer As New cUser`

26   Which two properties must be set to enable an ADO data control to provide information from a database?

    A. DataField and DataSource

    B. DataField and Recordset

    C. DatabaseName and RecordSource

    D. ConnectionString and RecordSource

27   To set up an ADO data control for editing data, which of the following must be true? Check all that apply.

    A. The CursorType must be either KeySet or Dynamic.

    B. The CursorType must be Static.

    C. The AllowUpdate property of the data control must be set to True.

    D. LockType must not be set to read-only.

28 What does the following line of code tell your program?

On Error GoTo 0

   A. Branch to an error handler when an error occurs.

   B. Continue execution on the next line when an error occurs.

   C. Turn off error handling for this procedure.

   D. Terminate the program when an error occurs.

29 In the following error-handling routine, what does the program do after the error is logged?

```
Exit Sub
ProcErr1:
    oErrorLog.LogError "frmMain", "SetFonts", Err.Number, _
    Err.Description
    Resume Next
End Sub
```

   A. Retries the line that caused the error

   B. Continues execution on the line after the error

   C. Exits the procedure

   D. Terminates the program

30 What property of a control must be set to enable context-sensitive help for the control?

   A. HelpContextID

   B. HelpTopicID

   C. WhatsThisHelpID

   D. HelpID

31   Which of the following code segments would display a particular topic in a help file?

A.
```
cdlHelp.HelpFile = "Test.hlp"
cdlHelp.HelpCommand = cdlHelpContents
cdlHelp.ShowHelp
```

B.
```
cdlHelp.HelpFile = "Test.hlp"
cdlHelp.HelpCommand = cdlHelpKey
cdlHelp.HelpContext = 120
cdlHelp.ShowHelp
```

C.
```
cdlHelp.HelpFile = "Test.hlp"
cdlHelp.HelpCommand = cdlHelpContext
cdlHelp.HelpContext = 120
cdlHelp.ShowHelp
```

D.
```
cdlHelp.HelpFile = "Test.hlp"
cdlHelp.HelpCommand = cdlHelpContext
cdlHelp.HelpContext = "Printing"
cdlHelp.ShowHelp
```

32   Which properties of a form must be set to allow WhatsThisHelp?

   A. WhatsThisHelp and WhatsThisHelpID

   B. WhatsThisButton and WhatsThisHelpID

   C. WhatsThisHelp and WhatsThisButton

   D. WhatsThisHelp and HelpContextID

33 In the following code, what happens if you do not precede the error-handling routine with the Exit Sub statement?

```
Exit Sub
InvoiceErr1:

If oErrorLog.LogError("Invoice", "cmdSave", Err.Number, _
Err.Description) Then
    Resume Next
Else
    Exit Sub
End If
```

A. The procedure exits when it encounters the `InvoiceErr1:` statement.

B. Nothing, since no error has occurred.

C. The LogError function is run even though no error occurs.

D. This causes an error, which causes the program to terminate.

34 What happens if your program encounters an error and the routine has no error handler?

A. The program displays a message and retries the operation.

B. The program terminates.

C. The program attempts to find an error handler in a higher-level procedure.

D. The program exits the procedure without displaying a message.

FINAL REVIEW

---

35   Which of the following code segments creates a read-only property?

    A.

```
Public Property Get AdminUser() As Boolean
AdminUser = m_bAdmin
End Property

Public Property Let AdminUser(bNewValue As Boolean)
m_bAdmin = AdminUser
End Property
```

    B.

```
Public Property Let AdminUser(bNewValue As Boolean)
m_bAdmin = AdminUser
End Property
```

    C.

```
Public Property Get AdminUser() As Boolean
AdminUser = m_bAdmin
End Property
```

    D. None of the above.

36   Which event of a control is used to retrieve developer settings?

    A. WriteProperties

    B. Save

    C. ReadProperties

    D. Read

37 What method is used to store developer settings for your control?

    A. The Store method of the UserControl object

    B. The Store method of the PropertyBag object

    C. The WriteProperty method of the PropertyBag object

    D. The WriteProperty method of the UserControl object

38 Which of the following is an advantage of an In-Process server? Check all that apply.

    A. It can run as a stand-alone application.

    B. There are more multithreading options than for an Out-of-Process server.

    C. It can handle more objects in a single project than an Out-of-Process server.

    D. It is faster than an Out-of-Process server.

39 To move from one ActiveX document to another, you use the NavigateTo method of which object?

    A. UserDocument

    B. App

    C. HyperLink

    D. Form

40 Which of the following settings of the Instancing property is the default setting for an In-Process server?

    A. Private

    B. SingleUse

    C. MultiUse

    D. PublicNotCreatable

41 What is the Object Model for a component?

A. The help file that describes the component

B. A definition of the relationship between classes in the component

C. A diagram of the component

D. A listing of the properties of the component

42 The Class Builder utility helps you do which of the following? Check all that apply.

A. Create collections for holding multiple instances of a class.

B. Create the properties, methods, and events of a class.

C. Write the documentation for a component.

D. Create a class based on an existing class.

43 If you set the Instancing property of a component to Private, where can the component be used?

A. In only one application at a time.

B. In any application.

C. Only in the server in which the component is defined.

D. Private is not a valid setting.

44 Which of the following *must* you specify when adding a component to the Visual Component Manager? Check all that apply.

A. Name

B. Keywords for identifying the component

C. Which applications use the component

D. File containing the component

45 Which of the following are ways to register a component? Check all that apply.

A. Copy the component to your project directory.

B. Run the component if it is an EXE server

C. Use the Regsvr32 utility.

D. Create a setup program to handle the registration.

46 Which of the following are valid settings for the RecordSource property? Check all that apply.

A. The name of a table

B. The name of another data control

C. The name of a query or stored procedure

D. A valid SQL statement

47 To use a query for the RecordSource, you should set the CommandType property to what?

A. adCmdUnknown

B. adCmdTable

C. adCmdText

D. adCmdStoredProc

48 Which of the following cursor types allow you to edit the information in the database? Check all that apply.

A. Static

B. Forward-only

C. Dynamic

D. Keyset

49   When using a data control, when is the information entered by a user saved to the database? Check all that apply.

   A. When the user moves from the current control to another

   B. When the user moves to another record

   C. When the user closes the form containing the data control

   D. When your code invokes the Update method of the recordset object

50   Which of the following code segments is correct for adding a record to the database?

   A.
```
With rsMember
    .Add
    !MemberID = lMemID
    !MemberName = sMemName
    .Update
End With
```

   B.
```
With rsMember
    .AddNew
    !MemberID = lMemID
    !MemberName = sMemName
    .Update
End With
```

   C.
```
With rsMember
    .AddNew
    !MemberID = lMemID
    !MemberName = sMemName
End With
```

D.

```
With rsMember
      .Edit New
      !MemberID = lMemID
      !MemberName = sMemName
      .Update
End With
```

51 What information *must* be specified in a search using ADO methods? Check all that apply.

    A. The field to be searched

    B. The search direction

    C. The starting point of the search

    D. The value to be searched for

52 When using ADO data access methods, which property do you check to determine if a search was successful?

    A. RecordFound

    B. NoMatch

    C. EOF

    D. RecordNumber

53 Which tool lets you edit the value of a variable? Check all that apply.

    A. Watch window

    B. Auto Data Tips

    C. Quick Watch

    D. Locals window

54   Which of following are advantages of compiling to native code? Check all that apply.

    A. Smaller executable size

    B. Faster program execution

    C. Eliminates the need for runtime libraries

    D. Faster compile times

55   What must be specified when you create a watch? Check all that apply.

    A. The name of the variable

    B. The name of your program

    C. The context of the watch

    D. The value to set for the variable

APPENDIX

**Study Question and
Sample Test Answers**

Unit 1 Answers

Study Questions

Assess the Potential Impact of the Logical Design on Performance, Maintainability, Extensibility, and Availability

1. False

2. Classes

3. Naming convention

4. Declare

5. String

6. False

7. Single quote, Rem

8. Option Explicit

9. Properties

10. Maintain and reuse

11. False

12. True

Design Visual Basic Components to Access Data from a Database

13. ActiveX server

14. UserControl

15. Code maintenance and error handling

16. True

Design the Properties, Methods, and Events of Components

17. Property Let

18. Property Get

19. Property Set

20. Internal variable

21. Public

22. False

23. RaiseEvent

24. Function

Sample Test Answers

1-1   B

1-2   A

1-3   A

1-4   D

1-5   C

1-6   A, C

1-7   A

1-8   C

1-9   B, C, D

1-10   C

1-11   B

Unit 2 Answers

Study Questions

Establish the Environment for Source Code Version Control

1. Version control

2. True

3. Add users

4. True

5. Log in to Visual SourceSafe

6. False

7. Check out

8. Track program changes and track who made them

9. Check in

10. True

Install and Configure Visual Basic for Developing Desktop Applications

11. True

12. Distributed Component Object Model (DCOM)

13. HTML Help (.CHM)

14. True

15. Project template

Sample Test Answers

2-1   A, D

2-2   B, C

2-3   A

2-4   C

2-5   D

2-6   B

Unit 3 Answers

Study Questions

Implement Navigational Design

1. Visible and Enabled

2. False

Dynamically Modify the Appearance of a Menu

3. Caption

4. Ampersand (&)

5. False

6. Checked

7. False

8. False

9. True

10. Visible

11. True

12. False

Add a Pop-up Menu to an Application

13. False

14. PopupMenu

15. False

16. True

17. Caption

18. False

19. False

Create an Application That Adds and Deletes Menus at Run Time

20. Name

21. False

22. Index

23. Load

24. True

25. Unload

26. False

27. WindowList

28. False

Add Controls to Forms

29. True

30. Left and Top

31. True

32. False

33. Visible

34. False

35. False

Set Properties for Controls

36. Height and Width

37. Upper-left

38. False

39. ForeColor and BackColor

40. True

41. True

42. Visible

43. Value

Assign Code to a Control to Respond to an Event

44. False

45. KeyDown, KeyPress, and KeyUp

46. KeyDown and KeyUp

47. MouseDown and MouseUp

48. True

49. True

Sample Test Answers

3-1   A

3-2   A, B, D

3-3   C

3-4   A, C

3-5   B

3-6   D

3-7   B

3-8   B

3-9   C

3-10 B

3-11   A, C

3-12   A

3-13   C

3-14   C

3-15   C

3-16   D

Unit 4 Answers

Study Questions

Display and Manipulate Data by Using Custom Controls

1. ImageList

2. Node

3. Report

4. Button

5. Picture

6. False

7. Clear

8. Key or Index

9. Text

10. Relationship, tvwChild

11. False

12. Relative and Relationship

13. MultiSelect

14. ColumnHeader

15. Text

16. SubItems

17. True

18. Style

19. ShowTips

20. Caption and Image

21. tbrButtonGroup

22. True

23. Key

24. ButtonClick

25. False

26. Panel

27. sbrText

28. Text and Picture

29. True

Create an Application That Adds and Deletes Controls at Run Time

30. True

31. Index

32. False

33. True

34. False

35. Load

36. Visible

37. True

38. UBound

39. False

Use the Controls Collection to Manipulate Controls at Run Time

40. False

41. False

42. For...Each

43. Name

44. TypeOf

45. True

46. False

47. True

48. False

Use the Forms Collection to Manipulate Forms at Run Time

49. Load

50. False

51. Name

52. False

53. False

54. Unload

Sample Test Answers

4-1   C

4-2   B

4-3   A, D

4-4	A
4-5	D
4-6	B
4-7	B
4-8	C
4-9	A, B
4-10	B
4-11	C
4-12	D
4-13	A, C
4-14	B, D
4-15	B
4-16	D
4-17	A, C

Unit 5 Answers

Study Questions

Write Code That Validates User Input

1. Option buttons, check boxes, combo boxes, and list boxes

2. KeyPress. KeyUp and KeyDown can also be used.

3. True

4. CheckBox

Create an Application That Verifies Data Entered at the Field Level and the Form Level by a User

5. Validate

6. False

7. CausesValidation, Validate

8. Field-level

9. True

10. Form-level

11. CausesValidation, False

12. Function procedure

13. True

Create an Application That Enables or Disables Controls Based on Input in Fields

14. Visible, False

15. Enabled, False

16. Locked

17. True

Write Code That Processes Data Entered on a Form

18. Initialize

19. Resize

20. Initialize and Load

Given a Scenario, Add Code to the Appropriate Form Event

21. Paint

22. False

23. Initialize, Load, Activate or Resize, Paint

24. Load, Show

25. QueryUnload

26. False

27. QueryUnload

28. QueryUnload and Unload

29. Deactivate

30. Terminate

Sample Test Answers

5-1	A, B, D
5-2	A, C
5-3	C
5-4	C
5-5	A
5-6	A, C, D
5-7	B, C
5-8	D
5-9	A
5-10	B
5-11	D
5-12	B, D
5-13	D
5-14	B

Unit 6 Answers

Study Questions

Add an ActiveX Control to the Toolbox

1. Components

2. False

Create a Web Page by Using the DHTML Page Designer to Dynamically Change Attributes of Elements, Change Content, Change Styles, and Position Elements

3. Dynamic Hypertext Markup Language

4. DHTML Application

5. False

6. OnClick

7. Value

8. False

9. Web browser

Use Data Binding to Display and Manipulate Data from a Data Source

10. False

11. DataSource

12. DataField

13. True

14. True

15. Text

16. False

Instantiate and Invoke a COM Component

17. False

18. Visual interface

Create a Visual Basic Client Application That Uses a COM Component

19. Reference

20. Object variable

21. Early binding

22. False

23. Set

24. CreateObject or Set

25. Late

26. False

27. Nothing

28. True

Create a Visual Basic Application That Handles Events from a COM Component

29. WithEvents

30. RaiseEvent

31. False

32. Write code for the event

Create Callback Procedures to Enable Asynchronous Processing Between COM Components and Visual Basic Client Applications

33. RaiseEvent

34. False

Sample Test Answers

6-1   A, D

6-2   B

6-3   C

6-4   D

6-5   A

6-6   C

6-7	B
6-8	D
6-9	A, C
6-10	C

Unit 7 Answers

Study Questions

Set Appropriate Properties to Enable User Assistance

1. Project Properties

2. App

3. .HLP

4. HelpContextID

5. F1

6. The control's container

7. True

8. Help Workshop

9. Index

10. HelpFile

11. HelpCommand

12. HelpContext

13. ShowHelp

14. Fixed Dialog

15. WhatsThisHelp

16. True

17. WhatsThisButton

18. WhatsThisHelpID

Create HTML Help for an Application

19. HTML Help Workshop

20. .CHM

21. True

Implement Messages from a Server Component to a User Interface

22. RaiseEvent

23. Raise, Err

24. Source

25. False

26. HelpFile and HelpContext

27. False

Implement Error Handling for the User Interface in Desktop Applications

28. Number

29. LastDLLError

Identify and Trap Runtime Errors

30. False

31. On Error Resume Next

32. On Error GoTo 0

33. True

34. Resume

35. Resume Next

36. Exit Sub or Exit Function

37. Resume [line label]

38. False

39. Number and Description

Handle Inline Errors

40. On Error Resume Next

41. Number, greater than 0

42. Clear

43. True

44. True

Sample Test Answers

7-1   B

7-2   C

7-3   B

7-4   C

7-5   A

7-6   B

7-7   C

7-8   C

7-9   B

7-10 C

7-11 B

7-12 A, B, C

7-13 A, C

7-14 C

Unit 8 Answers

Study Questions

Create a COM Component That Implements Business Rules or Logic

1. In-Process

2. Out-of-Process

3. False

4. Class

5. DLL or EXE

6. False

Create an ActiveX Control That Exposes Properties

7. Property Let

8. Property Set

9. True

10. BackStyle

11. Public

12. Sub or Function

13. Property Get, Property Let

14. RaiseEvent

15. False

16. Control Interface wizard

17. False

Use Control Events to Save and Load Persistent Properties

18. PropertyBag

19. False

20. WriteProperties

21. True

22. ReadProperties

23. PropertyChanged

24. Property Let

25. The property name and the default value

26. WriteProperty method, PropertyBag

27. Save, PropertyChanged

Test and Debug an ActiveX Control

28. True

29. Group

30. UserControl

31. Resize event

Create and Enable Property Pages for an ActiveX Control

32. Property Page wizard

33. False

34. Custom

Enable the Data Binding Capabilities of an ActiveX Control

35. DataBindingBehavior

36. False

37. DataField

38. Advanced button, Procedure Attributes

39. Properties that can be bound to a data source.

Create an ActiveX Control That Is a Data Source

40. False

41. DataSourceBehavior property

42. False

43. True

Use Code within an Active Document to Interact with a Container Application

44. PropertyBag

45. PropertyChanged

46. ReadProperties

Navigate to Other Active Documents

47. False

48. HyperLink

49. NavigateTo

50. GoForward and GoBack

Sample Test Answers

8-1   A

8-2   B

8-3   C

8-4   A, D

8-5   B, C

8-6   A, D

8-7   B

8-8   B

8-9   C

8-10   D

8-11   C

8-12   A

8-13   C

8-14   A, B, D

8-15   A, B

8-16   C

8-17   B

8-18   B

8-19   A, C, D

8-20   A, B, D

Unit 9 Answers

Study Questions

Debug a COM Client Written in Visual Basic

1. Toolbox

2. References or Components

3. False

4. Auto List Members

5. Auto Quick Info

6. False

7. Project group

8. Break In Class Module

9. True

Implement an Object Model within a COM Component

10. False

11. Collections

12. Object model

13. Class Builder utility

14. False

15. True

Set Properties to Control the Instancing of a Class within a COM Component

16. Instancing

17. Private

18. SingleUse or GlobalSingleUse

19. False

20. True

21. Persistable

Use Visual Component Manager to Manage Components

22. Visual Component Manager

23. False

24. Name and the file containing the component

25. Keywords

26. True

27. Find Items

28. Double-click

29. False

Register and Unregister a COM Component

30. Regsvr32

31. True

32. Setup

33. /u

34. /UnRegserver

Sample Test Answers

9-1   A, C

9-2   B

9-3   C

9-4   B

9-5   B

9-6   A, C

9-7   D

9-8   A, B, D

9-9   A

9-10   C

9-11   C

9-12   A, D

9-13   B, C, D

9-14   B

Unit 10 Answers

Study Questions

Access and Manipulate a Data Source by Using ADO and the ADO Data Control

1. ActiveX Data Objects

2. Your program and information in a database

Setting Up the ADO Data Control

3. ConnectionString and RecordSource

4. False

5. ConnectionString

6. False

7. RecordSource

8. Static

9. Dynamic and Keyset

10. CursorType

11. Optimistic and pessimistic

12. LockType

13. False

14. EOFAction

Working with Bound Controls

15. Displaying and editing

16. TextBox or Label

17. DataSource property

18. DataField

19. Text

20. False

21. True

22. CheckBox

23. False

24. DataGrid and MSHFlexGrid (or hierarchical flex grid)

25. Chart

26. DataSource

Extending the Capabilities of the ADODC

27. ADO methods

28. Recordset

29. AddNew

30. Cleared to enable adding information

31. True

32. Delete

33. False

34. True

35. Move the record pointer to another record

36. Find

37. The field to be searched, the comparison operation, and the value to be found

38. Next record, forward

39. SkipRecords

40. SearchDirection

41. Single or double quotes

42. EOF

Sample Test Answers

10-1   C

10-2   A, C, D

10-3   B

10-4   C, D

10-5   B

10-6   C

10-7   A, B, D

10-8   A

10-9   B

10-10   C

10-11   A

10-12   C

10-13   C

10-14   A

10-15   A, D

10-16   C

Unit 11 Answers

Study Questions

Given a Scenario, Select the Appropriate Compiler Options

1. False

2. Native code

3. P-code

4. True

5. Remove Integer Overflow Checks

6. False

7. Optimize for Small Code

8. False

9. Favor Pentium Pro and Remove Safe Pentium FDIV Checks

10. False

Control an Application by Using Conditional Compilation

11. #If

12. False

13. #ElseIf

14. All prior conditions are false

15. #Const

16. Project Properties, command line argument

17. True

Set Watch Expressions During Program Execution

18. Variable name or expression

19. Module and procedure

20. True

21. True

22. Auto Data Tips

23. False

Monitor the Values of Expressions and Variables by Using the Immediate Window

24. Question mark

25. True

26. Print, Debug

27. False

28. An assignment statement

29. The current procedure

30. Properties of the current form and its controls

31. False

32. Hierarchical tree

33. False

Implement Project Groups to Support the Development and Debugging Processes

34. Multiple Visual Basic projects

35. Startup project parameter

36. True

37. True

38. False

39. Properties

40. Methods

41. Close its user interface window

42. True

43. A watch on the variable

Given a Scenario, Define the Scope of a Watch Variable

44. False

45. The context setting when you create the watch.

46. The type of declaration statement and the location of the statement.

47. True

Sample Test Answers

11-1   A, B, D

11-2   A, D

11-3   A, D

11-4   B, C

11-5 A, D

11-6 B

11-7 C

11-8 B, D

11-9 B, D

11-10 A, B

11-11 B

11-12 C

11-13 A, C

11-14 A, C

Unit 12 Answers

Study Questions

Use the Package and Deployment Wizard to Create a Setup Program That Installs a Desktop Application, Registers the COM Components, and Allows for Uninstall

1. Testing the installation routine

2. .CAB

3. VB6Dep.ini

4. .DEP

5. False

Plan and Implement Floppy Disk-Based Deployment or Compact Disc-Based Deployment for a Desktop Application

6. True

7. Standard

8. Floppy disk

9. True

10. True

11. Disk drive of the floppy

Plan and Implement Web-Based Deployment for a Desktop Application

12. True

13. The most recent version of the program

14. True

15. Web publishing

16. URL of the Web site

17. HTTP Posting or FTP Transfer

Plan and Implement Network-Based Deployment for a Desktop Application

18. Disks

19. True

20. Folder

21. Location

Fix Errors, and Take Measures to Prevent Future Errors

22. Report errors

23. Error log

24. True

Deploy Application Updates for Desktop Applications

25. True

26. Packaging script

27. Version number

28. Revision

29. App

Sample Test Answers

12-1   B

12-2   B, D

12-3   B

12-4   B, C

12-5   A, C

12-6   A

12-7   C

12-8   B, C

Unit 13 Answers

Final Review Answers

13-1   C

13-2   A

13-3   B, C

13-4   C, D

13-5   B

13-6   A, B, D

13-7   C

13-8   D

13-9   C

13-10 A, D

13-11 C

13-12 B

13-13 A, D

13-14 B

13-15 B

13-16 A, B, D

13-17 B

13-18 C

13-19 C, D

13-20 C

13-21 C

13-22 C

13-23 B

13-24 A, C

13-25 B

13-26 D

13-27 A, D

13-28 C

13-29 B

13-30 A

13-31 C

13-32 C

13-33 C

13-34 C

13-35 C

13-36 C

13-37 C

13-38 D

13-39 C

13-40 C

13-41 B

13-42 A, B, D

13-43 C

13-44 A, D

13-45 B, C, D

13-46 A, C, D

13-47 D

13-48 C, D

13-49 B, C, D

13-50 B

13-51 A, D

13-52 C

13-53 A, D

13-54 B

13-55 A, C

Glossary

Access key   A key combination (such as Alt+F) that enables the user to open a main menu, or a single key that enables the user to select a menu item.

ActiveX document   A specialized Visual Basic application that can run within a Web browser.

ActiveX server   Any program that exposes objects to other programs for use while running as a stand-alone application.

Alias   Another name by which a procedure is identified for use in an application.

Asynchronous operation   Program execution in which multiple instructions can be run simultaneously.

Bookmark property   An identifier for a specific record in a recordset.

Breakpoint   A debugging tool that pauses the execution of the program at a specific point.

Callback procedure   A procedure in an application that can be called by a function in a DLL routine.

Child form   A form that is contained within a parent form.

Class   A structure that provides a definition of an object. A class defines the data (properties), tasks to perform (methods), and notifications (events) of an object.

Class modules   The code structures that implement classes in Visual Basic.

Collection   A grouping of similar objects, such as forms, recordsets, or controls.

Common Dialog control   A control that enables the programmer to easily create Open, Save, Help, Print, Color, and Font dialog boxes for programs.

Conditional compilation   Visual Basic compiles only parts of a program as they are needed.

Control array   A group of controls of the same type that have the same name. Members of the array are identified by the Index property. Arrays are used for easier processing of multiple controls.

Controls collection   A special collection that provides a reference to every control on a given form.

Dynamic-link library (DLL)   A file that contains object definitions for use by client programs. A DLL works as an In-Process ActiveX server.

Early binding   Declaring a specific object type is known as early binding of the object.

Encapsulation   The data about an object and the code used to manipulate the data are contained within the object itself. The data is stored as the properties of the object and the code as the methods of the object. Encapsulation enables the object data and code to stand alone, independent of outside routines.

Explicit declaration   A means of defining the data type of a variable by specifying the type in the declaration statement.

Forms collection   A special collection that provides a reference to every loaded form in an application.

Friend declaration   Enables the programmer to make a property or method available to other modules in the current project (the one in which the class is defined), without making the routine truly public.

Global variable   Another name for Public variable.

Hyperlink   A string that identifies a link to another document or Web page.

Implicit declaration   A means of defining the data type of a variable by placing a particular symbol at the end of the variable name.

In-Process server   An ActiveX server that is contained in a .DLL file and runs in the same process (memory) space as the client application.

Inheritance   Enables one object to be created based on the properties and methods of another object. With inheritance, it is not necessary to code the properties and methods that are derived from the parent object. The programmer has to code only new or modified properties and methods.

Invalid value error   An error that occurs when the programmer tries to assign a value to a variable that the variable is not capable of handling.

Jump   A link between two topics in a help file.

Late binding   Declaring a generic object variable is known as late binding of the object.

Local variable   A variable that can be used only in the procedure in which it is defined.

Logic error   An error that does not cause a program to crash but does cause a program to yield incorrect results.

Method   A procedure that provides an object with the ability to perform a task.

Modal form   A form that must be exited before other forms of an application may be accessed.

Module-level variable   A variable declared at the beginning of a form or code module that is available to all procedures in the module but not outside the module.

Multithreading   Processing multiple parts of an application in separate threads (typically on multiple processors).

Native code   Machine-level instructions that make up an application.

Object browser   A Visual Basic tool that lets the programmer see the properties, methods, and events of an object.

Open database connectivity (ODBC)   A specification that provides a consistent means to communicate with many types of databases.

Out-of-Process server   An ActiveX server that is contained in an .EXE file and runs in a separate process (memory) space from the client application.

P-code   An interpreted code that is between the English-like commands that programmers enter and the machine code that computers use.

Parent form   A form that provides a container for other child forms of the application.

Pop-up   A small window that contains additional information about a topic. The window "pops up" in response to a mouse click on a particular style of text.

Procedure   A self-contained segment of code that performs a specific task.

Programming interface   The structure through which programs communicate with one another.

PropertyBag   A storage device for maintaining information for an ActiveX document or ActiveX control.

Public variable   A variable that can be accessed from anywhere in the program.

Query   A SQL statement that is used to retrieve or modify data.

Recordset   An object that contains the information used by an application.

Registry   A database in Windows 95 and Windows NT that contains information about the settings of the computer.

Remote data   Data located in a database server, such as Oracle or SQL Server.

Runtime error   An error that occurs while a program is running.

Shortcut key   A key combination that directly invokes a menu option.

Status bar   A bar at the bottom of a form that provides the user with additional information about the application.

Synchronous operation   Program execution in which one instruction must be completed before the next instruction can be started.

Syntax error   An error in the wording of a line of program code.

Tool tip   A small window that provides additional information about a control. The tool tip pops up when the user rests the mouse cursor on the control for a few seconds.

Trapping an error   Handling an error within an application so the user does not see the original error information and so the program does not crash.

Watch   A debugging tool that tracks the value of a variable or expression.

Index

Note to the Reader: Page numbers in **bold** indicate the principal discussion of a topic or the definition of a term. Page numbers in *italic* indicate illustrations.